Education For All: A Landmark in Pluralism

Dedicated to
Lord Swann FRS FRSE
whose understanding, sensitivity and skills made it
possible to lay the foundation of cultural
pluralism in Britain.

Gajendra K. Verma

Education For All:
A Landmark in Pluralism

Edited by
Gajendra K. Verma

 The Falmer Press
(A member of the Taylor & Francis Group)
London . New York . Philadelphia

UK   The Falmer Press, Falmer House, Barcombe, Lewes, East Sussex, BN8 5DL

USA   The Falmer Press, Taylor & Francis Inc., 242 Cherry Street, Philadelphia, PA 19106-1906

© Selection and editorial material copyright Gajendra Verma 1989

First published 1989

British Library Cataloguing in Publication Data

Education for all: a landmark in pluralism.
  1. Great Britain. Multicultural education.
  I. Verma, Gajendra K. (Gajendra Kishore).
  1935-370.11′5
ISBN 1-85000-303-3
ISBN 1-85000-304-1 (pbk.)

Typeset in 10½/12 point Baskerville by
Alresford Typesetting & Design, Alresford, Hants

Jacket design by Caroline Archer

Printed in Great Britain by Taylor & Francis (Printers) Ltd, Basingstoke

Contents

Contents

Foreword

Lord Swann's report, *Education for All*, is the boldest, most comprehensive statement on the subject of multicultural education so far produced in Britain. It is uncompromising in its argument that multicultural education must be the basis of every child's schooling, not only those in minority groups. It is frank in admitting that racial prejudice and discrimination add an extra dimension of deprivation to the prospects of those already adversely affected by poor socioeconomic status. It is visionary in advocating a global perspective, and in seeking 'a good and relevant education for life in the modern world'.

In 1979, I established a Committee to investigate multicultural education in Britain under the chairmanship of Anthony Rampton, a London businessman with an excellent record of good multicultural relations in his own firm, who had also contributed to the wider community. The Committee was not an easy one to preside over — in a sense it was a microcosm of the problems of a multicultural society. Members differed on what the facts were, and on explanations of those facts. Much time was spent on wrestling with the issue of underachievement by West Indian children in the schools: how much was due to racial prejudice, how much to teachers' attitudes, some of them unconscious? The interim report identified racism as a very important element in explaining underachievement.

The final report, in Lord Swann's name (for he succeeded to the chairmanship in 1981) identified 'a large number of interrelated causes'. Among these are teachers' attitudes and pupils' aspirations. If expectations are low, children live down to those expectations. Research in a related area, the education of girls, shows quite marked differences in teachers' attitudes to boys and girls, and indicates that teachers devote more time to boys and ask them more questions.

Teachers' attitudes will be influenced by national educational goals. On the subject of multicultural education, Britain's goals have been unclear. In the 1960s, Roy Jenkins provided a classic definition of one kind of multicultural society — 'cultural diversity based on mutual tolerance'. Perceiving themselves to be tolerant, many Britons felt there was no need to embark upon legislation and administrative action to combat racism, as the federal government of the

United States had done. It would all work out all right. The decentralized education system in any case could not be ordered from the Department of Education and Science. Secretaries of State could exhort and persuade, but not command. So multicultural education was perceived as good or as bad as the local education authority.

Underlying this diversity of provision has been uncertainty about the objectives of multicultural education. It was straightforward enough to call for a curriculum and textbooks that reflected a modern world of independent states rather than an Imperial aftermath. I did so myself in the 1977 Green Paper that called for a core curriculum reflecting the cultural and ethnic diversity of our country and its interdependence with the wider world. Bringing it about, where resources were limited and became more so, and where few new teachers were being recruited because of falling rolls in the schools, was a much more difficult proposition. Argument continued too about the extent of multiculturalism in the syllabus. As Brian Bullivant says in his excellent chapter, how far should emphasis be placed on necessary common educational skills, how much on explaining diverse cultures? Parents often prefer the former, for practical reasons. In the USA, the diversity of ethnic groups was subordinated to the learning of a common language, English, and a set of core values, belief in the United States, her destiny and her constitution. Such an approach creates a sense of common citizenship, leaving the promulgation of ethnic cultures to the local community organizations. It is only now, faced with a large Hispanic minority speaking the same international language, that the US has had to face up to the possibility of two languages of instruction in its schools.

What has happened in Britain since the Swann Report? The requirement that teacher training courses must embody a multicultural approach, and will only get official approval if they do, seems to me a valuable step forward. Textbooks and teaching materials are improving, moving away from ethnic stereotypes. But the so-called 'educational reforms' proposed by our own Government trouble me. The National Curriculum could be a tool of multicultural education, but also it could squeeze out the creativity some schools have demonstrated in eliciting the riches of an ethnically diverse school population. More disturbing are the proposals for 'opting out' of a local education authority, which could become an excuse for segregated schooling, and the commitment to frequent testing, which can give a highly distorted picture of schools' achievements in 'adding value' to what children bring to them. The global approach so eloquently propounded by Professor Lynch could be another casualty of the proposed changes, which seem indifferent to the interdependence of the global village.

New educational technologies, on the other hand, offer some exciting possibilities. Open learning systems, in which mature men and women can participate, offer hope to people living in their own communities and fearful to emerge. Muslim women, for instance, are not easily attracted out of their homes, but can be approached through outreach staff, and perhaps through distance learning. Computers are colour and gender blind, and make learning possible at a pace chosen by the individual. The area of computer-assisted learning, especially in further education, deserves further study by those concerned with multicultural education.

Certain aspects of the subject are highly sensitive, but it is one of the strengths of this book that the authors tackle them. Millicent Poole and Judyth Sachs explore the evocative subject of 'rhetorical silences', a concept not unfamiliar to politicians. Brian Bullivant asks why some ethnic minorities, for instance the Chinese, seem to be able to overcome the disadvantages of their socioeconomic position and of moving into a new and alien culture. He describes them as governed by an 'ethnic success ethic'. Discrimination against them may owe more to envy than to arrogance.

Multicultural education in the societies studied in this book — Australia, Canada, the US, the UK — is a microcosm of world education. The objective of an international curriculum remains elusive, in spite of work done by the United Nations, the European Community and others. But in a planet whose problems are increasingly supranational rather than national, the attempt to achieve it must be made.

I welcome this book, and the Swann Report which inspired it, as milestones in the long march of the human race.

Shirley Williams

*Former Secretary of State for
Education; former Social Democrat
Party President*
December 1988

Chapter 1

Education for All: A Landmark in Pluralism

Gajendra K. Verma

The theme of this book has been inspired by the publication of the Swann Report (DES, 1985) under the title *Education for All*. The aim is to bring together a collection of chapters which are scholarly in orientation, but which have strong practical implications and offer strategies for rethinking, action or change in the field of race relations and education.

The papers that appear in this volume were selected because of their theoretical breadth and their pioneering of new interpretations in the education of children in a culturally plural society.

The origins of the Swann Report lie in the concern expressed since the 1960s by ethnic minority communities in Britain (effectively Afro-Caribbean and Asian) about the poor performance of their children within the educational system. This concern was voiced not only by ethnic minority communities but by teachers and educationalists, and also recognized in Government reports.

Studies, both large and small, showed that West Indian children in particular were overrepresented in schools for the educationally sub-normal. The Select Committee on Race Relations and Immigration called 'as a matter of urgency' for the setting up of an independent inquiry into the underachievement of West Indian children. The Government (in the person of Shirley Williams, then Secretary of State for Education and Science, who has written the Foreword to this volume) responded positively by setting up in 1977 a Committee of Enquiry into the Education of Children from Ethnic Minority Groups. Thus, *Education for All* is the outcome of such concerns and pressures.

The Government asked the Committee to look into the educational needs of children from all ethnic groups with priority given to children of West Indian origin. Therefore, the Committee looked into the educational needs of children from Chinese, Cypriot, Italian, Ukranian and Vietnamese origins as well as Liverpool blacks and the children of travellers. It must be admitted that the Committee's appraisal of these ethnic groups was rather superficial, the main thrust of the enquiry being on children from West Indian and Asian backgrounds.

Gajendra K. Verma

The terms of reference of the enquiry were:

review in relation to schools, the educational needs and attainments of children from ethnic minority groups taking account, as necessary, of factors outside the formal education system relevant to school performance, including influences in early childhood and prospects for school leavers;

consider the potential value of instituting arrangements for keeping under review the educational performance of different ethnic minority groups, and what those arrangements might be;

consider the most effective use of resources for these purposes; and to make recommendations.

In carrying out its programme of work, the Committee is to give early and particular attention to the educational needs and attainments of pupils of West Indian origin and to make interim recommendations as soon as possible on action which might be in the interests of this group.

Given the context of the enquiry, the Report deals with a wide range of educational, social and personal issues which confront *all* children within the educational system. A major contribution of the Swann Report to the educational debate is that it sees the issues of ethnic minority children closely tied up with the basic character of mainstream education. Multicultural education is, therefore, not just for schools with an ethnic minority presence, but for all schools. This implies that all schools need to be drawn into any national debate on education in a plural society.

Education for All has clearly established that many young people, particularly those of West Indian and Asian origins, were underachieving in school and, as a large consequence, were suffering from reduced opportunities in their lives after school. The Report made it clear that this underachievement was the result of a complex interaction of a number of factors, all of which had to be addressed. However, the Report was in no doubt that a major ingredient in their relative failure was discrimination — conscious and unconscious, personal and institutional — arising from their ethnic origins. It attempted to map out the kind of response required by the educational system to meet the needs and aspirations of all children.

Given the emerging 'pluralist' composition of British Society the Report stresses the educational benefits to be derived from an enhancement of racial and cultural diversity, and accepts that the maintenance of existing cultures need not be the schools' prime objective. It strongly advocates that the goal of cultural pluralism can be attained by addressing the achievement of equality of educational opportunity for all regardless of sex, race, creed, class, ethnicity and religion. Such a view may not be universally shared. However, the vision of a pluralist society is difficult to achieve so long as discrimination and inequality remain integral parts of the social, political and economic structure.

Rex, in Chapter 2, points out the confusions surrounding the terms such as equality of opportunity, multiculturalism and anti-racism. However, he places more faith in equality of opportunity and anti-racism as means of helping ethnic minority pupils to succeed in the educational system and gain access to a better quality of life. Multiculturalism, according to him, may have a place within the process of education, but it should not override equality of opportunity and anti-racism. He suggests that schools should seek to remove all obstacles, whether in selection/banding procedures, ethos, teacher pupil behaviours and expectations, that militate against ethnic minority success.

Acknowledging the contribution of the Swann Report, Rex expresses some reservations about its focuses. He is more critical, however, of the Government's cool response to its recommendations by not providing the financial support necessary for their implementation.

In the final analysis, Rex believes that the theme expressed in *Education for All* will bring some benefits, although it will not resolve all the problems faced by Britain's ethnic minorities.

Tomlinson (Chapter 3) fully endorses the call from the Swann Report to provide all children with 'a good, relevant, and up-to-date education for life in Britain and the world as it is today' (DES, 1985, p. 315).

Referring to the earlier DES consultative document *Education in Schools* (DES, 1977) which stated that 'the curriculum appropriate to our imperial past cannot meet the requirements of modern Britain', she seeks to trace the ethnocentric, sexist and racist strands of their origins particularly as manifest in the period 1870–1920. During that period mass education began to develop, this coinciding with the 'ideology of imperialism' reaching its zenith.

Tomlinson's argument is illustrated with references to papers on pedagogy, to contemporary textbooks and popular fiction, especially that directed at youth. Those textbooks as well as the adventure stories aimed at young male readers all reinforced the notion of the white man's supremacy over those under his imperial hegemony and who depended on him for civilization, justice, work and morality. Such views, the author argues, have become so deep-seated in public consciousness that, whatever the changes that have since occurred in the reality of the world, they continue to permeate British cultural values and beliefs to the detriment of Britain's ethnic minority population.

Tomlinson asserts that the battle to disabuse the British school population of these naively accepted views of the 'British Heritage' must be joined if today's youngsters are to be prepared for life in the modern world. Those changes in attitude will be all the harder to bring about because the erstwhile simplistic notions of British supremacy have become distilled over the last 100 years. These have (in varying degrees) influenced the minds and behaviour of the parent and grandparent generations. The author calls for more research into the curriculum process, particularly with a historical perspective, since in studying the past we can better arrive at an understanding of the present and the needs of today.

Poole and Sachs (Chapter 4) present a comparative critique of multicultural

Gajendra K. Verma

education policy initiatives in Australia and Britain. There are, they suggest, differences of focus in the orientation given to multicultural education in the two countries. In Australia, the focus is on 'giving recognition to cultural and ethnic diversity', whilst in Britain it is on 'race relations'.

Poole and Sachs see the British orientation arising out of the climate that gave rise to the creation of the Committee of Enquiry. They welcome the 'education for all' orientation given to the debate by Swann. Multicultural education in both Britain and Australia has tended to maintain the status quo rather than to bring about the social reconstruction necessary to 'achieve the access, equity and social justice denied at present to sections of society'.

Nonetheless, Poole and Sachs warn against the dangers of hiding behind rhetoric. If education for all is to give multicultural education a social reconstructionist impetus then it must become a policy translated into action.

In both countries evidence on achievement suggests that some minority groups are doing as well as or better than their 'non-immigrant counterparts'. Such progress, the authors suggest, is inevitable and multicultural education cannot claim the credit for this.

Poole and Sachs consider the concept of culture at some length, tracing differences in nuance in Australia and Britain. They argue that in both countries the interpretation of culture in the field of multiculturalism has been static in character; insufficient account is taken of the dynamics of culture.

If multicultural education is to be properly informed it must seek a model of culture that allows for the impact of 'gender, age, social class and place of residence' upon individual behaviour and performance.

Such a reappraisal of culture, taken in conjunction with a rigorous examination of 'teachers' knowledge' and the ways in which this is mediated by the individual's and the institutions' value systems would reinvigorate multicultural education. This would promote social reconstruction and bring about a true 'education for all'.

From the point of view of an Australian educationist, Bullivant (Chapter 5) argues that the Swann Report gives 'a sense of *déjà vu* — here we go again — and a feeling of irritation'. Moreover, he asserts, the issues it raises show that 'the problems of achieving harmonious inter-ethnic and race relations seem as intractable as ever'. Some of his sense of frustration he attributes to the imperfections of the world, some to the powerlessness of the social scientist to construct a framework that will provide solutions.

Referring extensively to a study commissioned and funded by the Australian Human Rights Commission, Bullivant examines a number of issues arising from his examination as to 'whether prejudice and discrimination, due to social class, race, ethnic and gender differences were disadvantaging the career decisions of students at the senior level of schooling in seven Melbourne high schools'.

He found evidence there and in other recent Australian studies that pointed to the same 'paradox of Asian performance' as Swann had found. Asian performance in Australia (and there, Asian included larger proportions of

4

Chinese than was the case in Britain) defied the conventional wisdom of perceived cultural and socioeconomic disadvantage. Many Asian youngsters were achieving more in school and in terms of entry to tertiary education than the Anglo-Australian groups. What was more the success that occurred had no correlation to socioeconomic status. Bullivant attributed that success to the 'ethnic success ethic' which motivated the youngsters to work hard in and out of school.

Home and in-school factors were contributory and Bullivant also pointed to the support given by the ethnic communities to the independent sector of education. Families wanted programmes that prepared pupils for advancement in mainstream society and not ones designed to make the world seem less alien to them.

One might have thought that the general tenor of Bullivant's findings offered grounds for optimism. Two dark clouds loom over them. One was the efforts of left wing teacher unions to suppress or halt private education perhaps in the cause of egalitarianism and/or perhaps in order to reduce redundancies in a contracting state system. (Bullivant speculates as to whether there was a parallel with the sectional interests that were instrumental in thwarting the desire of the Swann Committee to have research done into intra-ethnic group educational success factors.)

The second dark cloud and clearly a more perturbing one was the evidence emerging of a backlash to the 'ethnic success ethic'. This was apparent not only among Anglo-Australian youngsters (especially those from lower SES groups) but also among ethnic youngsters who were becoming imbued with negative 'Australian' attitudes and values.

The pluralist dilemma then, it would appear, was that as we begin to understand the rules and conditions that govern the game and devise strategies to meet those requirements, someone moves the goalposts and the process has to be begun all over again.

Bagley (Chapter 6) examines the relative contribution of the Canadian and British education systems to the education of ethnic minority children. He is firmly of the view that by accident of circumstance, the Canadian model is one that is more open. Being less competitive in character, the Canadian system appears to offer the child a greater measure of self-fulfilment. Factors in Canada contributing to this are identified, for example, its policy on immigration which targets on the admission of those with specific skills to bring to Canada. Canadian society is less class conscious. As a result it is a more fluid society in which it is easier to adapt and to come through.

Nonetheless, Bagley expresses concern about the quality of the education received in the Canadian system. It may be more open and, therefore, more accessible; but because less emphasis is given to competition and standard, the end product falls short of that achieved by the British system particularly at university level.

In his chapter on 'International Interdependence: Swann's Contribution' (Chapter 7) Lynch contends that the debate about the principles and practice of multicultural education has tended to be confined largely to a national or regional basis within the Western democracies. According to him one of the particular contributions of the Swann Report is that it takes account of 'the global dimension' of multicultural education. He argues that consideration of paranational issues and those affecting Third World countries in particular should have a bearing on the education of children to equip them for the modern world. He reminds us that although cultural diversity has been a 'fact of life' throughout the world for many centuries, the various conceptions given to the nation-state and its relations with minorities within it and those with other countries have tended to rely on a one-way establishment of cultural hegemony based on the maintenance of the status quo. This has been, and continues to be, to the disadvantage of minority groups.

Examining the contribution of national laws, international and regional agreements, such as the United Nations Declaration on Human Rights and the European Convention on Human Rights, Lynch comments that these do no more than provide an 'ethical baseline' on which education must build if cultural diversity is to flourish and if democratic societies are to match up to their ideals.

A truly multicultural education, according to Lynch, should work to provide equality of opportunity for all, regardless of race, creed, sex or class and to foster interest in, and respect for, cultural diversity locally, nationally, regionally and globally. By taking account of the global perspective in its approach to multicultural education, he concludes, the Swann Report represents 'a landmark in pluralism — a tiny first step for mankind in response to an ever more urgent problem'.

Craft (Chapter 8) presents a comprehensive and critical review of current practice, thinking and strategies relating to teacher education in a multicultural society. He argues strongly for the 'permeation' process of multicultural education. Multicultural education in teacher training should not be confined merely to certain option courses, where much of the time it would be preaching to the converted. Acknowledging the limited resources of time and finance in teacher training courses, he argues that much could be done 'simply by altering the range of exemplification to take account of cultural diversity'. Craft asserts that all teachers need an awareness and knowledge of Britain's cultural pluralism, in order that all pupils can be equipped for life in a multicultural society. The challenges that this situation poses should be seen, he concludes, 'not (as) a problem area, but (as) a new avenue of opportunity for teacher education, and one that it would be irresponsible to ignore'.

Cohen (Chapter 9) presents a questionnaire study conducted among first year student-teachers from four different UK higher education institutions. The questionnaire sought to obtain a measure of subjects' ethnocentricity and their 'knowledge of ethnic minorities', to gauge their perceptions of and feelings towards 'visible' ethnic minority groups and their reactions to the concepts of assimilation/integration and cultural pluralism.

From the results Cohen draws what he calls 'tentative' conclusions:

(i) that the majority of his sample of student teachers held perceptions towards ethnic minority people that were positive or neutral in character; only a small proportion of the sample showed antagonistic or hostile attitudes towards ethnic minority groups;

(ii) only a small proportion of the student group had 'wide-ranging' contacts with visible ethnic minority people, yet the majority of the student group subscribed to the cultural-pluralist standpoint;

(iii) considerable ignorance was found of the cultural trappings and beliefs of ethnic minority groups;

(iv) those student teachers showing higher degrees of prejudice tended to have no or only limited experience of visible ethnic minority people and tended to come from areas where few if any such people live.

If his sample were representative of the body of student teachers entering training, then they represented a conducive audience, given the right sort of programme.

Troyna (Chapter 10) seeks, in the aftermath of *Education for All*, to consider the educational response to racial inequality, particularly in what he terms 'predominantly/all-white areas'. He contends that the Report has failed to stimulate effective strategies for tackling the issues arising in those areas.

Charting the efforts of the multicultural education and anti-racist education movements, he points to the progress, though rather limited in his view, that both have made in dealing with the issues as they arise in multiethnic areas. Elsewhere, he contends, there has been little change and education has not made the efforts that it should have. He argues that the anti-racist approach is the better suited to meet that challenge. Nonetheless, he is mindful of the jaundiced view with which it is received in some quarters and suggests that this is in part because of attempts to discredit the movement and in part is self-inflicted.

The issues of racial inequality should not be presented to youngsters in isolation. Instead, they should be presented in the wider context of other disadvantages, notably classism and sexism. Youngsters should not be laden with guilt about 'their racism', but should be brought to see it as part of the power struggle for resources. To treat the problem in any other way would only serve to maintain and harden prejudices.

He refers to an action study conducted in an FE college in an all-white area and feels that the lessons learnt from it could have an important part to play in shaping the way ahead.

Mittler (Chapter 11) suggests that the goal of *Education for All* 'is now at the heart of both (special educational needs and multicultural education) movements and that a joint approach to its realization might be productive'.

Both the product of committees of enquiry, Warnock and Swann stimulated much public and professional debate; they directed attention to children and young people denied equality of opportunity by the educational system and society.

Both reports have important implications for all children not merely for the groups of particular concern; they were at pains to point these out. Both reject the 'deficit' models approach when seeking to explain the needs of children whom the educational system had marginalized. Solutions were best found within a mainstream educational framework ('whole school' approach).

The whole school approach has important implications for teacher education — in both initial and in-service training. Initial training has a key role to play in providing a properly oriented general background for the teaching force and for producing specialists within the various special needs areas. In-service training's role lay in updating existing knowledge and skills and especially at the school level, in the process of communicating these to colleagues. The reports have implications for teaching styles, course content and assessment, teacher-pupil and home-school relationships.

Both reports have not had the degree of commitment one might have expected from central government, especially in the provision of resources. However, Mittler argues, many local initiatives within individual LEAs and schools offer some grounds for optimism, although the 1988 Education Reform Act might appear to stifle some of them.

Mittler calls for special needs and ethnic minority constituencies to come together and 'make a common cause to work for *Education for All*. In that way, he considers, they can best draw attention to their particular and separate requirements within that framework.

Cornford's contribution (Chapter 12) is a revised version of a paper first published as an annex in the Swann Report. He reviews the problems encountered in research into issues as complex and sensitive as those relating to ethnic minority educational achievement.

Quite apart from drawing attention to the dearth of 'first class' researchers working in the field, Cornford examines the politics of research initiatives, the negotiations of access with schools and communities and the issues of data collection — the problems of accuracy and confidentiality and the liberty of the individual.

In this context he also points out the absence of any systematic collection of data — either nationally or locally, that would provide a base that would enable informed judgments to be made on the scale of needs identified from studies.

He makes a strong case for an end to ad hoc research policy. Studies should be on a larger scale than many presently undertaken and he calls too for more standardized research strategies. In this way, localized studies tackling issues in depth could lend themselves to comparison/greater generalization.

In this chapter, suggestions are also put forward for areas worthy of further exploration.

Parekh (Chapter 13) sets out to analyze factors bearing on the production of reports by 'Independent Committees or Commissions of Enquiry appointed by governments' and then, in light of these, to analyze aspects of the Swann Report. Such reports are 'paradoxical documents' being the product of committees appointed with a particular brief to meet.

Committees of enquiry are only set up when an issue of concern has been the subject of public debate and about which no clear cut views and opinions have emerged. Their work is constrained and guided by their remits. This itself is conditioned by 'a distillation of the consensus thrown up by public debate. . . and cannot be ideologically neutral'.

The composition of the Committee is determined by the government of the day. Some members, because of their public or political status carry more weight than others. Members have other commitments which, like time and money, act as constraints.

Arguments are inherently inconclusive and so 'alliances get formed and deals struck'. As a result, the report reflects 'the balance of power and (is) generally a compromise between contending points of view'.

The roles of the chairman and of the civil servants servicing the Committee are critical. A chairman will have to be 'sound' and the civil servants will be well aware of the 'departmental stance' on the issues discussed.

Since the report is a public document, it has to run the gauntlet of presentation by the media where it will be subjected to simplifications, vulgarization and varying degrees of (deliberate) misinterpretation.

When the report is completed the Committee comes to the end of its life. Its report rests in the hands not only of the media but also of the government.

Parekh in his chapter looks at aspects of the Swann Report against that backdrop. These include the setting of the terms of reference, the role and performance of various elements within the Committee, the issues of genetic intelligence, home background, the character of the educational model proposed — multicultural or anti-racist and the abortive attempt to commission a special research study into the degree of influence of home and school factors on academic success or failure within different ethnic groups.

Concluding, Parekh argues that because of the interplay of those various factors the Committee's report 'is necessarily a messy and yet skilfully produced compromise'.

Before inviting the reader to pursue the chapters contained in this book, it would be appropriate to reflect on the Swann Report and to venture an assessment of its contribution to the debate on pluralism.

First and foremost, it seems to me that the Report highlights the imperfections of social science research. Whether these are largely methodological in character — so many approaches are brought to bear on the issues of this era — or whether the infinite variety of individual perspectives on and experiences of life and the social processes is inevitably problematic.

The Report offers, in my view, a very balanced verdict on the inconsistencies in the data available and of their interpretation on matters relating to the education of ethnic minority children. And yet in face of these, it has tried to be pragmatic and, at the same time, visionary.

The title of the Report *Education for All* offers the direction that things should take if we are to develop a truly plural society. By a truly plural society I mean, and I think this comes out fully in the Report, one in which the full range of cultural experiences, expectations and aspirations of the myriad of individuals that make up our society are given recognition by others. The Swann Report challenges not only individuals and individual ethnic groups but also the LEAs, the DES, community relations groups and other interested parties to come together to strive to achieve a better, fairer and juster society.

Looking back on the Report some four years since it was published one is prompted to ask whether it has achieved as much as one would have hoped. Has the government's response been as full as might have been expected? Have people come together? Has the Report promoted a debate?

Four years on, it is still too early to make a full assessment, but I would venture to suggest that the Report's impact has not been negligible. The Report may not represent the tablet of stone that the impatient may have wished for, yet could one have expected it to be one? Has it moved the government? Answers here would depend largely on one's political/ideological stance.

Experiments and debate go on in the name of pluralism. People meet together to exchange points of view and to discuss the issues; and fresh issues have emerged since the Report was published. Whether all the initiatives that have been undertaken since are directly attributable to the Report is unlikely. Yet the debate should be better informed because of it.

What *Education for All* offers, what it represents is indeed a landmark towards better things. It took account of the bearings that had already been discerned, disposed of some, firmed up others and pointed the way ahead. In that sense *Education for All* represents a landmark in pluralism and one with which I am proud to be associated. The chapters presented in this book come from a variety of sources and represent the thoughts and views of writers at work in different continents. All address issues or aspects relating to pluralism as perceived in those countries and are viewed through or from the landmark that the Swann Report has provided. In themselves they reflect perspectives on one of the major challenges facing late twentieth-century societies at home and abroad.

Reference

DEPARTMENT OF EDUCATION AND SCIENCE (1985) *Education for All: Report of the Committee of Enquiry into the Education of Children from Ethnic Minority Groups* (The Swann Report), Cmnd. 9453, London, HMSO.
DEPARTMENT OF EDUCATION AND SCIENCE (1987) *Education in Schools,* London, HMSO.

Chapter 2

Equality of Opportunity, Multiculturalism, Anti-racism and 'Education for All'

John Rex

Three distinct or distinguishable ideals are posited in the debate about the education of immigrant or ethnic minority children in British schools. These are equality of opportunity, multiculturalism and anti-racism. Too often they are confused or lumped together under the single label 'multicultural education'. In the case of the Swann Report (DES, 1985) they are all discussed but then subordinated to the evasive and perhaps misleading notion of 'education for all'. It is desirable, therefore, if we are to clarify the debate and assess the possibility of implementing the Swann recommendations, that we should say what all these ideals mean and what would have to be done to realize them.

The goal of equality of opportunity does not imply the most radical egalitarianism. The radical egalitarian position would be that which envisages that all children have equal abilities and that if there is equality of outcomes this must be because of environmental conditions of some kind. To correct such inequalities it would be necessary to manipulate the environment not merely of the extra-familial world but the family environment itself, or at least to seek to remedy inequalities arising in the home by remedial work in schools.

Few social scientists, however, would defend such a radical position. Nearly all would accept that there are some hereditary differences of ability and other differences due to subtle and intractable environmental causes. The most that can be done, therefore, is to ensure that other environmental situations are not imposed on these, reinforcing existing differences of performance or even giving advantages to the less able and disadvantaging the able.

The notion of equality of opportunity which it is realistic to discuss is that which refers to the elimination of differences in the opportunities offered to children of different class, racial and religious backgrounds. The British education system is a severely competitive one oriented to the attainment of certificates, and, however much it may be necessary to have *another* debate about the desirability of this system, the issue of equality of opportunity is that of ensuring that children of different class, ethnic and racial backgrounds have the same chances of success in selection and examination.

The issue of social class complicates the debate about equality of opportunity for ethnic minority children. What most of those who are concerned with ethnic equality wish to ensure is that a child should have the same chance whatever his/her ethnic background. But, if such a chance were ensured, the ethnic minority child would enjoy an advantage over the native British working class child because it is an empirical fact that educational life chances are unequal as between social classes in Britain. Of course, the situation is more complex still because ethnic minority children are also divided in class terms, but it may well be the case that belonging to an ethnic minority group has an effect of a similar kind on all classes. If the inegalitarian effects of ethnicity and reactions to ethnicity are eliminated, therefore, it might well be the case that minority children would be at an advantage over their British working class classmates. Inevitably, therefore, the raising of the question of equality of opportunity for minority children raises a parallel question with regard to class. Equal opportunity policies for ethnic minorities point the way to more general equal opportunity problems which deal with social class. We will deal here with the conditions necessary for the attainment of equality of opportunity for ethnic minority children recognizing that this other debate will inevitably be opened up. The danger is that if the need for this is not recognized there would be a racial backlash amongst working-class parents.

There are, in any case, many problems in education which the promotion of equality of opportunity does not solve and this must be recognized. If we ensure that ethnic minority children have an equal chance of being in the 20 per cent of children who attain 'A' or 'O' levels, there is still the question of what happens to the children who are in the other 80 per cent. In theory all these children are given an education which enables them to attain the fullest possible development, given their abilities and the notion of equality of opportunity would imply that ethnic minority children should have no additional obstacles placed in the way of their development. The issues here, however, are subtle and difficult. Remedial education, for example, is in theory an aid to equality of opportunity, but the classification of children as 'remedial' can mean a labelling process by means of which discrimination is practised against particular groups. There is also little doubt that many other processes of streaming, setting and banding can have similar discriminatory effects. Wherever such processes operate the ideal of equality of opportunity demands that ethnicity as such should not prevent an individual child from achieving the most favourable outcome.

From what has been said here it should be clear that the ideal of equality of opportunity is a limited one, but it is also realistic. If it is confused with other educational ideals the likelihood is that something less than equality of opportunity will be achieved. Thus if someone says that he or she is only interested in equality of outcome or with the 'education of the whole child', this could mean that the real existing disadvantages in a competitive system were not seriously scrutinized. Equality of opportunity, of course, is not all that could be asked of an education system. It can also be judged by other educational standards. But, within the existing system in Britain, equal chances in a competitive system are vital for the ethnic minority child.

Before we return to a detailed consideration of the obstacles which have to be overcome, we should now consider the definition and practical meaning of the other two ideals, 'multiculturalism' and 'anti-racism'.

Multiculturalism is now a widely accepted ideal in the educational system and it would appear to refer to the provision of education in the language and culture of minority children along with their education in the language and culture of the host society. How far is this an ideal to be sought after apart from the question of equality of opportunity?

Many immigrants, it should be noted, do not expect, and sometimes do not want, their children to be educated in their own minority culture. Having made the decision to migrate they want to ensure above all that their children get on in the society of settlement. Arguably too much stress on their cultural difference might act as an obstacle to this process of 'getting on'. For such immigrants education in the minority culture can only be a secondary goal. Given that their children get the opportunity to learn English and to learn about British culture and institutions, they may still be concerned that their children and the children's relations with their home should not be scarred by a rapid process of change and may wish that they receive assistance in helping to maintain and transmit their own minority culture. This, however, is a far cry from asking that their children should receive an alternative education in schools.

A much stronger demand for the maintenance of minority culture is likely to be made if there is a real prospect of return to the homeland. In this case the parents will want to ensure that their children are not at a disadvantage when returning home. This is often the case with Turkish immigrants in Germany and in other countries where a minority consists of migrant rather than immigrant workers. Not surprisingly the European Economic Community has seen at least mother-tongue maintenance as a right of migrant workers which it calls on member states to guarantee.

In some countries, however, the notion has gained ground that the society of settlement should itself be transformed into a multicultural society. Thus, in Canada, after the case for bilingualism and biculturalism had been recognized in Quebec, the rights of multiculturalism were envisaged as extending to other immigrant communities. A similar argument has been put forward in Britain particularly with regard to the Afro-Caribbean, South Asian and East African Asian minorities. It is no longer argued that immigrants must conform to a monolithic British culture. What is encouraged instead is what Roy Jenkins as Home Secretary called 'cultural diversity' coupled with mutual tolerance.[1]

I have argued elsewhere that the concept of multiculturalism is all too easily misinterpreted unless it is coupled with the notion of equality of opportunity. There are, unfortunately, many who argue for multiculturalism because they believe in a segregated and unequal society. In this sense the South African doctrine of apartheid represents multiculturalism par excellence.

In order to clarify the notion of multiculturalism as I wish to use it, it is useful to distinguish between the public and the private domains. The public domain refers to the world of politics, employment and the market place. It is governed in Britain by a long fought for civic culture based upon the idea of equal rights. In some other countries this has meant that each ethnic group has a defined share in the control of public resources. This is the case in Quebec and in Belgium. But in Britain all individuals are thought of as entitled to equal access to those resources and positions of power.

There cannot, in the conception of a multicultural society employed here, be any question of undermining this public pattern of equality. Nor realistically can we talk of, say, Afro-Caribbean or South Asian minorities having a defined share of control. The danger is that if we were to go down this path the minorities would be given an unequal share, and that what we should have is a system of apartheid. It is true that some minority politicians do campaign for special representation as in the case of the Black Sections movement in the Labour Party, but this does not mean that these politicians are right. Unwittingly they are working for a differentiated society which will be unequal.

Of course the notion of equality of opportunity in the public domain does not mean that we should rule out the monitoring of occupancy of positions of power and authority. The object of such monitoring, however, is purely to see to it that there are objective signs of an equal opportunity policy functioning. If minorities are not represented in appropriate percentages then the various processes of selection and appointment must be checked to see whether discriminatory obstacles of an overt or covert kind stand in the way of minorities. This is quite different from what happens in societies which have an agreement about the division of power in the public domain.

If, however, there is only one culture in the public domain and that culture is the culture of equal opportunity, there is no reason at all why any society should insist that the norms which govern familial and community life, including such matters as marriage arrangements and religious practices, should be the same for all. Multiculturalism here recognizes that the maintenance of separate culture patterns is essential to the psychological sense of identity of the various minority groups. According to its tenets every group has the right to practise its own communal culture and all should learn to respect the culture of others.

There are, of course, difficulties in maintaining the distinction between public and private domains. In particular the education system seems to straddle the two domains. It is at once the means through which moral values of a communal kind may be transmitted and the means whereby children are selected for adult roles. A multicultural education policy will therefore be concerned both with encouraging variety and tolerance on the private level and with ensuring that the common culture of equal opportunity is maintained in the selection processes. To put this in another way, the ideal of multiculturalism must be pursued along with that of equality of opportunity.

The third ideal which we have to discuss is that of anti-racism. This is a very popular term and one which is very loosely used. Sociologists in the past had distinguished between racism and racialism, maintaining that racism referred to *theories* of racial inequality and that racialism referred to *actions* of a hostile or discriminatory kind. The notion of anti-racism suggests opposition to both of these. 'Racism' refers to actual racist attacks, to the denigration of the other race, to unfair discriminatory practices and to statements, theories and beliefs which lead to the perception of the other race as unequal.

The actual meaning of anti-racist educational policies is one which has emerged as a result of dissatisfaction with what is popularly called 'multicultural education'. There are two aspects in which such policies have failed to give satisfaction to minority communities. On the one hand, as we have seen, multiculturalism may be advocated without any consideration of whether it is coupled with equality of opportunity. Another way of putting this would be to say that it does not deal with racial discrimination. Those who advocate anti-racist education, therefore, often mean that policies should ensure that racial discrimination is prevented or that there should be equality of opportunity regardless of race or ethnicity. Secondly, however, anti-racism has a moral purpose going beyond multicultural education. It seeks to ensure that the actions, the beliefs, the words, and even the thoughts of one section of the community, are not hostile and unfair to other sections. To this end it calls both for specific programmes of moral and political education and for a reconsideration of all teaching practices and material which might propagate racism.

A society is conceivable in which the central political beliefs which are supported by the authorities are anti-racist. In such a society teachers might be required to instil anti-racism as a part of moral and political education and there might be a deliberate attempt to raise consciousness and increase awareness of covert forms of racism. Where this is not the case the advocacy of anti-racist policies in education and of racism awareness training takes the form of a political struggle in which opponents of racism seek to change the beliefs and practices of others against opposition and without explicit support from central government or from the leaders of political parties. It is because this is largely the case in Britain that the struggle for anti-racist education does not win support of the kind which is accorded to multicultural education taken by itself or even to equal opportunity policies.

So far we have been considering ideals and trying to make them explicit. What we now have to do is to indicate what precise policies would be necessary in schools to implement the three ideals. As we shall see, they overlap in part, but it is also interesting to note that each adds certain policies of its own to the common core. What will be advocated here as a policy of 'multicultura education' in the broadest sense will involve all the policies which are required to realize the three ideals.

John Rex

The first consideration in bringing about equality of opportunity is that of choice of school. Ideally, of course, all schools should be capable of producing equal results. In practice, however, there is a considerable difference in quality between schools, particularly between those in the inner city and those in the suburbs. This raises the question of bussing and, more generally, of catchment areas.

Bussing in Britain has not proved to be acceptable either to parents in the 'white' suburbs or to ethnic minority parents. Whatever gains may be made by a small number of minority children bussed to better suburban schools, the policy also involves serious losses in that, given its artificial nature, it draws attention to minority children as a problem and may serve to reinforce racial hostility. What has to be done, therefore, is to work towards the elimination of discrimination and segregation in housing and at the same time to bring about greater equality in standards between schools.

In some cases the problem has not, however, been simply due to educational segregation following housing segregation. Catchment areas may in fact be so devised that, say, all Afro-Caribbean children are directed to the same schools when it would be quite possible to redraw the boundaries so that some of them at least had the opportunity of attending racially mixed schools. Still worse there have been some suggestions that such children might be concentrated for schooling purposes even though they are relatively dispersed in the population. Obviously all allocation schemes require careful scrutiny and it is vital that parents should be able to appeal against allocations and exercise a degree of freedom of choice.

The next very important set of considerations relates to the use of English and minority languages. From the point of view of equality of opportunity it is essential that children be equipped as early as possible with a good command of English, since that is the language in terms of which their educational performances will ultimately be judged. At the same time minority languages may be used to facilitate early education and their maintenance may be of value in establishing a harmonious relationship between home and school.

The following are policies with regard to language which appear to be necessary:

1 Instruction of non-English speaking children at the point of the entry into the system, not in order to segregate them permanently, but in order that they should not be prevented at an early stage from learning to learn by a situation of linguistic and cultural shock.
2 Instruction in mother tongue so that children should not have to pay the price of not being able to communicate with their parents for any success which they may have in education. This is necessary not simply to promote multiculturalism, but because of its relevance to equality of opportunity.
3 The early introduction of English as a second language with adequate arrangements to ensure that time spent on acquiring English does not prevent progress in normal school subjects.

4 Second stage English instruction to ensure that children are given not merely
   minimal English, but sufficient command of the language to enable them
   to cope with study at whatever level they are otherwise capable of reaching.

What we are arguing for here is the promotion of effective bilingualism with
emphasis being placed on a command of the language which is necessary for
educational achievement. This is obviously the case with Asian children whose
home language is not English but it is also the case with Afro-Caribbean
children from Creole speaking homes. It could well be the case that these latter
children suffer severe culture shock on being immediately forced in school
to operate in standard English and that their mobility to make the transition
from Creole to English results in their being classified as disruptive or backward.

   If language is an important element in promoting equality of opportunity
so also is culture. Obviously all children will need to learn about British culture
both in the sense of the public culture discussed above and as the culture of
the majority in the society of settlement. At the same time, however, there
is a real danger in a situation in which the child's own home-culture is either
denigrated or lost entirely. In such circumstances children may have the
psychological resources and the sense of identity which is necessary for successful
educational progress. Arguably the relative success of Asian children in schools
has to do with the psychological security provided by a strong home culture
and that in this respect they enjoy an advantage over Afro-Caribbean children
and British working-class children whose home culture is less secure and
distinct.

   If then minority culture is of value to children entering a competitive
educational system the question arises whether subject matter relating to this
culture should be included in the syllabus. In principle it clearly should be
so that children are not deprived of their own inheritance and can see that
it has recognition within the curriculum and within the value system of British
society. What has to be avoided, however, is paternalistic teaching of minority
cultures at a low level (Williams, 1979) which could have the effect of
denigrating rather than strengthening them. Ideally children should receive
this part of their education from those who believe in it, preferably themselves
drawn from the minority. If this cannot be done it might be best for this type
of education to be provided in supplementary schools run by the community
but subsidized by the state.

   It is necessary if minority cultures are to be taken seriously that they should
be taught not only in the low-status uncertificated parts of the syllabus but
in the prestigious certificated part. The child's self-respect will be enhanced
and he will be more strongly motivated to succeed if it is clear that the culture,
language and history with which he is associated by his group membership
should have equality of status with, say, French language, literature and history.
There is considerable scope within the GCSE system for the teaching of Asian
languages, history and culture and of Afro-Caribbean history and culture.
This development is important obviously from the point of view of

multiculturalism and anti-racism. It is also important from the standpoint of equality of opportunity.

Given that the minority child in school operates in conditions of linguistic and cultural security the next essential is that he/she should be fairly treated in all the processes of selection, streaming, banding and setting which are a normal part of procedures in secondary education in particular. There is a considerable amount of evidence and the Eggleston report (1986) emphasizes that stereotypical judgments of an implicitly racist type operate during these processes. What has to be done is that the outcome of all selection processes should be monitored and if it appears that minority children do less well than white British children investigations should be made of the causes of their disadvantage. At the same time teachers who operate the processes should be educated regarding the dangers of racist stereotyping.

Several other factors important from the standpoint of anti-racism are also highly relevant to the promotion of equality of opportunity. Obviously if a minority child is attacked or abused or if his culture is denigrated in the curriculum he or she cannot be expected to achieve high standards. To this end educational policies should ensure:

  (i) the elimination from the syllabus in all subjects of all those elements derived from an earlier historical period in which the culture of minorities is denigrated and a positive emphasis in the syllabus on the histories and cultures of their countries as an important part of the education of all children;
 (ii) a positive commitment on the part of the school to the elimination of racism through the syllabus as a whole, through specific teaching against racism and through school practices which treat racism as a disciplinary offence;
(iii) the employment of qualified school-teachers from the minority groups and a guarantee that they will be promoted on merit.

The list of points mentioned above dealing with the allocation of school places, the linguistic needs of minority children, the support of minority cultures, the use of fair processes of selection and a deliberate attack on racism constitute a comprehensive policy of equality of opportunity. Arguably this is also a policy of multiculturalism and anti-racism. We should, however, also consider the implications of a policy which puts its primary emphasis on these other ideals.

A policy of multiculturalism would emphasize the desirability of fostering other cultures for its own sake, apart from the question of equality of opportunity. It would do so both because of the psychological benefits which it brings to minority children and because it is thought that our society should in some sense be multicultural. It would imply the provision of special education in minority cultures at all levels in the school and the revision of all teaching material in all subjects to ensure that it was not tied to a single monolithic majority culture. If the aim was to create a multicultural society and not simply to help the minority child the full multicultural syllabus would be taught to all children in all schools and not simply to minority children or in schools with large numbers of such children.

Multiculturalism specified in this way would not be universally supported either in the majority or in the minority communities. Many white British parents in white suburban schools, for example, would regard education about Sikhism, Islam or Afro-Caribbean culture as irrelevant to their own children's education and on the other hand some Asian and West Indian parents might feel that their children were held back from learning things which were essential to achievement in British society (Stone, 1981). Nonetheless, there is considerable support for multicultural education and its supporters do make the demands listed in the previous paragraph.

It needs to be emphasized again, however, that the support which exists for multicultural education includes that of many who are quite content that minorities should be offered something different or inferior, or that majorities should be given an exotic caricature of minority culture. The numbers of those who support multiculturalism in a situation of equality of opportunity is much smaller and it is to be expected that the policies which they prefer will run into considerable opposition. It is not an obvious goal in itself and is perhaps less so than the goal of equality of opportunity.

Anti-racism is the third ideal we have to consider and it is possible to envisage a policy in relation to the position of minority children in schools which puts this rather than equality of opportunity or multiculturalism at the centre of our thinking. As we saw above, however, it has many implications. It implies opposition to racial attacks, to the deliberate denigration of other races and ethnic groups, to syllabus material which has the effect of denigrating them, to biases based on stereotyping in selection processes and to the conscious and unconscious use of racial assumptions in any thinking, policy making or statement. To cure a society or its educational system of all signs of racism is therefore a considerable undertaking.

The major task of an anti-racist programme in education should be the elimination of conscious and unconscious discrimination in provisions of allocation and selection, that is to say a fight against what sociologists used to call *racialism*. Such a programme would deal, not with thoughts and ideas, but with actions which were to the detriment of minority children. Of course it might be shown that stereotypical thinking was one of the causes of discrimination and that a process of teacher education in 'racism awareness' was necessary, but it is essential to emphasize that the object of anti-racist policy is ultimately the control of actions and not thought-control.

With this said, it must nonetheless be recognized that traditional syllabuses in an imperial metropolis inevitably contain much explicitly and implicitly racist material and, once this is acknowledged, it will be necessary to review all textbooks and teaching material with a view to bringing about a gradual improvement in what is taught. A programme to achieve this needs to be carried out subject by subject and on a national basis. It is best not left to the ad hoc inspirations of local teachers who might well lack the necessary authority to bring about change and whose efforts in this direction might simply provoke a backlash from teachers accustomed to the old books.

'Racial awareness' or, better, 'racism awareness' training of teachers is another aspect of anti-racist policy. Properly organized and sensitively practised, such training can do much to produce critical awareness of the dangers of racism. What has to be avoided however is a situation in which teachers are treated as delinquents who are in some sense being punished for their racist crimes. An essential ingredient of a programme of this kind is that it is based upon some degree of consensus and that it is backed by established authority.

Racial attacks and racial abuse would necessarily become offences under an anti-racist policy, whether they occurred amongst pupils, amongst teachers or amongst administrators. Again, however, it is necessary to point out that such programmes are more likely to be effective if there is a clear consensus behind them and if they have the support of established authority. One could imagine for example an effective programme of action being taken where a minority of children had started a campaign of 'Paki-bashing' against Asian children. In this case the offenders would be publicly punished and the notions of the offence made clear. What is less likely to be effective is a programme designed to catch out teachers and administrators for some slip of the tongue deemed by some to be racist. There is evidence of anti-racist policy being implemented in this way in some London boroughs and it has, in the event, done more harm than good to the cause of anti-racism.

It may seem to some that the above paragraphs are unduly tentative in supporting policies designed to achieve the objectives of anti-racism. This, however, is not the case. There is every reason for supporting anti-racism as an objective in education. What has to be avoided, however, is a naively idealistic sociology which assumes that structures are best altered by changing ideas at random. The effect of proceeding in this way is simply to exacerbate hostility and to allow the opponents of anti-racism to show that they have authority on their side.

One way in which anti-racist policy can gain in authority is by the explicit insertion of teaching against racism as a part of the syllabus. It is generally recognized that, apart from training in literacy, in languages and in science, an important part of the core curriculum should be that which is concerned with moral and political education. The syllabuses for such education in a liberal society should in general involve an open-ended exploration of alternative ideas (amongst other things a programme of multiculturalism demands that such syllabuses should be open-ended). But just as there is a consensus that murder or the deliberate inflicting of pain on others are not matters up for debate, so, on the political level there should be no debate about the desirability of anti-racism. So, within the syllabus of political education to which all children should be subject the teaching of anti-racism and of the ways of combating racism should play a central part. Learning about anti-racism should be seen as part of a process of socialization into membership of British society.

Multicultural education itself also serves the ends of anti-racism. If it is conceived not simply as a means of helping minority children to maintain their culture, but as part of the education of all children then the effect must be that those children learn to understand and respect others who have different cultures and characteristics. Together with explicit teaching against racism such education in minority cultures can do as much as anything to create an anti-racist or non-racial society.

What we have seen here is that the problems of the minority child in the British educational system involve three problem areas and three overlapping ideals. This was not, however, the way in which these problems were approached by the Rampton and Swann committees which were set up to deal with these problems (DES, 1981 and 1985).

There were two sets of problems which led to the appointment of the Rampton Committee. These were the problems of West Indian underachievement and that of the presence in British schools of Asian children with distinctly different languages and cultures. Clearly these were different problems and only racist assumptions could justify their being treated as one.

The Rampton Committee was in no sense a radical body, even though it was not a normal establishment body. It was chaired by Anthony Rampton of the Lambeth Community Relations Council and included those whom the government saw as being key figures in race relations work. Amongst those appointed were a number of black members, none of whom could be said to be a known radical.

The Committee first of all agreed that West Indian children were doing badly in school and then split between those who said this was due to the racism of the school and those who said it was due to the failure of the West Indian family and community. The eventual report was a compromise between the two groups, leaning slightly towards the side which blamed the schools.

The new Conservative government which received the report saw it as dangerously radical and leaked a story to this effect to the *Times Educational Supplement*. Additionally, and for personal reasons, Rampton resigned and it was left to the incoming Secretary of State for Education and Science, Sir Keith Joseph, to decide on the future of the Committee. His response was to appoint a neutral respected establishment figure in Lord Swann as the new Chairman. Several members resigned and several new ones were appointed.

What the Committee could have done was to put aside the debate about underachievement and get on with the business of deciding:

1 What factors in the educational system militated against equality of opportunity for minority children.
2 To what extent Britain was a multicultural society and whether it required special and different education for minority children.
3 To what extent British society was racist and whether anything could be done about this in the schools.

In fact the Committee was still preoccupied with the multicultural debate and that remained central. Critics of Rampton had questioned the statistics offered in its report, claiming that if such factors as parents' occupation and education were controlled, the alleged differences would disappear. West Indian immigrants in Britain, it was argued, came from overwhelmingly poor backgrounds and the differences in their children's performance reflected this (Reeves and Chevannes, 1982). To such criteria the Swann Committee responded by arguing that even where controls were introduced differences remained.

Addressing the underachievement problem, the Committee rejected the idea that the differences reflected differences in IQ and argued that differential performances for all children was associated with differences in socioeconomic status. Minority children were seen as sharing in the general disadvantage of working-class children, but they were doubly disadvantaged because they had to face racial discrimination and prejudice. Such discrimination and prejudice arose outside the school as well as within it. The schools could affect the outside world by creating a new generation which was less prejudiced, but the prime aim of anti-racist educational policy should be to eliminate prejudice within the school itself. This was something which could be tackled by what the Committee at first called multicultural education, but then came to call 'Education for All'.

So far as racism is concerned the Swann Report distinguished between malign prejudice and harmless likes and dislikes. Malign prejudice occurs when someone is evaluated on the basis of assumed characteristics in advance and by implication without adequate information on which to base a rational judgment. It is the task of education to overcome prejudice.

Racism is seen as entering the educational system through teachers' stereotypes, but it is often covered up by a claim on the part of teachers that they are 'colour-blind'. It is recognized that sometimes overt prejudice is not the issue, but that the whole system functions to produce inequality (institutional racism). The school has also to encounter the general climate of racism in the society. It has to prevent racial attacks and racial name-calling.

All in all, the Swann Committee admits the pervasiveness of racism in society in general and in schools. Its discussion at this point appears to point to the need for a specifically anti-racist strategy as the centre of a policy for minority children in schools. The question is whether this anti-racist strategy is sufficiently included in the proposed policy of education for all.

The question of multiculturalism is discussed in the two opening chapters of the Swann Report. As the Report sees it, British society must not be thought of as a plural society in which groups contend against one another for power; nor should it be seen as an assimilationist society. As it says:

> We consider that a multiracial society such as ours would function more effectively and harmoniously on the basis of pluralism which enables, expects and encourages members to participate fully in shaping the society as a whole within a framework of commonly accepted values, practices and procedures whilst also allowing and,

where necessary, assisting the ethnic minority communities in maintaining their distinct ethnic identities within their common framework.

What the report has to say on multiculturalism and the multicultural society then is very much in accord with what has been argued earlier in this chapter. It couples the cultivation of difference with the maintenance of a core of common political values.

What the Swann Report does now is to argue that the overcoming of disadvantage, anti-racism and multiculturalism are all best accomplished in a programme which it calls 'Education for All'. The reasons for the choice of this all-inclusive title are to emphasize that the policy is desirable not only on specific grounds (for example, overcoming disadvantage) but on general educational grounds and that it is a policy affecting the education of all children.

'Education for All' includes the following elements:

1 It involves emphasis on the international dimension of education.
2 It seeks to take advantage of the cultural variety of Britain and to use this for educational purposes.
3 It involves education against racism.
4 It aims at the elimination of any racist procedures in school practice.
5 It involves applying these educational policies to *all* schools and not simply to inner city or immigrant majority schools.
6 It nonetheless requires that the specific needs of minority children should be met.
7 It calls for a systematic review of the syllabus to eliminate racism and encourage multiculturalism.
8 It accepts the necessity of political education in schools including racism as a topic.

One issue on which the Swann Report takes a surprising stand however is its opposition, in its section on language, to any form of bilingual education, to teaching of other subjects in mother-tongue, or indeed to mother-tongue teaching as such in schools. What it does do is to accept the place of minority languages in the curriculum, leaving mother-tongue maintenance to the community.

Taken as a whole the Swann Report may be said to deal with the implementation of all three of the ideals which we have discussed in the first part of this chapter. It does deal with equality of opportunity although it discusses this largely in terms of the alleged underachievement of West Indian children. It deals with multicultural education in the strange form of arguing that all children must learn about minority cultures. And, finally, it firmly accepts that there is racism both within schools and in society outside and emphasizes political education which makes racism and anti-racism an explicit topic.

The main weakness of the report lies in its failure to accept the necessity of using minority languages in school and its consequent vague proposals for teaching English with the aid of support teachers. Clearly non-English speaking children will suffer if their needs are not met more systematically. If constructive language proposals were added to the report's recommendations it would go far to setting out at least in general terms a programme for the realization of our three ideals.

It is unfortunate that the report decides to cover up the Radical nature of what is proposing under the rather empty title *Education for All*. All this seems to suggest is that hitherto 'all' have not received education or that education has only been thought of as for some. Probably this title was chosen in order not to be provocative and to win general support by suggesting that the arguments for the programme were educational rather than political. It is possible to appreciate this argument in the light of some of the provocative anti-racist policies pursued by some of the London boroughs which have produced a backlash, but there is no getting away from the fact that a programme designed to deal with the problems of the minority child in schools has to be political.

The one remaining question to be asked about the Swann Report is simply 'Will its findings and recommendations be taken seriously?' So far it looks as though the government has no intention of making extra financial resources available for this purpose. If this continues to be the case, however, it may still be asked whether something cannot be done within the existing resource constraints. The answer to this question is a positive one and the initiatives taken by local authorities in developing multicultural policy statements and having them discussed are at least a beginning. A movement for multicultural, equal and anti-racist education has been started and, even without central leadership, this movement will have an effect on our schools.

Unfortunately the situation is far short of one in which the authority of government is placed firmly behind a programme for 'multicultural education' or 'equality of opportunity' or 'anti-racism' or 'education for all'. Government statements in response to Swann have been evasive and have not given any resources towards the implementation of its programme. At the other extreme, moreover, some local authorities governed by black and Left councils have embarked on programmes of anti-racism of a naive punitive kind which have produced a considerable backlash against them. It is possible that these extreme programmes may be a necessary phase and that eventually there will be local authorities which pioneer policies along the lines suggested in this chapter and, partially at least, covered by the Swann recommendations.

Note

1 Roy Jenkins, speech on the extension of the Race Relations Act, 23 May 1966.

References

DEPARTMENT OF EDUCATION AND SCIENCE (1981) *West Indian Children in Our Schools: Report of the Committee of Enquiry into the Education of Children from Ethnic Minority Groups* (The Rampton Report), Cmnd. 8273, London, HMSO.

DEPARTMENT OF EDUCATION AND SCIENCE (1985) *Education for All: Report of the Committee of Enquiry into the Education of Children from Ethnic Minority Groups* (The Swann Report), Cmnd. 9453, London, HMSO.

EGGLESTON, J. (1986) *Education for Some: The Educational and Vocational Experiences of 14–17 year old Members of Minority Groups,* London, Tavistock.

REEVES, F. and CHEVANNES, M. (1982) 'The underachievement of Rampton', *Multi-Cultural Education*, London, Fontana.

WILLIAMS, J. (1979) 'Perspectives on the multicultural curriculum', *The Social Science Teacher*, 8, 4.

120844

Chapter 3

The Origins of the Ethnocentric Curriculum

Sally Tomlinson

Since the publication of the Swann Report (DES, 1985) the focus of multicultural education in Britain has moved from issues concerning the education of ethnic minority pupils, to issues concerning the education of all pupils who are growing up in an ethnically diverse society. Although the Report provided evidence that many schools regarded issues of multicultural education, global awareness and race and racism as remote or irrelevant to their curriculum (*ibid.*, pp. 243–314), there is now evidence that a number of all-white LEAs, and those with few or concentrated numbers of ethnic minorities, are realizing the importance of beginning to change their curriculum in a multicultural direction and to assess the values and beliefs which underpin their educational activities.

In particular, DES provision of Educational Support Grants over the years 1986/88 has resulted in the setting up of a variety of curriculum projects in all-white areas[1], — and 'teaching and planning of the curriculum in a multi-ethnic society' was included as a national priority area for in-service teacher education in 1986 (DES, 1986). This has encouraged many teachers to review their professional activities, giving consideration as to how best to reflect a culturally and ethnically diverse Britain, and to help pupils become realistically aware of the rest of the world.

Chapter 6 of the Swann Report — the core chapter discussing the meaning of 'Education for All' — was clear that 'offering all pupils a good, relevant, and up-to-date education for life in Britain and the world as it is today' (DES, 1985, p. 315) would involve considerable change in a school curriculum which reflected ethnocentric[2] values and attitudes inappropriate both to the changed nature of British society and to Britain's place in the world. This view echoed that put forward in 1977 by the DES that:

> The curriculum appropriate to our imperial past cannot meet the requirements of modern Britain. (DES, 1977, p. 4)

The recognition that the curriculum was, and still is, in many ways influenced by the beliefs and values of a period of imperial enthusiasm and a final expansion of the British Empire—a period which coincided with the development of mass education[3]—has, however, been afforded little discussion. Yet it was during this period of Empire, that many aspects of what is now regarded as 'British culture' came to be reflected in the school curriculum, underpinned by a set of values still regarded by many as 'traditional' British values. Some of these values were and are highly questionable in terms of democracy, tolerance and social and racial justice. They reflected a dominant world-view which was not 'traditional' at all but was created from the 1880s by dominant social and political elites and spread, by education and by imperial propaganda (MacKenzie, 1984, p. 2) into popular consciousness. This world-view was one in which imperialism, a revived militarism, and unpleasant racial beliefs derived from social Darwinism fused to create a popular consciousness that the British 'race' had a particular superiority *vis-à-vis* the rest of the world. Several historians of British society have dated the period from the 1880s to the 1950s as a time when a 'core ideology' of imperialism emerged, characterized by values of moral superiority, race patriotism and xenophobia (Field, 1982; MacKenzie, 1984). Readers of popular newspapers in the Britain of the 1980s could hardly doubt that feelings of moral superiority and offensive views of other nations are still part of 'traditional' British values.[4]

It is this world-view, and these inappropriate values, reflected in parts of the school curriculum, which the Swann Committee characterized as ethnocentric, and which led the committee to declare a concern with 'bringing about a fundamental reorientation of the attitudes which condition the selection of curriculum materials', to help pupils 'analyze critically and rationally the nature of British society in a global context' (DES, 1985, p. 324).

There is currently, however, much tension between those who believe that there is an unproblematic British heritage—a set of values which should be unquestionably reflected in the school curriculum, and those who consider that it is now time to disentangle the curriculum from the imperial past. To the latter, there is undoubtedly a need to develop a curriculum based on a more appropriate, but as yet undefined, set of values. The tension was demonstrated in a statement by Sir Keith Joseph, on his last day as Secretary of State for Education (20 May 1985) in which he commented on government educational policy for an ethnically mixed society.

> British history and cultural traditions are, or will become, at least part
> of the cultural heritage of all who live in this country . . . schools should
> be responsible for trying to transmit British culture—enriched as it
> has been by so many traditions. (Joseph, 1986, p. 8)

Some reaction to this unproblematic view of British culture was that 'many black people and no few whites regard the majority culture as based upon and upholding prejudiced and discriminatory structures and behaviour' (Klein, 1986).

Clearly, these opposing views cannot be reconciled without a wider understanding of the values implicit in popular notions of British culture and heritage and their reflection in education and the school curriculum. This is a task both curriculum theorists and exponents of multicultural education have avoided, perhaps because too close a scrutiny of 'the stories we tell ourselves' (Inglis, 1985) about our cultural heritage would be too uncomfortable.

This chapter briefly examines some influences on the state school curriculum in the late nineteenth and early twentieth century — a period when a consciousness of Empire and a popular imperialism was at its height, and a value system was emerging based on a militaristic patriotism and a 'national pride' which by definition excluded non-whites, colonials and foreigners. The influence of public school values on the developing school curriculum, textbooks which reflected an imperial purpose and patriotic fervour, and juvenile literature which became an early mass medium for disseminating imperial values, are discussed. The aim of this chapter is to begin to probe the strength of imperial values and beliefs, which, by underpinning the school curricula and educational activities, have influenced several generations of white adults in twentieth-century Britain, including parents of children currently in our schools. As many people, including many teachers, are not aware of the extent of the British Empire, a list of territories acquired over a 300 year period, and dates of autonomy of these territories, is included as an appendix.

History, Values and Curriculum

Educationalists have to be careful when linking historical and contemporary events. Silver (1977) and others have rightly pointed out the dangers of 'raiding history' to prove contemporary points. However, curriculum theorists have, until relatively recently, been more inclined to neglect an historical dimension in their work, than to raid history, and few have attempted to link the values underlying current curriculum content with the past.

Raymond Williams, one of the most perceptive analysts of cultural values and education, laid the foundations for a study of history, values and the curriculum. He wrote in 1965 that:

> an educational curriculum expresses a compromise between an inherited selection of interests and the emphasis of new interests. At various points in history even this compromise may be long delayed and will often be muddled. The fact about our present curriculum is that it was essentially created by the nineteenth century. (Williams, 1965, pp. 171–2)

His view was that, in order to discuss education sensibly, an examination of the cultural choices involved in the selection of curriculum content must be examined in historical terms, in order to understand the influences on choices, and the emphases, omissions and distortions present within a particular curriculum. Lawton (1975) used Williams' insights to argue that developing a curriculum involves not only crucial cultural choices, but also political choices. Theoretical debate about the reflection of cultural values in a curriculum must question who controls and influences the selection of curriculum knowledge, and which social groups or controlling elites have the power to influence curriculum decisions. Lawton described a curriculum as 'essentially a selection from the culture of a society — certain aspects and ways of life, certain kinds of knowledge, attitudes and values, are regarded as so important that their transmission to the next generation is not left to chance' (Lawton, 1975, p. 6) but *who* makes the 'selection' is of course of the greatest importance. Because the school curriculum is a transmitter of cultural values, curriculum study must focus on the dominant ideas and values which come to be reflected in schools and question the origins of these values. This means that an historical dimension to contemporary curriculum study is vital.

There is currently some interest in remedying past neglect of the historical dimension, and empirical study and analysis of curriculum from an historical perspective is now being undertaken (Goodson, 1988; Goodson and Ball, 1984). A systematic understanding of how curriculum is negotiated over time, what values become acceptable and reflected in the curriculum at particular times, and whose interests are served by the selection and retention of certain values, is becoming possible through a study of curriculum history. Historical work can establish who influenced the emergence and establishment of particular educational activities, and what values are reflected in these activities. Certainly the changes required to alter the ethnocentric nature of the English school curriculum, as suggested by the Swann Committee, cannot be brought about without an historical understanding of the nature of the values currently underpinning the curriculum.

Public School Influence

One way in which the values of a dominant social and political elite came to influence mass education in Britain was via the public schools. There is little doubt that the values of the late nineteenth-century public school curriculum filtered into the developing state elementary and secondary school curriculum of the early twentieth century, and that these values uncompromisingly reflected an ideology of imperialism. Mangan, a historian of Empire, recorded his view that 'the British Empire was run by public schoolboys' and that the curriculum values imbibed by public schoolboys eventually influenced all school pupils (Mangan, 1980).

Much imperial propaganda in late nineteenth century British education was concerned with a growing awareness of empire among public schoolboys, and the deliberate cultivation of a militaristic imperialism in public schools by heads and teachers. By the turn of the century a close relationship had developed between the public school curriculum, service to the Empire, and a glorification of imperialism. Lawson-Walton, an exponent of the duties of government to its empire, wrote in the *Contemporary Review* in 1899 that, since the energies of the British race had given them their empire, and as 'British rule...of every race brought within its sphere, has the incalcuable benefit of just law, tolerant trade, and considerate government' (p. 306) it was the duty of public schools to provide competent rulers and administrators. Many public school headteachers saw this as an important duty, and were willing to educate not only future imperial administrators, but generals, missionaries, educationists and traders. Mangan (1980 and 1986) in his studies of the images of Empire in Victorian and Edwardian public schools, has documented the committed and single-minded imperialism of some headteachers. For example, H.W. Moss, Head of Shrewsbury School from 1872 to 1908, believed fervently that God had entrusted England with the task of creating a Christian Empire to be held together by military means. He set up one of the first public school Cadet Corps, with drill, shooting, camps and reviews by serving officers to lay the foundation of the boys' training for their imperial mission. Moss also supported the general developing militarism of the period, suggesting that public schools should directly train army officers so that 'boys with brains and character would be available for the preservation of English dominions in time of war' (Mangan, 1986, p. 119). J.E.C. Welldon, the Head of Harrow, was another enthusiastic propagandist for Empire. He read a paper to the Royal Colonial Institute in 1895 on 'Imperial aspects of education' in which he argued that the public schools must produce the governors, generals and statesmen to run the Empire. 'The boys of today are the statesmen and administrators of tomorrow—In their hands is the future of the British Empire'. Welldon also believed unquestioningly in the moral superiority of white people to govern their 'racial inferiors' and to demand 'instinctive obedience' from non-white imperial subjects, and he was an exponent of the popular view that much imperial strength was derived from the games field—'In the history of the British Empire it is written that England has owed her sovereignty to her sports' (Welldon quoted in Mangan, 1986, p. 121).

Another head who reflected the values of imperial government, militarism, moral and religious superiority over the imperial subjects, and the healthy discipline acquired on the games field was H.H. Almond, Headteacher of Loretto School, Edinburgh, from 1862–1903. He delivered an annual lecture on 'The divine governance of nations' in which he asserted that God's purpose for the British was to guide world history, and the major purpose of a public school education was to create the 'neo-imperial warrior—untroubled by doubt, firm in conviction, strong in mind and muscle' (Almond quoted in Mangan, 1980, p. 120). Public school headteachers were able to spread their imperial cultural values via their overt and their hidden curriculum; sermons, prize day speeches, school magazine editorials all provided means of reinforcing these values, and they were also able, in a boarding school setting, to restrict access to alternative views, and influence an adolescent educational elite to the point where the values were internalized strongly enough to provide a lifelong basis for action. Mangan describes the public school values of the time as based on four spheres of social and political consciousness. There was, among the elite groups governing Britain and the Empire, a need to establish in their young an ideal of selfless service, a sense of racial superiority, a sense of imperial chauvinism and an uncritical acceptance of the rightness of these views and values (Mangan, 1986, p. 116).

The imperial training required by the upper classes did, however, take a very practical turn. It was not possible to run an Empire on a classical education, particularly if trade and exchange of goods were involved. A mathematics textbook — first published in 1874 — deplored the fact that 'many persons who are supposed to have received the best education which the country affords, are in matters of numerical information ignorant and helpless, in a manner which places them in this respect far below members of the middle class' (Colenso, 1892, preface).

Arithmetical training for future imperial rulers required them to complete such examination questions as:

Question 14: A rupee contains 16 annas and 12 pice: Find, in French money, the annual interest, at 3.5 per cent, on 5217 rup. 3 an. 6 pi. — exchange 2.63 francs per rupee. (Colenso, 1892 p. 188.) (The answer for those slow to calculate, is 480 fr. 24.5 cents.)

For future engineers of the Empire, question 28, examination paper 15 of this textbook, required boys to work out the following:

Question 24: Of the whole cost of contracting a railway, 5/7 is held in shares, and the remaining £400,000 was borrowed on mortgage at 5 per cent. Find what amount of gross annual receipts — of which 40 per cent will be required for the working expenses of the line, and 8 per cent for a reserve fund — will yield to the shareholders a dividend of 4.5 per cent on their investments. (Colenso, 1892 p. 206) (The answer to this sum is £125,000.)

The importance of the values underpinning the public school curriculum was not only that they pervaded the schooling of imperial and later commonwealth administrators, but that these values percolated from the public schools to other schools — the higher elementary schools and the state grammar schools. By the end of the First World War the 'notion of Empire' had become part of the consciousness of the state education system. Values which comprised elements of nationalism, militarism and racial arrogance, combined with beliefs in superior moral and Christian benevolence towards imperial subjects had become incorporated in the school curriculum offered to the majority of the nation's children (many of them to grandparents of children at school in the 1980s). Some evidence of this percolation into an elementary school curriculum in early twentieth century Britain, is provided by Roberts' account of a childhood in Salford, *The Classic Slum* (1971). Roberts detailed the way in which the state school teachers copied their public school 'superiors' in fostering an ethnocentric view of imperial greatness, and led the middle and working classes towards a 'staunch patriotism' based extensively on racial superiority. 'The public school ethos,...distorted into myth,...set standards and ideals...for slum boys' (*ibid.*, p. 127). The schools provided models for the rest of the education system, and their values become part of the values embedded in state school curricula and extra-curricular activities. The work of MacKenzie and others (MacKenzie, 1984 and 1986) has strikingly demonstrated the many aspects of juvenile life affected by public school ideas of Empire. Certainly by the 1920s, the symbols and rituals of imperial life had become part of the state curriculum — school loyalties were manipulated for imperial ends, magazines and speech days extolled the activities of boys in the Empire and imperial campaigns. Roberts also noted that children welcomed the flag-waving, processions, bands, uniforms and royal visits, as a relief from routine, often accompanied as they were, by free patriotic mugs, buns and chocolate (Roberts, 1971, p. 23). Humphries, in a study of early twentieth century working-class youth (1981) remarked that the ideology of imperialism made a direct appeal to some values of working-class boys, as it reflected any number of existing cultural 'traditions', for example, fighting, gang warfare over street territory and assertions of masculinity. Fighting, racism and sexism were certainly still part of the 'traditional values' espoused by the working-class boys studied by Willis (1977) later in the century. However, the major importance of the cultural values and influences disseminated from the upper to the lower classes, via education, was that the 'lower classes' were encouraged to believe in their economic, political, social and racial superiority to the rest of the empire, 'the domestic underclass could become the imperial overclass' (MacKenzie, 1984, p. 254) and all classes could unite in a comforting national, patriotic solidarity. The strength of this solidarity is demonstrably still with us in the late twentieth century, and goes some way towards explaining the xenophobia and racism which are still part of the 'British heritage'.

School Textbooks

Ideological justification for imperial expansion, colonial wars and conquest, and the continued subjugation of those whom Rudyard Kipling so eloquently described as 'lesser breeds without the law' was reproduced on a large-scale in late Victorian and early Edwardian textbooks and juvenile literature. Many of these texts were reprinted and continued to be used in schools into the 1950s. An example of such a text is Seeley's *The Expansion of Empire* (first published 1883) which set out a simplistic and persuasive account of the benefits of the British Empire to both British subjects at home and overseas, but especially at home. He glossed over the military conquest and exploitation required to obtain such an Empire and became best known for his quotation that 'we have conquered half the world in a fit of absence of mind'.

There have been few historical studies of school textbooks and imperial values (but see Chancellor, 1970; Bratton, 1981; MacKenzie, 1984). Those who are currently concerned with an examination of racism in children's literature and school textbooks, and in the production of anti-racist literature, have not yet made systematic attempts to link the values underlying the texts which influenced the grandparents and parents of present-day pupils, and relate these to the values implicit on current texts (but see Klein, 1986). Nor has there been much debate about the policies required to deal with textbooks and literature that encapsulate ideas and values, accepted by schools as normal until the 1950s, but now widely regarded as inappropriate. The ad hoc policies of some LEAs, schools and individuals, intended to deal with racist textbooks and fiction, particularly by the removal of materials from libraries, has led to accusations of censorship and provided an easy political target. The removal of some anti-racist textbooks from schools may be a necessary policy, but, as one historian of the British Empire has noted, 'moral revulsion may not be the best way, to understand the path of Empire' (Lloyd, 1984, p. ix) and there may be ways of using the textbooks of empire to demonstrate how certain values came to be incorporated in the texts, what they demonstrated about the 'British heritage' and why they are no longer appropriate.

One task of the study of school textbooks and educational materials must also be to discover the process by which historically specific values are transferred into, and perpetuated as 'facts' or 'right answers' in particular texts and to do this it is necessary to study the pedagogy of the historical period. Curriculum content, if simplified and taught didactically, can quickly become unalterable and accepted as truth. Reflections of imperialism in educational materials came at a time when new pedagogic techniques were developing in state schools, and new methods of instruction were being urged on teachers via a powerful school inspectorate and teachers' manuals. One 'new' method thought particularly useful in the early twentieth century, for teaching working-class pupils, was the simplification of concepts — particularly those used in history and geography, so that 'children would not be harassed by complicated issues' (Board of Education, 1927). This early promulgation of what would now be regarded as a 'low expectation' did have the effect of injecting an uncritical approach to textbooks in both teachers and pupils.

The teaching of history and geography, and the reflection of imperial values in the textbooks used, provided a major influence on pupils in the early twentieth century which many teachers still find difficult to question. Inglis, an uncompromising critic of current curriculum values, has pointed out that 'thousands of teachers at all levels...believe that many of the commonly accepted answers to old questions are incredible falsehoods' and in particular 'the history we told ourselves for half a century will not do, and was always disgusting' (Inglis, 1985, p. 108). Whether labelled as incredible falsehood or ideology, there is no doubt that late Victorian and Edwardian imperial values became strongly reflected in school textbooks and the values have proved extremely resistant to change.

History, first introduced into the public school curriculum by Arnold at Rugby, was gradually introduced into state schools but did not become compulsory in senior elementary and secondary schools until 1900. Geography was more popular, being taught in most elementary and secondary schools from the 1890s, which was a period of increased publication of both history and geography textbooks. This was also the period when 'a single ideological slant was introduced into all school texts' (MacKenzie, 1984, p. 177). This 'slant' was a convergence of ideas of patriotism, militarism, respect for the monarchy, support for imperial expansion and dominance, and racial superiority. In the textbooks, the past was skewed to fit the current ideas. For example, issues such as The American Civil War, and slavery, were glossed over, moral responsibility for conflict was shifted to colonial countries, omissions and half-truths encouraged pupils to believe that the territorial and commercial wars fought to acquire the Empire were unavoidable but led ultimately to benefits for the conquered, colonized countries.

A popular history textbook issued by the Board of Education in 1902 (Finnemore, 1902) suggested that lessons on 'Great Englishmen' was a suitable method of teaching history to higher elementary classes. In this text the presentation of the 'natives' who fought to resist imperial rule as possessed by evil ill-feeling towards benevolent and just rulers, was a persistent theme, and their cruelty during rebellions, particularly to English women and children living in the colonies, was stressed. Clive of India 'made the English supreme over that vast country' (*ibid.*, p. 188), and Sir Henry Havelock and Lord Roberts suppressed the Indian mutiny in which 'English women and children were called upon to suffer horrors and tortures to which one cannot give a name' (*ibid.*, p. 237). The emotive language of this book—the 'pluck, endurance and heroic bravery' (*ibid.*, p. 255) of the British troops, always contrasted with the 'fiends incarnate' who were resisting imperial rule, was part of the hidden curriculum intended to instil attitudes in school pupils towards imperial subjects overseas.

The supposed beneficial effects of British rule was also a constant theme in both history and geography textbooks, which has continued to be reflected in textbooks used relatively recently. One geography textbook, used in Britain until the 1960s, stressed the beneficial and civilizing influence of Britain's role in helping Africa to modernize:

> Under the guidance of Europeans, Africa is steadily being opened up...doctors and scientists are working to improve the health of the Africans, — missionaries and teachers are educating the people...the single fact remains that the Europeans have brought civilization to the peoples of Africa, whose standard of living has, in most cases, been raised by their contact with white people. (Stembridge, 1956, p. 347)

This paternalistic view in which the Empire was presented as devoted to the civilization and well-being of subordinate races, was certainly promulgated in many history and geography textbooks until changes in approach, content and method in these subjects developed in the 1960s. The sense of racial and cultural superiority generated by the values implicit in these textbooks was passed on to a receptive white majority in Britain.

Juvenile Literature

It was not only in textbooks that images of moral, racial, political and technological superiority of the white races appeared. From the 1880s an expansion of popular publishing and the creation of a wider readership came at the same time as the development of mass education and wider literacy. One publishing market which proved popular, until well after the Second World War, was the juvenile literature market — children's journals, magazines and, later, comics.[5] From the 1880s, much of this literature took the form of an adventure tradition 'replete with militarism and patriotism, in which violence and high spirits became legitimized as part of the moral force of a superior race' (MacKenzie, 1984, p. 199).

The adventure literature was mainly designed for boys, and many of the fictional tales were set in public schools which provided another avenue by which public school imperial values could influence state school pupils. Roberts wrote of the way in which he and his friends in back-street Salford became 'avid for the fictional world of the (public) school' (1971, p. 127) and noted particularly the influence of 'Greyfriars', the public school invented by Frank Richards as a setting for serialized stories in the popular journals *Magnet* and *Gem*. The public schoolboy hero became an influential figure with whom several generations of state schoolboys identified. Rudyard Kipling's *Stalky and Co.* (1899) which extolled the high spirits, patriotic pride and intrepid self-reliance of a group of public schoolboys destined to be military leaders of Empire, was serialized on British television in the 1980s.

An increasing number of boys' adventure journals were produced from 1880, which presented an imperial world-view suffused with nationalistic, militaristic and racial ideas, incorporated into adventure stories which also appealed to romantic emotions. Bratton (1986) has noted that in many journals 'an overwhelming surface impression is that of a blatant reiteration of racial pride, militaristic values and a coarse enthusiasm for conflict' (p. 77). Intellect was not prized — physical powers and action were important — and in some stories:

> the world becomes a vast adventure playground in which Anglo-Saxon superiority can be repeatedly demonstrated *vis-à-vis* all other races, most of whom are depicted as treacherous and evil. (MacKenzie, 1984, p. 204)

The Tarzan stories, written by Edgar Rice Burroughs, are probably one example of this view of the world. These stories have had a powerful impact throughout the century, being continually presented on film, and later on television, and serialized extensively in magazines and comic strips. In the stories, Tarzan's breeding, and aristocratic European background, which enabled him to become an educated gentleman in the 'jungle' are continually stressed against the 'treacherous savage natives' he is constantly fighting. His breeding apparently allowed him to kill black people with deliberate cruelty.

In *Tarzan the Untamed* (Burroughs, 1919) Tarzan could not 'resist the pleasures of black-baiting, an amusement and a sport in which he had grown even more proficient'. In this story 'black-baiting' included torturing fellow-humans before killing them.

Other stories, however, stressed the romance of Empire, and many school textbooks as well as juvenile fiction included the word 'romance' in their title. For example, T.C. Jacks' *Romance of Empire* series and the Seeley Service *Library of Romance*, included such titles as *The Romance of Modern Pathfinders, The Romance of Savage Life* and *The Romance of Missionary Heroism*. In all the literature, the personal bravery of heroic individuals was a constant theme, which was also extended to include an individual identity for England. In naval adventure stories in particular,

> England is a gallant little nation whose power and conquests are obviously the reward of merit, since all her opponents are bigger and uglier than she is...the British tar is superhuman in his bravery, endurance and discipline,...the officers are wonderfully good at inspiring their men, and able to carry out audacious manoeuvres under the noses of lumbering or befuddled foreigners. (Bratton, 1986, pp. 83–4).

There are parallels here with the values implicit in the propaganda produced during the Falklands conflict in 1982.

Of all the imperialistic boys' adventure magazines produced in the 1880s, *Union Jack* was perhaps more influential than most. Its second editor, G.A. Henty, wrote over eighty boys' adventure stories himself, and employed well known writers of the period to write for the magazine, including Conan Doyle, Jules Verne and Robert Stevenson. Henty, like other boys' writers in the late nineteenth and early twentieth century, had personal experience of colonial warfare and war reporting. He also had strong racial and militaristic views, and his schoolboy heroes exhibited both class snobbery and racial prejudice. Their superior morality was associated with their public school education and their Nordic complexions; many of Henty's stories were both anti-black and anti-semitic. Non-whites were presented as unfit to govern themselves, and the energy and self-reliance of Northern Europeans was contrasted with the lethargy, fatalism and ignorance of non-whites. To be white and British provided a moral and ethical base-line for judging all other nations, and races, who were always found wanting. *Union Jack* ceased publication in 1933, *Magnet* and *Gem* during the second World War, but other publications came to replace these, particularly the comics *Rover* (1922), *Wizard* (1922), *Skipper* (1930) and *Hotspur* (1933) in which an imperial world view and notions of national and racial superiority continued to be present.

> Long after contemporary realities and intellectual thought had moved on, the same complacent self-confidence, sense of national and racial superiority, and suspicious xenophobia continued to be the principal characteristics of children's literature. (MacKenzie, 1984, p. 224)

Conclusion

The Swann Committee made a brave attempt to grapple with some of the dilemmas inherent in a change of curriculum from 'one appropriate to our imperial past' to one which would be more appropriate for a twenty-first century multi-ethnic society. But the information and new ideas available to the Committee were limited and the important Chapter 6 could only point in a very general way to the 'new approach' required in schools.

There is now a good deal of multicultural, anti-racist curriculum development work in progress around Britain, although it is still more likely to be targeted at ethnically-mixed rather than all-white areas. Many of the problems experienced by the curriculum developers are the result of strong underlying values and assumptions implicit in much educational material. These values centre on deeply-entrenched beliefs in the superiority of white people, and a deep distrust of foreigners and non-whites. Rather than dismiss these beliefs as 'irrational' it is possible to trace past influences on the curriculum to assess the point at which specific ethnocentric, racist values entered both the curriculum and teacher consciousness.

This chapter has attempted to demonstrate that the development of mass education, and the filtering of ideas and values from public to state schools, coincided with the height of a popular imperialism, which was particularly reflected in school textbooks and juvenile literature. The intensity of ethnocentric beliefs in the glories of Empire, white superiority, and a militaristic 'patriotism', were uncritically reflected in textbooks and other literature; and were reinforced by pedagogic techniques which encouraged simplification of complex moral issues, and unthinking acceptance of value-laden curriculum content.

The importance of these imperial values and beliefs is two-fold. Not only are they still reflected, although in changed or rationalized ways, in much current curriculum material, and thus influence the present generation of school children, they have undoubtedly influenced the grandparents and parents of children currently in schools. The task of changing the value-base of the curriculum has to take account of the ethnocentric views held by parents, for as MacKenzie (1984) has pointed out 'the values and beliefs of the imperial world settled like a sediment in the consciousness of the British people' (p. 258).

Disturbing the sediment will be one of the major challenges to the education system in the future.

Notes

1 For example ESG supported curriculum projects have been set up in Wiltshire, Shropshire, Norfolk, Cumbria and Derbyshire.
2 To be ethnocentric means to view the world totally from one point of view and to some extent all education systems are ethnocentric.

Sally Tomlinson

3 The period 1870–1920 is taken in this chapter as the time when mass education developed, and an ideology of imperialism was at its height.
4 For example, in the week of 21 April 1987, *The Sun* ran a series of articles denigrating the French and Germans.
5 J.S. Bratton has pointed out (in MacKenzie, 1986) that to attempt to quantify the presence of imperialism in the thousands of juvenile publications of the Victorian and Edwardian periods would be impossible, but selections from the literature can demonstrate the way in which fiction encapsulated and transmitted imperial values.

Appendix: Territories of the British Empire

Name of state or colony	Date of acquisition	Date of autonomy and/or leaving the Commonwealth
Aden (South Yemen)	1839	1967
Anguilla	1650	—
Antigua	1632	—
Australia (various territories)	1788–1859	1852–1890
Bahamas	1629	1973
Bangladesh (East Pakistan)	1757–1842	1947
Barbados	1625	1966
Belize (British Honduras)	1638–1802	1982
Bermuda	1609	—
Botswana (Bechuanaland)	1884	1966
British Antarctica	1819–1832	—
British Indian Ocean territories	1815	1960
British Somaliland	1884–1887	1960
British Virgin Islands	1672	—
Brunei	1888	1983
Burma	1826–1885	1948
Canada (various territories)	1670–1849	1847–1871
Cayman Islands	1670	—
Cyprus	1878	1960
Dominica	1763	1978
Egypt	1882–1914	1922
Falkland Islands	1833	—
Fiji	1874	1970
Florida	1763	1783
Gambia	1661–1713	1965
Ghana (Gold Coast)	1821–1901	1957
Gibraltar	1704–1713	—
Granada	1763	1974
Guyana (British Guiana)	1796–1815	1966
Heligoland	1807–1814	1890
Hong Kong	1842	(Due for secession 1997)
India	1757–1842	1947

Ionian Islands	1815	1864
Iraq	1948–1923	1932
Ireland (Irish Free State)	1169–1606	1921–1949
Jamaica	1655–1670	1962
Kenya	1887–1895	1963
Kiribati (Gilbert Islands)	1892–1918	1979
Lesotho (Basutoland)	1868	1966
Malawi (Nyasaland)	1889–1891	1904
Malaysia	1786–1882	1957–1963
Malta	1800–1814	1964
Mauritius	1815	1968
Minorca	1708–1713	1782–1783
Montserrat	1632	—
Nauru	1919	1968
New Zealand	1840	1852
Nigeria	1861–1903	1960
Pakistan (separated from India)	—	1947–1972
Palestine (Israel)	1917–1923	1948
Papua New Guinea	1884–1919	1975
Pitcairn Islands	1838–1887	—
St. Christopher Nevis	1624–1628	1983
St. Helena, Ascension Isles, Tristan da Cunha	1661–1816	—
St. Lucia	1814	1979
St. Vincent, Grenadines	1627	1979
Seychelles	1814	1976
Singapore	1819–1824	1963–1965
Solomon Isles	1893–1900	1978
South Africa (various states)	1795–1902	1872–1910
South West Africa (Namibia)	1915–1919	1960
Sri Lanka (Ceylon)	1815	1948
Sudan	1898	1954
Surinam (Dutch Guiana)	1651	1668
Swaziland	1890–1902	1968
Tanzania (Tanganyika and Zanzibar)	1870–1919	1961–1964
Tonga	1900	1970
Transjordan (Jordan)	1917–1923	1946
Trinidad and Tobago	1802–1815	1962
Turks and Caicos Isles	1638	—
Tuvalu (Ellice Isles)	1892–1918	1978
Uganda	1888–1895	1962
United Kingdom (England, Wales, Scotland, Ireland)	1707–1801	—
United States of America thirteen colonies	1636–1732	1776
Vanatu (New Hebrides)	1887–1906	1980
Western Samoa	1919	1901–1970
Zambia (Northern Rhodesia)	1889–1900	1964
Zimbabwe (Southern Rhodesia)	1888–1893	1980

Source: Adapted from Lloyd, T. O. (1984) *The British Empire 1558–1983.* Oxford, Oxford University Press, pp. 405–11.

References

BOARD OF EDUCATION (1927) *Handbook of Suggestions for the Consideration of Teachers and Others Concerned with the Work of Public Elementary Schools*, London, Board of Education.

BRATTON, J.S. (1981) *The Impact of Victorian Children's Fiction*, Beckenham, Croom Helm.

BRATTON, J.S. (1986) 'Of England, home and duty: The image of England in Victorian and Edwardian juvenile fiction' in MACKENZIE, J.M. (Ed.), *Imperialism and Popular Culture*, Manchester, Manchester University Press.

BURROUGHS, E.R. (1919) *Tarzan the Untamed*, New York,

CHANCELLOR, V. (1970) *History for Their Masters — Opinion in the English History Textbook*, Bath, Adams and Dark.

COLENSO, J.W. (1874) *Arithmetic — Designed for the Use of Schools*, (2nd ed 1892), London, Longman Green and Co.

DEPARTMENT OF EDUCATION AND SCIENCE (1977) *Education in Schools — A Consultative Document*, London, HMSO.

DEPARTMENT OF EDUCATION AND SCIENCE (1985) *Education for All: Report of the Committee of Enquiry into the Education of Children from Ethnic Minority Groups*, (The Swann Report), Cmnd. 9453, London, HMSO.

DEPARTMENT OF EDUCATION AND SCIENCE (1986) *Local Education Authority Training Grants Scheme. 1987/88*, Circular 6/86, London, HMSO.

FIELD, J.H. (1982) *Towards a Programme of Imperial Life — The British Empire at the Turn of the Century*, Oxford, Oxford University Press.

FINNEMORE, J. (1902) *Men of Renown — A Concentric Historical Reader*, London, A. and C. Black Ltd.

GOODSON, I.F. (1988) *School Subjects and Curriculum Change*, Lewes, Falmer Press.

GOODSON, I.F. and BALL, S.J. (1984) *Defining the Curriculum: Histories and Ethnographies*, Lewes, Falmer Press.

HUMPHRIES, S. (1981) *Hooligans or Rebels*, Oxford, Oxford University Press.

INGLIS, F. (1985) *The Management of Ignorance*, Oxford, Blackwell.

JOSEPH, K. (1986) 'Without prejudice — education for an ethnically-mixed society' reprinted in *Multicultural Teaching*, 4, 3, pp. 6–8.

KIPLING, R.S. (1899) *Stalky and Co.*, London.

KLEIN, G. (1986) 'Open letter to Sir Keith', *Multicultural Teaching*, 4, 3, pp. 4–5.

LAWSON-WALTON, J. (1899) 'Imperialism', *Contemporary Review*, LXXV.

LAWTON, D. (1975) *Class, Culture and the Curriculum*, London, Routledge & Kegan Paul.

LLOYD, T.O. (1984) *The British Empire 1558–1983*, Oxford, Oxford University Press.

MACKENZIE, J.M. (1984) *Propaganda and Empire — The Manipulation of British Public Opinion 1880–1960*, Manchester, Manchester University Press.

MACKENZIE, J.M. (Ed.) (1986) *Imperialism and Popular Culture*, Manchester, Manchester University Press.

MANGAN, J.A. (1980) 'Images of empire in Victorian-Edwardian public schools', *Journal of Educational Administration and History*, 12. 1.

MANGAN, J.A. (1986) 'The grit of our forefathers: Invented traditions, propaganda and imperialism' in MACKENZIE, J.M. (Ed.), *Imperialism and Popular Culture*, Manchester, Manchester University Press.

ROBERTS, R. (1971) *The Classic Slum*, Manchester, Manchester University Press.

SEELEY, J.E. (1883) *The Expansion of Empire*, London, Macmillan.

SILVER, H. (1977) 'Nothing but the past or nothing but the present', *Times Educational Supplement*, 1 July.

STEMBRIDGE, J. (1939) *The World — A General Regional Geography*, London, (1956 edit).

WILLIAMS, R. (1965) *The Long Revolution*, London, Pelican Books.
WILLIS, P. (1977) *Learning to Labour: How Working Class Lads Get Working Class Jobs*, Farnborough, Saxon House.

Chapter 4

Education for All: Social Reconstruction or Status Quo?

Millicent E. Poole and Judyth M. Sachs

The chapter compares and contrasts the major policy recommendations found in the multicultural policy documents promulgated by educational authorities in Australia and Britain. Accordingly, we first present an historical synthesis of Australian policy initiatives in multicultural education alongside those proposed in Britain (in the Swann Report (DES, 1985)) with the view to examining the intent of such policies. Second, we identify common themes and omissions ('rhetorical silences') found in key policy documents in both countries. Third, we consider multiculturalism as educational reform. Fourth, we suggest issues which need to be considered if multicultural education is to be oriented towards social reconstruction rather than the maintenance of the status quo.

Palliative or Policy?

Compared with the American experience, multicultural education as a state policy for accommodating ethnic relations in Australia and Britain was late in starting. What is apparent within Australian and British policy documents and scholarly writing, as Grant and Sleeter (1985) have noted, is that multicultural education seems to mean different things to different people. They argue:

> Writers are most explicit about its meaning when discussing purpose and goal; when discussing its application at the level of policy, teacher education or classroom practice, they will tend to assume the reader will know what conceptions of multicultural education they have in mind. (p. 110)

In what follows, significant policies generated in both countries will be presented against Grant and Sleeter's claim. The analysis will be on the basis of multiculturalism as policy. In order to do this the orientations of multicultural policy will be identified as well as their content.

At the most general level, the distinction between Australian and British policy can be found in the different emphases given to race relations and the education of ethnic minorities. On the one hand, British policy has been characterized by race relations while on the other, Australian policy has been concerned with the recognition of cultural and ethnic diversity. In both cases, the education of minority groups has passed through similar phases, namely 'assimilation' and 'integration'. Some Australian scholars have gone so far as to say that multiculturalism in Australia emerged in part due to the failure of assimilationist and integrationist perspectives to maintain social cohesion and guarantee equality of opportunity, while sustaining overall Anglo-Celtic bourgeois hegemony.

In Australia, it was through the enthusiasm and charisma of a Labour politician, A.J. Grassby, that multiculturalism was placed on the political agenda. With the publication of *A Multicultural Society for the Future* (Grassby, 1973) the attention of the Australian public was drawn to the present and future composition of Australian society. Catch cries and exhortations such as 'Australia is a multicultural society' and 'Australia is one of the most cosmopolitan societies on earth' and 'we should strive to become a family of the Nation' (*ibid.*) became part of the public consciousness. The nascent vision of Grassby later found expression in the submission to the Australian Immigration and Population Paper entitled *Australia as a Multicultural Society* (1977) by the Australian Ethnic Affairs Council (AEAC).

Premised on three key concepts — social cohesion, equality and cultural identity — the preferred direction for multiculturalism was outlined. The justification for a multicultural Australia was on demographic grounds. According to AEAC, Australia is 'composed of ethnic communities (which) are the carriers of different cultures, but these communities do not form distinct regions nor distinct socio-economic strata' (p. 6). For the AEAC 'multiculturalism means ethnic communities getting into the act' (p. 17). However, while the intent was clear, the AEAC did not specify which act — the political, economic, social or cultural — or how this would be achieved. As Bullivant (1985) noted, 'the normative intent is quite obvious' (p. 17), insofar as prescriptions for social reconstruction in the form of legislation were not forthcoming.

Responses from some authorities, however, were quite specific. The Ethnic Affairs Council (1977), for example, maintained that policies and programs concerned with education for a multicultural society should be directed at *all* children, not just those from non-English speaking backgrounds and should be evident throughout the curriculum. Six recommendations were made. Three were concerned with language education: teaching English as a Second Language, community language programs and bilingual education; others, with ethnic schools. Recommendation 6 stood out in terms of its vision for all children. This recommended that

> Schools should be given incentives to develop ethnic-studies programs
> and to infuse the curriculum in general with the reality of the pluralist
> nature of Australian society, with the object of both enhancing the
> self-esteem of students of ethnic origin and giving *all* children a more
> authentic view of the nature of society. (p. 12)

Multiculturalism as a policy for ethnic relations gained political legitimacy
through the publication and presentation in parliament in 1978 of the *Report
of the Review of Post-Arrival Programs and Services for Migrants* (The Galbally Report).

Galbally was commissioned to examine and report on the effectiveness
of the Commonwealth's programs and services for those who have migrated
to Australia. The terms of reference were to:

(a) examine welfare and other programs and services including in the fields
of health, housing, education and employment insofar as these bear on
the social welfare of migrants;
(b) take account of the extent to which programs and services are being
provided by other levels of government and non-government organizations
(p. 1).

This report provided the impetus and basis for educational initiatives in
multicultural education at both Federal and State levels through the endowment
of funds. Within this report recommendations were made such that:

> . . .our schools and school systems should be encouraged to develop
> more rapidly various initiatives aimed at improving the understanding
> of different histories, cultures, languages and attitudes of those who
> make up our society. . .(Galbally, 1978, p. 106)

The Galbally Report signalled the direction which multiculturalism would take
in Australia. This, Galbally argued, would be in the form of greater
understanding:

> . . .through greater allocation of resources to the teaching of histories,
> cultures and languages (both English and other languages), through
> the development of bilingual teaching, through better teacher education
> in these fields. . .through development of curriculums and essential
> materials and through greater involvement of parents and the
> community. (*ibid.*)

Educational initiatives for multicultural education in Australia so far
presented are congruent with Grant and Sleeter's (1985) education for the
culturally different. Grant and Sleeter argue that such programs are targeted
toward minority groups, aimed at providing standard school fare, the aim
being to increase students' access to the mainstream and language as a bridge
into mainstream culture (p. 100).

In 1978, through the commissioning of the McNamara Report, the
Australian Schools Commission (an independent authority set up by the
Whitlam government to dispense Commonwealth education funds) entered
into the multicultural arena. Through the publication by the Committee on

Multicultural Education of *Education for a Multicultural Society* (1978), advice was presented on the educational recommendations of Galbally.

For the purposes of this chapter, two issues are crucial: first, the notion of 'core values'; second, the issue of intercultural understanding. Central to the theory of multiculturalism advocated by the Australian Schools Commission is the notion of core values:

> It becomes important. . . to recognize that within the diversity of Australian society is a common thread. It is not only in literature, nor traditional lore, but in the acceptance by all communities, however diverse, of some common values. These are likely to include a belief in parliamentary democracy, in equality of opportunity, in educational and economic activity and to the right to a private life and choice of occupation. (Australian Schools Commission, 1978, p. 7)

A second area is stressed, that of intercultural understanding to be achieved 'through programs or studies which aim at presenting to all our students an opportunity to study (their) historical, social, aesthetic, literary and cultural backgrounds and traditions' (pp. 11–12). The emphasis here is somewhat different from Galbally in that all students are to benefit from such an education. Grant and Sleeter (1985) refer to this type of program as 'multicultural education', insofar as it is targeted for all students and advocates that teachers help students develop ethnic identities, knowledge about different cultural groups, respect for others' rights to be different and competency in more than one cultural system (p. 101). According to the Australian Schools Commission (1979) such programs include international and intercultural studies as well as community language programs, English as a second language and bilingual education programs (p. 12).

The British experience has been somewhat different from the Australian, insofar as they have emphasized race relations. This can be seen with the establishment of a Committee of Enquiry in 1979 under the chairmanship of Anthony Rampton. In 1981 his Committee produced an interim report of its findings (DES, 1981). Their most significant finding was that West Indian children as a group were 'underachieving' in relation to their peers, not least in obtaining the examination qualifications needed to give them equality of opportunity in the employment market and to enable them to take advantage of the post-school opportunities available'. The Committee also concluded that racism, intentional or unintentional, could not be held solely responsible for the underachievement of West Indian children. Rather, it was the interplay between negative teachers' attitudes and an inappropriate curriculum that helped to explain the underachievement of West Indian students. Four years later, Rampton's vision was elaborated by Swann through the production of *Education for All* (DES, 1985). The main finding of this report, which echoes that of Rampton, is that West Indian students are not competing as equitably as their white classmates, but that this could not be attributed to genetically-based IQ.

British initiatives evident in the Swann Report emphasize changes in behaviour and attitude as well as urging the government 'to demonstrate its commitment to the development of education for all by ensuring that necessary additional resources are made available. . .'. The necessity to align resources to policy initiatives was thus realized by both Galbally and Swann.

While Swann recognizes the occurrence of varying approaches to multicultural education in Britian, he makes the observation that there is general confusion as to 'the precise meaning and content of multicultural education' (p. 221). He goes on to add that 'the type of multicultural education found in a particular LEA seems determined by the nature of the types of ethnic communities there' (p. 222). Where initiatives in multicultural education are evident Swann claims 'they can be seen as the direct result of perhaps one teacher's particular enthusiasm and interest' (p. 221). He further adds the 'extent to which it is built into a school or LEA "strategy" can be rather tenuous' (p. 221). The adaptation of multicultural educational policy was thus more *laissez-faire* and derived from local initiatives than was the case in Australia where the initiatives came from the federal arena and then were taken up by state education authorities without contextualizing them. That is, a similar version of multicultural education advocated by the Commonwealth government in Australia was to be found in state multicultural policies. There was little or no attempt to adapt the policy for local conditions to account for demographic or historical differences.

In Australia, more recently, the Australian Council on Population and Ethnic Affairs (ACPEA, 1982) has continued to stress what Bullivant (1982 and 1986) refers to as 'naive' or 'romantic' multiculturalism. Such approaches to multiculturalism fail to demonstrate that 'political and structural issues rather than purely cultural differences were at the bottom of the discrimination and lack of job opportunities experienced by immigrants and their children' (Bullivant, 1982). In *Multiculturalism for All Australians* (ACPEA, 1982) the familiar 'ideals' of social cohesion and cultural identity and equality of opportunity and access are presented (p. 12). Cultural identity figured strongly focusing on:

- intercultural understanding, tolerance of and respect for cultural patterns other than one's own;
- improved communication between members of one cultural group and those of others;
- maintaining and nurturing the cultural and linguistic heritages within society. (*ibid.*, p. 18)

At the state policy level in Australia there has been a similar emphasis on 'cultural' rather than structural interpretations of multicultural education with the three 'ideals' of social cohesion, cultural identity and equality of opportunity providing the political and ideological backdrop for policy statements. In what follows statements from the Australian Capital Territory, Queensland, New South Wales and South Australia will be examined as exemplars of official versions of multicultural education policy in Australia which are in marked contrast with the decentralized structure evident in British LEAs.

Australian Capital Territory

In the Australian Capital Territory (ACT) multicultural education policy was first promulgated in 1979 in a statement from the Multicultural Education Working Party. While this document does not define what multicultural education is, the ACT policy does provide a philosophical statement rationalizing multiculturalism. The sections of this statement are listed *inter alia:*

1.1 The ACT Schools Authority accepts that multicultural education requires:
- an acknowledgement that Australia is a pluralist rather than a homogeneous society and that the various ethnic groups are able to make significant contributions to the mutual benefit of all members of the community;
- a perception of cultural diversity within the Australian community that includes cognizance of the special position of Aborigines;
- a recognition by teachers and educational administrators that multicultural education is not an additional or optional subject, but an ethic which should permeate all curriculum areas;
- a commitment by teachers to programs which allow groups to maintain their ethnic identity, customs and self-esteem;
- the continuing development within schools of attitudes of tolerance in all children towards others whose languages and lifestyle differ from their own.

The ACT Schools Authority not only recommends the teaching of community languages but also makes a distinction between multicultural education and the teaching of English. In paragraph 2.1:

> While accepting the necessity for multicultural education,...English is the major language of communication in Australia and that situation is likely to continue.

What is apparent in the ACT policy are the 'cultural' rather than 'structural' assumptions upon which the policy is based. Once again, the policy emphasizes the familiar catch-cries of 'tolerance', 'respect', 'ethnic identity', which both Grant and Sleeter (1985) and Bullivant (1982) have described as human relations and naive multiculturalism respectively.

Queensland

Queensland's multicultural education policy is to be found in *Education for a Multicultural Society: A Discussion Paper* (Queensland Department of Education, 1979) prepared by the Working Party on Multicultural Education.

While it is not appropriate to provide an historical analysis of the genesis of the Queensland document here, it is significant to note that the Queensland Working Party was constituted in response to the Australian Schools Commission Report (ASC, 1978), and at a time when social studies was under severe criticism by fundamentalist Christians (Smith and Knight, 1978 and 1982). The influence of that report is obvious in the Discussion Paper later promulgated. In the Queensland document, multiculturalism is used as a term to describe demographic diversity. The philosophical basis for justifying initiatives in multicultural education include:

(a) Australia is a multicultural society;
(b) education for a multicultural society is a philosophy which permeates all aspects of a school's activities and embraces all children;
(c) education for a multicultural society assists children to develop a personal identity, supports their ethnic identity and contributes to the national identity; and,
(d) education for a multicultural society is the concern and responsibility of all schools, all teachers, all students and all school communities. (p. v)

What is interesting about the Queensland policy document is its failure to define multiculturalism and multicultural education, and a tendency to use these terms interchangeably, confusing programs with a theory of society. Thus the general aim of the multicultural education program:

is to provide opportunities for students in government and non-government schools in Australia to study the languages, traditions and cultures of the many ethnic groups making up the Australian population and to encourage a climate of respect for, and sensitivity to, different cultural backgrounds. (p. vi)

The Queensland policy document has also been criticized for its assimilationist orientation. When one notes the following extracts, this claim has credence. For example:

Even when the school does attempt to provide cultural maintenance opportunities, its program must be flexible enough to allow minority groups to opt for preparation for life in the mainstream society as opposed to cultural maintenance. If this is their wish. (p. 12)

and,

that balance between the desire of cultural minorities to maintain their own cultures and their need to operate within the mainstream culture is not easily resolved. Congruence between the values, beliefs and goals of minority culture parents and those of the school is desirable, but not always possible. (p. 12)

The Queensland policy has no commitment to foster change, or to enhance the life-chances of minority group students. Rather, the policy has as its intent the enculturation of Queensland children into mainstream society with little or no social dislocation.

New South Wales

Multicultural education policy in New South Wales was first promulgated in 1979, with a rewrite in 1983 which offers a version not markedly different from its precursor.

The aims presented in the 1983 document are congruent with those found in the Australian Schools Commission Report (ASC, 1979). The general aim of multicultural education in New South Wales:

> seeks to develop knowledge, skills and attitudes appropriate to the multicultural nature of Australian society. This will be achieved in part through the process of incorporating *multicultural perspectives to curriculum*, as well as other processes and programs. (p. 3)

In the formulation of specific aims, the cultural stand remains. This is obvious in the following:

> In formulating aims and objectives of multicultural perspectives to curriculum schools should consider:

- identifying the cultural needs of students, the school, the community and the nation;
- incorporating a diversity of cultural perspectives existing within the school and its community . . . ,
- countering cultural bias in school practices and teaching/learning materials . . . (p. 3)

By developing such aims, multicultural education in New South Wales will provide the stimulus for initiatives which:

- develop an understanding and appreciation of the multicultural nature of Australian society past and present;
- assist students to function effectively in an ethnically diverse society;
- foster a sense of personal worth in *all* students through an understanding or appreciation of their Australian and ethnic identities . . . (p. 3)

Once again, the emphasis of multicultural education in New South Wales is for intercultural understanding. Little attempt is made to redress educational inequalities experienced by minority group students. As well, multicultural education is weak insofar as it is a philosophy that permeates the curriculum rather than a strategy for enhancing life chances.

South Australia

The official South Australian position on multicultural education was late in starting when compared to most other states. However, South Australian education authorities were quick to acknowledge the diversity of Australian society with the publication of resources and kits for teachers. Published in 1982 by the South Australia Department of Education *Diversity and Cohesion* signalled the orientation to be taken. The aim of multicultural education was to create a cohesive society but not at the expense of cultural diversity. Within the policy the notion of common values was advocated:

> For groups from widely divergent backgrounds to co-exist happily and productively within a framework of common values, while still preserving languages and cultures, the diverse and changing nature of Australian society must be recognized, accepted and valued by all Australians.

With the emphasis placed on 'the acquisition and understanding of the common values of Australian society; . . . and the appreciation, understanding and tolerance of cultures represented in Australia, including the Anglo-Australian culture'. The position advocated in South Australia resembles multiculturalism as human relations in Grant and Sleeter's (1985) typology. That is, its purpose is the prevention of conflict between members of different ethnic groups, the development of tolerance and of a positive self-image.

From the review of four Australian state education authorities and the Swann Report, several points need to be made. First, in nascent versions of multiculturalism in Australia and Britain emphasis has been placed on intercultural understanding. Second, others have features in common with the human relations (Grant and Sleeter, 1985) approach. In both contexts there has been no attempt within Australian or British society, even at the level of rhetoric, to provide any explanations for inequality in access or outcomes. Third, what is apparent within all of these policy documents is that little or no use is made of social science theory for guidance as to how a multicultural society might be achieved, a point we will take up later in this chapter. Nor is there much evidence of what Grant and Sleeter (*ibid.*) call education that is multicultural or social reconstructionist. In essence, despite claims to the opposite, multicultural education is seen in terms of school programs where students can feel better about themselves and others rather than coming to an understanding of the dynamics of a multicultural society. This is despite the fact that equality of opportunity is one of the key issues underpinning the rhetoric of policy documents in both countries.

Fourth, such programs as those described are based on 'liberal' assumptions that education has the potential to contribute to the reconstruction of a new social order, that a new society can be attained provided that certain prescribed courses of action are followed. Bullivant (1982 and 1986) and Jayasuriya (1984), for example, both make the point that this position ignores two question-begging assumptions: that the education system can first bring about changes in the wider society and, second, that access of ethnic groups to participation on an equal basis in political, legal, economic and civil activities will be achieved through maintaining a balance between core values and shared values

(Bullivant, 1983), i.e. notions of social reconstruction. These assumptions are further questionable as they imply that schooling per se, and the emphasis on cultural concerns in the curriculum in particular, can overcome the difficulties children from disadvantaged backgrounds face in schools and which prevent them from gaining access to power and privilege. Finally, as Bullivant (1982 and 1986) and Jayasuriya (1984) both point out, programs based on intercultural understanding do little either to enhance the life chances of minority children or to maintain social cohesion.

Rhetorical Silences

Following our examination of multiculturalism as a state policy for ethnic relations, we identify three issues which have been dealt with differentially in policy documents in Australia and Britain. These are: (a) the presentation of the culture concept; (b) the emphasis placed on racism; and (c) questions related to achievement. The differential treatment of these themes in the policy rhetoric of the Australian and British contexts we refer to as 'silences' or omissions, and we argue that cognizance needs to be given to these in future educational initiatives in multicultural education.

Conceptualization of Culture

The emphasis placed on culture within Australian policy documents and the Swann Report demonstrates their divergent views. In the Swann Report, for example, one of the citicisms of multiculturalism has been the emphasis on 'culture'—a term which is itself rarely clearly defined and is thus open to a myriad of interpretations—and which is often seen as avoiding the more central issues of race, prejudice and power (DES, 1985, p. 204). While similar criticisms may be directed towards the conceptualization of culture in Australian multicultural education, there have been some attempts to define the concept.

However, in many instances, the concepts of culture used, as Bullivant correctly noted (1981b), are out of date or otherwise inadequate. Reliance on such conceptions and definitions of culture serves political purposes insofar as multiculturalism and associated concepts of culture are reduced to vacuous political slogans, diverting attention away from a critical examination of the dynamics and tensions currently present within Australian society. The ambiguity surrounding such terms Rizvi (1985) argues leads to passive acceptance of the status quo and the masking of irreconcilable interests.

Generally, policy documents in Australia have used descriptive definitions to present a status quo view of individuals within society. This tendency has found currency in the widespread use of omnibus or all-encompassing definitions of culture which equate culture with heritage or ethnicity.

In policy terms, culture was first equated with heritage by Grassby (1973), who acknowledged the importance of culture within a multicultural society. However, for Grassby, culture is seen in 'more normative and aesthetic terms of historical customs, folk heritages and community groups: ethnic groups are claimed to be synonymous with cultural groups' (p. 13).

Galbally's (1978) notions of culture relied on an omnibus definition of culture to provide a 'theoretical' underpinning. For Galbally culture is defined thus:

> We believe it is a way of life, that complex 'whole' which includes knowledge, belief, art, morals, law, customs and any other capabilities and habits acquired by man as a member of society. (p. 104)

Later in the report the equating of culture with heritage is more obvious:

> ...our schools and school systems should be encouraged to develop more rapidly various initiatives aimed at improving the understanding of the different histories, cultures, languages and attitudes of those who make up our society.

and,

> ...the most significant and appropriate bodies to be involved in the preservation and fostering of cultures are the ethnic organizations themselves...(p. 110)

Not only do such extracts equate culture with heritage, culture is seen as 'something' static and reified, and the preserve of 'ethnic organizations' and not groups of individuals. Furthermore, Galbally recommends that in order to foster their own cultures 'ethnic groups...will need to use community resources (such as libraries) to enable them to do this as effectively as possible' (p. 111). The ambiguities of the loose use of culture inherent in the above give credence to Bullivant's claim that the culture concept here is theoretically incompetent (Bullivant, 1982).

A similar concern with culture as heritage was preferred by the Ethnic Affairs Council (1977) through their encouraging ethnic groups to develop their culture—their languages, traditions and arts—so that these can become living elements of the diverse culture of the total society' (p. 17).

Like Galbally, the Australian Schools Commission (1979) favoured and adopted the following notion of culture:

> The most common and popular usage of culture in education which equates culture with a social group's heritage, that is traditions, history, language, arts and other aesthetic achievements, religion, customs and values. (p. 68)

Such definitions of culture as presented provide an erroneous notion that culture equals heritage. The problem is, as Bullivant (1986, p. 20) argues, that 'to equate culture with heritage is a dangerous oversimplification as it ignores the adaptive and evolutionary nature of a group's culture'.

It is surprising that the Swann Report failed to acknowledge or to define such elementary notions of culture. Swann refers to 'cultural preservation' and 'cultural development' (DES, 1985, pp. 322 and 323) but fails to define what constitutes 'cultural'. Implicit within his document is the equating of 'culture' with 'life style'. Such a conception of culture is limiting both theoretically and in policy terms.

In Australia, at the state level, the concept of culture has been central in the overall conceptualization of multicultural education. For example, the conception of culture as presented within the Queensland Multicultural Co-ordinating Committee paper *Education for a Multicultural Society: Policies and Practices* (1982) provides a more comprehensive yet idiosyncratic version of culture than alluded to in the Swann Report. Its breadth makes it an omnibus type definition, but it goes further than a descriptive type of definition. Culture so defined:

> embraces all aspects of shared life within a community; is manifest in patterns of language and thought, in forms of activity and behaviour and in the artefacts of a people; embraces particular attitudes, values and beliefs; is neither static nor absolute; provides a model for relating to, perceiving and interpreting experiences and the environment; promotes in the individual a sense of belonging to a particular way of living associated with the historical experience of the particular group of people to which he/she belongs. (p. 6)

However, this definition is a 'grab-bag' of everything which through its so-called comprehensiveness describes everything but analyzes nothing, except maybe the behaviour and resultant artefacts of groups of people. These definitions embrace, as Saunders (1982) notes, behaviour in an all inclusive sense as well as the values underlying that behaviour. The implication here is that the relationship between the two is such that values are determined by behaviour.

What all definitions so far presented fail to take into account is the dynamics of the actor/structure relationship. This is a crucial point because it masks both the context of action and the power dimensions within Australian and British society. Swann (DES, 1985, p. 204) alludes to this point but fails to develop it. By so doing, the culture concept remains inadequate for explaining the articulation of social groups within Australian and British society, whereby culture is used as a commodity (Apple, 1982) to exclude some members of society from access to prestige and power. The consequence of such conceptions and the failure to examine the relationship between actor and structure in Australian and British society is that multicultural education will remain a weak adjunct to the curriculum focusing on the expressive aspects of culture and will neglect the political and material aspects of Australia's and Britain's culture(s) which can help to explain inequality.

Culture as such becomes detached. As Bruner (1966) noted:

> what is imparted often has little to do with life as it is lived in society, except insofar as the demands of the school are of a kind that reflect indirectly the demands of life within a technological society. But these indirectly imposed demands may be the most important feature of the detached school. (p. 152)

While culture is not specifically defined within the New South Wales Department of Education's policy or support documents, culture is presented as being synonymous with ethnic and is not comparable with 'other overlapping identities such as those related to age, sex, occupation, social class and place of residence' (Ethnic Studies Support Document, 1983, p. 1). Furthermore, within this document the claim is made that cultural traits delineate ethnic groups (p. 4). The logic of this is, as Eipper (1983) argues:

> the term ethnic group is synonymous with cultural group; ethnic means cultural; ethnicity is culture. (p. 437)

Such notions of culture and ethnicity have obvious ideological appeal for policy makers, as they are not adequate for the task of analyzing social conflicts in economically and politically complex pluralist societies and serve to obfuscate these complexities, thus tending to maintain the status quo rather than seek to address questions related to social reconstruction.

The state, through policy documents, thus legitimates a preferred version of culture; a discourse of exclusion (Foucault, 1972). Such discourse obscures political, economic and class relations within Australia and Britain and instead focuses on a neutral, descriptive version of culture which serves to underpin the status quo.

Racism

In Australia, the second silence has related to the issue of racism, especially its public forms. Racism has not been raised in debate or policy to the extent that it has recently in Britain, especially in relation to educational and social issues. This is somewhat surprising given the evolution of Australian race relations, for example, the 'White Australia' policy in force until the 1970s (see Lovegrove and Poole, 1975). McQueen (1972) more than any other Australian historian, has noted this silence (p. 93). Examining the connection between racial attitudes and the labour market, McQueen argues that Australians have avoided their 'racist heritage for too long even to the point of denying its existence. Silence has been a source of sustenance to racism and it has not gone away just because we have not had to articulate it'. Poole (1985a) asserted that the lessons of history and of social science research on intergroup relations seem to have been overlooked by Australian policy-makers, and any attempts to remind them such as those in recent times by the historian

Professor Blainey have led to public outrage and moral indignation. Policy has been lifestyle oriented and major issues such as racism, sexism and class bias have been marginalized (Jayasuriya, 1985) or left as 'silences'.

In Britain, greater emphasis has been placed on the role of education in challenging and countering racism, both within schools and in the wider society. The need to 'identify and seek to challenge racism — both the misunderstandings and stereotypes which encourage its persistence, and its many manifestations which deny quality of access and opportunity to all groups' (DES, 1985, p. 319) was seen as a task for schools in preparing young people to live constructively in a multiracial British society.

The definition of racism in Australia and Britain has been given less attention than 'culture' and the rhetoric is different to attach to policy. Racism 'consists of an interaction between three separate components: an uneven distribution of power and influence; discriminatory practices, procedures and customs; and the prejudiced beliefs and attitudes of individuals, both conscious and unconscious' (*ibid.*, p. 369). Four reasons presented as to why racism should be dismantled and replaced by equality and justice are:

(1) Racism is morally wrong, since it involves benefits for some people at the expense of others.
(2) Racism is against the long-term self interest of all, since it is bound to lead eventually to social unrest.
(3) Racism gives to all people a false view of their own identity and history.
(4) Racism prevents ethnic minority people and the host community from learning from each other's cultures, history and experience, and prevents them from genuinely cooperating as equals on the solution of common problems. (*ibid.*, p. 370)

Such assertions carry much moral and social force but how they are to relate to educational policy remains unclear.

A key focus, however, in both British and Australian policy documents is attitude change and the encouragement of positive attitudes towards a multicultural (Australian) and multi-racial (British) society. Equipping young people with knowledge about their own and other cultures is seen as a step schools can take towards the reconstruction of inaccurate myths and stereotypes. Australian policy documents highlight tolerance and acceptance of cultural diversity. The Swann Report contains terms such as 'negative prejudice'. 'unintentional racism'. In both countries the roots of racism are seen as relating to skin colour, religion and lifestyle but, more importantly, to economic circumstances (for example, rising unemployment, restructuring of the labour market and the shrinkage of unskilled jobs, pressures and competition for upward mobility, jobs and housing). Again, the role that education can be asked to play in the racism debate has to be carefully considered as schools are only one institution in society and cannot, on past experience, compensate for society (Bernstein, 1972).

Millicent E. Poole and Judyth M. Sachs

The focus on racism in the British context has been challenged. O'Keeffe (1985), for example, argued that the Swann Report's focus on racism as an 'all-white' and a British problem is misdirected:

> a huge industry has been erected, a hate-relations complex... The contradiction between the successful economic life of advanced capitalism (with its growing and manifest functional indifference to the race or gender of its economic agents) and a misanthropic intellectual culture (turning grotesquely between the poles of guilt and envy). (p. 72)

He sees the Swann Report as having little that is interesting or convincing to say on what the race problem is, what causes it and what can be done about it. O'Keeffe sees racial prejudice, poverty and despotism as the standard experiences of history and sees the report as 'soft, sub-Marxist... riddled with moral and cultural relativism' (p. 70).

In an analysis of racial issues in Canada, *Equality Now*, Moodley (1984) points to the dangers of giving salience to race as a mark of deprivation, in contrast to an apolitical multiculturalism:

> Positive multiracialism is a dangerous supplement to a praiseworthy multiculturalism because it heightens invidious racial perceptions where multiculturalism is rightly silent on the question of race. (p. 799)

Both British and Australian educational policy could perhaps benefit from critical reflection on the salience and silence respectively given to the concept of racism in the equality and equity debate.

Achievement

In the British context, racism has been closely linked to the achievement of children in schools. For example, the interim report 'West Indian Children in our Schools' presented evidence that:

> racism, both intentional and unintentional, has a direct and important bearing on the performance of West Indian children in our schools. (cited in DES, 1985, p. 9)

The evidence showed a strong trend to underachievement of pupils of West Indian origin on the main indicators of academic performance. Yet such studies did not, by and large, take account of socio-economic factors which might have operated. Nor did they sufficiently highlight the within group variance.

In Swann, the argument is presented that the education system appears to have different expectations of various minority groups:

> West Indian children will be good at sports but not 'academic'; Asian children will be hardworking and well motivated but likely to have unrealistically high career aspirations; Chinese children will be

reserved, well behaved, and likely to be 'under pressure' at home from having to help in the family business in the evenings. (*ibid.*, p. 15)

Swann argues, on the basis of some NFER research, that teachers may directly affect pupils' achievement or behaviour.

The achievement data for Asian pupils in England, however, were quite different and raised important questions concerning the relationship between racism and achievement: 'Most of the studies point to performance levels on the part of Asians that either match or exceed those of indigenous peers' (*ibid.*, p. 64). Asians tend to do well in examinations, except in English, although there is variation in the performance of different sub-groups (for example, children of Bangladeshi origin show lower achievement levels).

The Swann Report examines a number of factors associated with achievement concluding that the problem is 'very complex with no single cause, but rather a large number of interrelated causes' (*ibid.*, p. 68). Factors considered included 'adverse environmental circumstances', 'genetic' inheritance, the structure and ethos of families and schools, and the failure of educational authorites to respond to changing needs. What is surprising in this analysis are the conclusions reached as the evidence presented is at best tentative and somewhat contradictory. Yet the report states:

> We are left in no doubt that the ethnic minority communities are, on average, markedly more socially and economically deprived than the white majority, though to an extent and in a manner that varies as between different groups. Secondly, this extra deprivation is almost certainly due, in substantial part, to racial prejudice and discrimination. And, lastly, this extra level of deprivation in turn contributes substantially to underachievement at school. (*ibid.*, pp. 75–6)

O'Keeffe (1985) discusses some of the inconsistencies in the Swann analysis on achievement and asks whether it might not be better policy to try and uncover common sources of failure since many white children fail too:

> Putting it another way, should we not look at what characteristics many white children have, and many Asians and some West Indian children have, which promote educability (in the case of non-whites, in the face of much prejudice)? We can say, if we like, that the presence of prejudice is a critical variable when characteristic X is absent but not when it is present. Wouldn't it make more sense, however, to say that characteristic X, and not prejudice, is the critical variable? (p. 74)

Swann raises many important issues relating to achievement but the overall impression given is that schools are being asked to undertake major social reconstruction on a potentially divisive and imprecise basis ('racism') where the real issues surrounding access, equity and social justice are largely avoided (for example, class, gender, culture: in social terms; and streaming, school organization, resources, and teachers' knowledge, in educational settings).

In a review of Australian research on the achievement of immigrant groups in Australia, Poole (1981) concluded:

> Currently, in terms of access and outcome measures, minority groups are not, on average, disadvantaged, except in relation to achievement outcomes in language-related areas. Aspiration levels of immigrants tend to be high, with parents supportive of their children's schooling. However, there are other factors to be taken into account, such as social class and family resources (intellectual and economic), differences in commitment to schooling between and among different immigrant groups, and some evidence of differing cultural expectations for immigrant boys and girls. Overall, the evidence suggests that social class factors rather than minority group membership tend to inhibit equality of educational opportunity. (p. 254)

A more recent review undertaken by the Australian Council for Educational Research (Sturman, 1985) concluded:

> The general pattern is for students with non-English-speaking backgrounds to remain longer at school than other students, although variations across the different immigrant groups are evident. This pattern is extended across all social classes and one of the more interesting findings was that immigrant students of lower socio-economic status had relatively high aspirations and, at least with respect to school participation, seemed more able to achieve these aspirations than was the case for Australians or immigrant students from English-speaking backgrounds. However, there was some evidence that despite high retention patterns for immigrant Australians there was still some ability wastage, and that the high levels of retentivity were not as evident for female immigrant students.
>
> The results of research concerning school achievement are less easy to summarize. There is no doubt that some immigrant groups suffer disadvantage in performance at both the primary and secondary level (especially at the primary school level), although this disadvantage is far less evident for numeracy than for other areas. (pp. 53–4)

What is interesting in the research findings reviewed in Swann and those reviewed by Poole and Sturman is the realization that some minority groups are doing very well, equal to or better than their non-immigrant counterparts (for example, Asians). This emerging variability among groups suggest that educational policy may need to be targeted to specific groups rather than to minority groups generally. In addition to certain cultural factors which might be operating, there are also class and gender differences emerging in the achievement literature in both countries and these need to be given more salience in policy formulation. Moodley (1984) has outlined some of the predicaments that unsophisticated racial affirmative action can produce and advises caution with policy advocates for ethnic groups:

> A flourishing ethnic relations industry, from special consultants to intercultural communicators in a state-sponsored bureaucracy, has now reached the stage of developing an interest in its self-perpetuation and further expansion, regardless of need. Needs can also be manufactured and one of the consistent requests. . .(concerns) more funds for assessing, meeting and stimulating additional needs. (p. 803)

Such advocacy may achieve short-term gains but lead to long-term problems if a more balanced picture of achievement needs does not present class and gender as equally important aspects to be considered in policy formulation so that all children can maximize their potential. School achievement should not be the end point in monitoring access, equity and social justice. Rather, access to and performance in the labour market should be monitored in government policy so that education for all translates to life chances and options for all, beyond schooling.

Multiculturalism as Educational Reform

Education has been advocated as the vehicle for reforming a culturally diverse society. As Popkewitz, Tabachnick and Wehlage (1982) have noted,

> The 1960s were a time of ferment for most institutions. . .schools were asked to respond to the social and political issues that commanded the nation's attention: the civil rights movement called for improved education for minority children, and political changes created a demand that could help establish a sense of community and of moral cohesion. When criticism of the ability of schools to solve personal and social problems undermined faith in the existing institutions, educational reform became a potent symbol for responding to the nation's social predicaments. (p. 3)

The development of multiculturalism as a state policy for ethnic relations in Australia and Britain can be seen in this light as a means of reducing racial tension, promoting social cohesion, and contributing towards equality of educational opportunity. However, the ideology underlying the rhetoric of multicultural education obscured the relationship between reform and the underlying values of Australian and British society.

According to Popkewitz *et al.* (*ibid.*, p. 8) 'social institutions perform certain agreed upon functions to achieve social goals'. The discourse and practice of multiculturalism as being ideological insofar as the structural mechanisms of inequalities between groups are obscured, as observed by Henry and Lingard (1982) is a case in point. Furthermore, Sharp (1980) argues (in relation to Australian society) that the humanistic assumptions common to multicultural education, and liberal reformism more generally, fail to recognize the patterns of power distribution. Multicultural education as promulgated within the discourse of policy thus fails to address the possibilities of improving the life chances and choices of ethnic and other minority groups (Jayasuriya, 1985; Poole, 1985b; Sachs, 1988)

Multiculturalism as a concept in Australian and British policy documents has served as a slogan to legitimize reform. The terms 'social cohesion', 'equality of opportunity', 'ethnic identity' and 'cultural diversity' are slogans each of which, as Popkewitz *et al.* (1982) argue, 'symbolize(s)' to educators a variety of emotions, concepts and values, just as terms like 'democracy' and 'national security' symbolize the values and aspirations of political groups (p. 21).

As reform programs, multicultural initiatives at the school level become superficial and resistant to the intentions of policy discourse. Smith and Sachs (1980 and 1981), for example, in their evaluations of regionally based multicultural programs in Australia corroborate this. Reform programs then may thus best be described as 'services and strategies' which as Warren, Rose and Bergunder (1974) observe:

> make minor adaptations of existing structures and programs while at the same time setting in motion processes of organizational cooptation and the preventing—blunting—repelling sequence. (p. 170)

Such strategies concentrate on the allocation of resources but do not address structural reform. Through processes such as the 'preventing—blunting—repelling sequence', programs are modified at the school level in such a way that the practice of multiculturalism often has little match with policy intentions. In this way, schools continue to be agents of social control engaged in the maintenance of the status quo insofar as reform has become a symbolic act that conserves rather than changes (Popkewitz *et al.*, 1982). The failure of multicultural programs, then, to consider the redistribution of income and power effectively means that the key concern of multiculturalism is the advocacy of 'life style' rather than 'life chances' (Jayasuriya, 1985; Poole, 1985b; Sachs, 1988), thereby avoiding an examination of major questions relating to social reconstruction.

Schools have thus been asked to bear the burden of educational reform, which is illusory. As Bernstein (1972) argued: 'education cannot compensate for society' insofar as 'the power relationships created outside the school penetrate the organization, distribution and evaluation of knowledge through the social context' (p. 116). Schools as such are weak institutions for social reconstruction.

Whether such educational reforms are attempted at the Federal, State, local, or school-based levels, social reform is still within a framework of social control rather than personal or group empowerment. Questions related to participation become, as Warren, Rose and Bergunder (1974) argue, a palliative rather than a catalyst for social change involving the redistribution of power and resources.

Towards Multicultural Education for Social Reconstruction

In both Britain and Australia a key issue is not only whether multicultural policies are to be developed to maintain the status quo or to bring about social reconstruction, but towards whom such policies should be directed. For example, within Australian multicultural education policy there are tensions with respect to the audience for multicultural programs. On the one hand, the early policy documents such as Grassby, ACPEA and the Ethnic Affairs Council all advocated a version of multiculturalism for all Australians, while on the other hand the Galbally Report and the Australian Schools Commission envisaged a 'compensatory' approach for children from ethnic minority groups.

However, the Swann Report has argued strongly for the notion 'education for all'. Their claim is:

> We believe it is essential to change fundamentally the terms of the debate about the educational response to today's multi-racial society and to look ahead to educating all children, from whatever ethnic group, to an understanding of the shared values of our society as a whole as well as to an appreciation of the diversity of lifestyles and cultural, religious and linguistic backgrounds which make up this society and the wider world. (DES, 1985, p. 316)

Swann is correct in advocating this and promoting the notion of a 'good education for all'. However, fundamental concepts need to be further developed if the Swann rhetoric is to make progress beyond that attained in Australian multicultural education policy implementation.

We conclude by identifying issues which we believe should be promoted in Britain and Australia if 'multicultural education' and 'education for all' are to be oriented towards social reconstruction rather than the maintenance of the status quo. We advocate: (a) removal of the silence concerning 'culture'; and (b) an examination of 'teachers' knowledge and discourse' concerning multiculturalism and equality.

Culture

As was indicated earlier the concept of culture has been relatively under-used as an analytic construct within multicultural education policy and practice. We believe that, in order for the development of multicultural education to occur along social reconstructionist lines, the concept of culture and its conceptualization is critical in policy. Essentially, the concept of culture advocated here is first an ideational one (Goodenough, 1971)—derived from cognitive anthropology, having as its major theoretical assumption the knowledge individuals use to interpret experience and generate social behaviour. Second, we support Keesing's (1978) proposal for a political economy of knowledge. This notion is used as our point of departure. Such a view takes as its problematic the degree and nature of diversity in individual interpretations of the political constraints on the distribution of knowledge in the community, both from within and without; and the ways in which symbolic meanings mystify, rationalize, disguise and perpetuate existing political and economic relationships.

By subscribing to such a view the differential access to, and knowledge of, the various microcultural systems (which is a significant aspect of power relations in all societies) can be of major focus. Furthermore, this orientation facilitates an examination of cultural competencies possessed by individuals in different social, economic and culture milieux. Our justification of this view of culture is based on the proposition that lack of appropriate competencies effectively inhibits the life chances of individuals. As Gibson (1976) argued, individuals who do not have access to a repertoire of knowledge and the associated appropriate behaviour, which they can draw upon in various situations, are constrained. Within the context of multicultural education, culture is a concept that can be used to analyze power relations with a pluralist society. As all anthropologists have properly agreed, culture is learned. If some groups in society do not have access to certain bodies of knowledge and competencies then they will continue not to have access to power and to prestige which possession of these 'commodities' facilitates.

An attempt to move beyond what was referred to as a discourse of exclusion is found in the work of Bullivant (1981a, 1981b, 1982 and 1986). Bullivant (1981b) sees culture in quasi-cybernetic terms as a communicable body of knowledge and ideas, which social groups accumulate over time, add to and modify, as the survival needs of the groups alter in response to the changing environmental pressures. Bullivant (1982) makes a further claim that: 'Such a definition can be applied as much to the culture of the wider society as to that of each of its constituent ethnic groups' (p. 56). He then goes on to argue:

> Whatever their affiliations, people must be equipped with the kinds of knowledge and conceptions which will make them competent to give meaning to and cope with the present and anticipated future problems of their existence.

By developing a political economy of knowledge the insight such as Clarke, Hall, Jefferson and Roberts (1981) provide is elaborated and strengthened. They claim that the experience of everyday reality shapes social consciousness and that the different experiences gained by different classes lead to different social consciousness. As Clarke *et al.* (1981) put it:

> A culture includes the 'maps of meaning' which make things intelligible to its members. These 'maps of meaning' are not simply carried around in the head: they are objectivated in the patterns of social organization and relationship through which the individual becomes a 'social individual'. (p. 53)

From this perspective culture is a dialectical process insofar as it is not something solely objective and external to the individuals who comprise a particular society, class or group. Rather, culture is learned, communicated and shaped through individual attempts to master and participate in the life of the group (Bates, 1986, pp. 9/10). Culture, then, is not static but rather contested and reconstructed through the process of social interaction and through the attempts of individuals to make sense of their lives.

In terms of multicultural educational practice, such a conception of culture can be used to emphasize power relations and dimensions of structural inequality, rather than merely focus on behaviour and material aspects of group life (Sachs, 1986). Furthermore, the culture concept becomes central in the endeavour of multicultural education becoming a vehicle for the education of all.

Teachers' Knowledge

In terms of the translation of policy initiatives into teachers' 'professional discourse' little attention has been paid to the nature and content of teachers' knowledge. We believe that in order to promote the notion of social reconstruction through the curriculum and multicultural education, an understanding of teacher culture is necessary.

Sachs (1988) argues that teacher culture is constructed in particular kinds of circumstances so that some patterns of thought and action are more likely to characterize schools than others. These are teaching as a labour process, structural constraints on teaching, bureaucratic structures and professional preparation and socialization. This is important because it identifies the mechanisms by which teachers' knowledge is constituted (Sachs, 1987a).

In this section several issues will be raised which have bearing on and require consideration within the practice of multicultural education. The major concept to be developed here is that of the 'practicality ethic' (Doyle and Ponder, 1977). It is important that the complexity of the 'practicality ethic' is not underrated. While it is primarily based in the experience of teachers in classrooms, it is not restricted to these experiences alone, but is shaped by a teacher's life in the school, the system and beyond. Elbaz (1983) draws attention to the scope and range of teacher knowledge and argues:

> this knowledge encompasses first hand experiences of student learning styles, interests, needs, strengths and difficulties and repertoire of instructional techniques and classroom management skills. The teacher knows the social structure of the school and what it requires of teachers and students for survival and success; she knows the community of which the school is part, and has a sense of what it will or will not tolerate.

This is similar to Clandinin's (1985) claim that the knowledge is not only experiential, but is value-laden, purposeful and orientated to practice. Furthermore, teacher knowledge encompasses beliefs about teaching, knowledge, students and the catchment community which partly shape their teaching 'styles'. This point is important theoretically because it breaks with the notion that while teachers are institutionally incorporated, they are not necessarily ideologically incorporated.

Nevertheless, the idea that the practicality ethic provides the central core of teachers' culture is appropriate for this chapter as it provides a foil for the individualistic and relativistic notion that 'every teacher is different'. At the level of the subject this is clearly the case, but schools are characterized by patterned sets of activities and events. Teachers within the institution are far less complex social and cultural entities than they are as social agents. This understanding is captured by Freedman, Jackson and Boles (1983):

> *the work situation* of elementary school teachers intrinsically creates a culture whose aspects are overwhelmingly shared by *all* the teachers at this level, no matter what their present teaching situation or what background they have brought to teaching. . . Every one of us shares basic concerns and problems (emphasis added). (p. 261)

Further research by Hatton (1985) has demonstrated that no matter what teachers do, they are strongly influenced by the hidden pedagogy. This section can be drawn together by the proposition that, if the 'practicality ethic' dominates teacher work as the literature indicates then educational and other 'theoretical' knowledge has no intrinsic privileged status. That is, when faced with a choice between the acceptance of theoretical knowledge and the maintenance of 'practical' practice, teachers are likely to reject the former or colonize it. That is, they are likely to use the procedures of 'revitalization' movements (Wallace, 1961) insofar as their activities are a deliberate, organized, conscious effort by members to construct a more satisfying culture or 'bricolage' (Levi-Strauss, 1963) in that they draw upon the stock of knowledge which is at hand. While they draw upon a previously determined set consisting of theoretical and practical knowledge, and associated technical means, nevertheless, these restrict the possible solutions to problems in classrooms, and reformulate 'theory' into 'practical' forms that 'work'. This is what Bernstein (1972) has referred to as decontextualizing knowledge, such that its meaning in a discourse is lost as it is inserted into a different set of interpretative frames.

When policy makers and curriculum developers understand the full complexities of the institution and content of teachers' knowledge, then key concepts will be able to be used to their full analytic value.

Conclusion

We have argued the need for policy makers to come to terms with the construct of culture and teachers' knowledge and discourse in multicultural education policy and practice if social reconstruction is to occur rather than the maintenance of the status quo. In conclusion, we state that we believe that inequality does not lie within individuals but rather is to be found within groups. The psychologistic tendency to see the remedy for social and cultural inequalities in individual terms rather than in the nature of group and social relationships and structures is to be avoided. Such reductionism can often lead to the promoting of culturally relativistic slogans and policies. These policies, while seemingly liberal and just at the surface level, can lead to unacceptable practices and consequences which cannot be justified on moral or ethical grounds and which in themselves may lead to social disintegration and away from shared common core values.

References

ACT SCHOOLS AUTHORITY (1978) *Multicultural Education in the Australian Capital Territory*, Canberra, Australian Government Publishing Service.

APPLE, M. (1979) *Ideology and Curriculum*, London, Routledge & Kegan Paul.

AUSTRALIAN COUNCIL ON POPULATION AND ETHNIC AFFAIRS (1982) *Multiculturalism for All Australians*, Canberra, Australian Government Publishing Service.

AUSTRALIAN ETHNIC AFFAIRS COUNCIL (1977) *Australia as a Multicultural Society*, Canberra, Australian Government Publishing Service.

AUSTRALIAN ETHNIC AFFAIRS COUNCIL COMMITTEE ON MULTICULTURAL EDUCATION (1981) *Perspectives on Multicultural Education*, Canberra, Australian Government Publishing Service.

AUSTRALIAN INSTITUTE OF MULTICULTURAL AFFAIRS (1980) *Review of Multicultural and Migrant Education*, Melbourne, Australian Institute of Multicultural Affairs.

AUSTRALIAN INSTITUTE OF MULTICULTURAL AFFAIRS (1982) *Evaluation of Post-Arrival Programs and Services*, Melbourne, Australian Institute of Multicultural Affairs.

AUSTRALIAN SCHOOLS COMMISSION EDUCATION COMMITTEE ON MULTICULTURAL EDUCATION (1978) *Education for a Multicultural Society* (The McNamara Report) Canberra, ASC.

AUSTRALIAN SCHOOLS COMMISSION (1979) *Multicultural Education Program: Information Bulletin No. 1*, Canberra, ASC.

BATES, R. (1986) *The Management of Culture and Knowledge*, Geelong, Deakin University Press.

BERNSTEIN, B. (1972) 'Education cannot compensate for society' in RUBINSTEIN, D. and STOREMAN (Eds) *Schooling for Democracy*, London, Penguin, pp. 105–16.

BRUNER, J.S. (1966) *Towards a Theory of Instruction*, Cambridge, MA, Harvard University Press.

BULLIVANT, B.M. (1981a) *Race, Ethnicity and Curriculum*, Melbourne, Macmillan.

BULLIVANT, B.M. (1981b) *The Pluralist Dilemma in Education: Six Case Studies*, London, George Allen & Unwin.

BULLIVANT, B.M. (1982) 'Power and control in the multi-ethnic school: Towards a conceptual model', *Ethnic and Racial Studies*, 5, 1, pp. 53–70.

BULLIVANT, B.M. (1985) 'Educating the pluralist person: Images of society and educational responses in Australia', in POOLE, M.E., DE LACEY, P. and RANDHAWA, B. (Eds) *Australia in Transition: Culture and Life Possibilities*, Sydney, Harcourt Brace Jovanovich.

CLARKE, J., HALL, S., JEFFERSON, T. and ROBERTS, B. (1981) *Resistance Through Rituals*, London, Hutchinson.

DEPARTMENT OF EDUCATION AND SCIENCE (1981) *West Indian Children in Our Schools: Report of the Committee of Enquiry into the Education of Children from Ethnic Minority Groups* (The Rampton Report) Cmnd. 8273, London, HMSO.

DEPARTMENT OF EDUCATION AND SCIENCE (1985) *Education for All: Report of the Committee of Enquiry into the Education of Children from Ethnic Minority Groups* (The Swann Report) Cmnd. 9453, London, HMSO.

DOYLE, W. and PONDER, G. (1977) 'The practicality ethic in teacher decision making', *Interchange*, 8, 3, pp. 1–11.

EIPPER, C. (1983) 'The magician's hat: A critique of the concept of ethnicity', *Australian and New Zealand Journal of Sociology*, 19, 3, pp. 428–45.

ELBAZ, F. (1983) *Teacher Thinking: A Study of Practical Knowledge*. London, Croom Helm.

FOUCAULT, M. (1972) *The Archaeology of Knowledge*, New York, Random House.

FREEDMAN, S. , JACKSON, J. and BOLES, K. (1983) 'Teaching: An imperilled profession' in SHULMAN, L. and SYKES, G. (Eds) *Handbook of Teaching and Policy*, New York, Longman.

GALBALLY, F. (1978) *Migrant Services and Programs, Report of the Review of Post-Arrival Programs and Services for Migrants*, Canberra, Australian Government Publishing Service.

GIBSON, M. (1976) 'Approaches to multicultural education in the universityted states: Some concepts and assumptions', *Anthropology and Education Quarterly*, vii, 4, pp. 7–18.

GOODENOUGH, W.H. (1971) 'Multiculturalism as normal human experience', *Anthropology and Education Quarterly*, 7, 4, pp. 4–6.

GRANT, C. and SLEETER, C. (1985) 'The literature on multicultural education: Review and analysis', *Educational Review*, 37, 2, pp. 97–118.

GRASSBY, A. (1973) *A Multicultural Society for the Future*, Canberra, AGPS.

HATTON, E.J. (1985) 'Equality, class and power: A case study,' *British Journal of Sociology of Education*, 6, 3, pp. 225–72.

HENRY, M. and LINGARD, R. (1982) 'Multiculturalism: Rhetoric and reality', *New Education*, 4, 2, pp. 75–90.

JAYASURIYA, L. (1984a) 'Into the mainstream', *Australian Society*, March, pp. 25–7.

JAYASURIYA, L. (1984b) 'Multiculturalism: Ethnicity and Equality', *Education News*, 18, pp. 42–3.

JAYASURIYA, L. (1985) 'Multiculturalism: Fact, policy and rhetoric' in POOLE, M., DE LACEY, P. and RANDHAWA, B. (Eds), *Australia in Transition: Culture and Life Possibilities*, Sydney: Harcourt, Brace, Jovanovich.

KEESING, R. (1978) 'Review of *Meaning in Anthropology* by Basso, H. and Selby, H.', *American Anthropologist*, 80, pp. 132–3.

LEVI-STRAUSS, C. (1963) *Structural Anthropology*, New York, Basic Books.

LOVEGROVE, M. and POOLE, M. (1975) 'Groping towards tolerance: The Australian experience' in VERMA, G. and BAGLEY, C. (Eds) *Race and Education Across Cultures*, London, Heinemann, pp. 170–213.

McQUEEN, H. (1972) *A New Britannia*, Victoria, Penguin.

MOODLEY, K.A. (1984) 'The predicament of racial affirmative action, a critical review of *Equality Now*', *Queen's Quarterly*, 91, 4, pp. 795–806.

NEW SOUTH WALES DEPARTMENT OF EDUCATION (1979) Minister for Education, *Multicultural Education Policy Statement*, Sydney, Australian Government Publishing Service.

O'KEEFFE, D.J. (1985) 'Swann-song of prejudice. Thoughts on "Racism in Schools"', *Education Encounter*, pp. 70–5.

POOLE, M.E. (1981) 'Educational opportunity for minority groups: Australian research reviewed', in MEGARRY, J., NISBET, S. and HOYLE, E. (Eds) *World Yearbook of Education*, London, Roger Page, pp. 254–80.

POOLE, M.E. (1985a) 'Australian multicultural policies: Future prospects', in POOLE, M.E., DE LACEY, P. and RANDHAWA, B. (Eds) *Australia in Transition: Culture and Life Possibilities*, Sydney, Harcourt, Brace, Jovanovich, pp. 59–69.

POOLE, M.E. (1985b) 'Pathways and options for ethnic adolescents' in POOLE, M.E., DE LACEY, P. and RANDHAWA, B. (Eds) *Australia in Transition: Culture and Life Possibilities,* Sydney, Harcourt, Brace Jovanovich, pp. 192–203.

POPKEWITZ, T., TABACHNICK, B.R. and WEHLAGE, G. (1982) *The Myth of Educational Reform: A Study of School Response to a Program of Change,* Madison, WI, University of Wisconsin Press.

QUEENSLAND DEPARTMENT OF EDUCATION (1979) *Education for a Multicultural Society. A Discussion Paper Based on the Report to the Council of Directors of the Queensland Department of Education,* Brisbane, Australian Government Publishing Service.

QUEENSLAND MULTICULTURAL COORDINATING COMMITTEE (1982) *Education for a Multicultural Society: Policies and Practices,* Brisbane, Australian Government Publishing Service.

RIZVI, F. (1985) *Multiculturalism as an Education Policy,* Geelong, Deakin University Press.

SACHS, J. (1986) 'Putting culture back into multicultural education', *New Community,* 8, 2.

SACHS, J. (1987) 'The constitution of teacher knowledge: A literature review', *Discourse,* 7, 2.

SACHS, J. (1988) 'Teachers' conceptions of the culture concept', unpublished PhD thesis, University of Queensland, St. Lucia.

SAUNDERS, M. (1982) 'Education for a new society', *New Community,* X, 1, pp. 64–71.

SHARP, R. (1980) 'The culture of the disadvantaged: Three views', *School and Community News,* 4, pp. 17–23.

SMITH, R. and KNIGHT, J. (1978) 'Macos in Queensland: The politics of educational knowledge', *Australian Journal of Education,* 22, 3.

SMITH, R. and KNIGHT, J. (1982) 'Liberal ideology, radical critiques and change in education: A matter of goals', *British Journal of Sociology of Education,* 3, 3.

SMITH, R. and SACHS, J. (1980) *One Notion, Many Conceptions: Context Evaluation of Brisbane South Region Multicultural Education Project,* Sydney, Australian Government Publishing Service.

SMITH, R. and SACHS, J. (1981) *A Step in the Right Direction: Process Evaluation of Brisbane South Region Multicultural Education Project,* Sydney, Australian Government Publishing Service.

SOUTH AUSTRALIA DEPARTMENT OF EDUCATION (n.d.) *Multicultural Education: A Curriculum Directorate Information Brochure,* Adelaide, Australian Government Publishing Service.

SOUTH AUSTRALIA DEPARTMENT OF EDUCATION (1982) *Diversity and Cohesion,* Adelaide, Australian Government Publishing Service.

STURMAN, A. (1985) *Immigrant Australians and Education,* Melbourne, ACER.

WALLACE, A. (1961) *Culture and Personality* (1st edn) New York, Random House.

WARREN, R., ROSE, S. and BERGUNDER, A. (1974) *The Structure of Urban Reform.* Lexington, MA, Lexington Books.

Chapter 5

The Pluralist Dilemma Revisited

Brian M. Bullivant

In any sexually reproducing species, equality of individuals is a natural impossibility...The just society...is one in which sufficient order protects members, whatever their diverse endowments, and sufficient disorder provides every individual with full opportunity to develop his genetic endowment, whatever that may be. (Ardrey, 1970)

From the perspective of an antipodean educationist working in a very different demographic and ethnocultural context from that of Britain, the Swann Report (DES, 1985) provides both a sense of *déjà vu* — here we go again! — and a feeling of irritation. The *déjà vu* will be familiar to most people who have been trying for years to find solutions to resolve the tensions inherent in race and ethnic relations. We do not seem to be able to get beyond conventional wisdom: pat maxims such as 'equality'; well-trodden paths such as recommendations for more teacher training; and seemingly unassailable statistics such as those that virtually assume minority ethnic groups' lack of academic achievement. The big questions remain unanswered; the problems of achieving harmonious interethnic and race relations seem as intractable as ever.

This feeling is exacerbated when one recalls Troyna's comment (1984) about what has occurred in Britain:

> ...despite repeated demands for the re-appraisal of curricular, organizational and pedagogic procedures along multicultural lines and the decision by a growing number of black parents and community groups to establish their own 'supplementary schools' to provide their children with the skills presumed to be lacking in formal educational institutions, the DES, LEAs and their individual schools stubbornly resisted any changes at least until very recently. (p. 76)

Are we to assume that the DES, LEAs and possibly other organizations such as teacher unions are being merely neglectful or are co-partners in a hegemonic conspiracy to 'keep ethnics in their place'? If the same question were posed of the situation in Australia, either answer could be sustained.

Our feeling of irritation also stems partly from an overactive conscience: we (the social scientists and 'experts') surely should be able to solve these problems and right society's ills. Yet nagging doubts still persist: 'What if harmony is not a realizable human condition?' 'What if equality is a chimera of figment of overstained utopian imagination?' 'What if there are forces operating in societies composed by sexually reproducing species that defy all our rational solutions?' 'What if there is more to sociobiological explanations of social equality than meets the eye?'

Faced by these kinds of speculations our erstwhile confidence in being able to find the solutions through sheer perseverance is sorely tested, but we are not alone. As Lord Swann comments (1985) 'Achievement of potential, it is clear, is an immensely difficult and long-term socioeconomic problem, and one must doubt whether any human society has yet come anywhere near to solving it' (p. 4). Yet this is nothing new, having been said years before in A.H. Halsey's (1972) pessimistic conclusion that 'the essential fact of twentieth century educational history is that egalitarian policies have failed' (p. 6). *Déjà vu* again! Why don't we explore beyond the trite and the conventional and try to discover whether there are principles operating in society which may defy all our egalitarian aims?

The Conventional Wisdom in Lord Swann's Paper

Such reflections stem from the contrasts that can be made with the British situation which are implicit in the 300-page report of a major research project we completed in 1986 for the Australian Human Rights Commission (Bullivant, 1986b and 1987). During the research many conventional assumptions about educating ethnic minorities were rigorously examined and some found to be baseless.

For example, it examined sufficient evidence to cast strong doubt on the claims that improving minority children's self-esteem would increase their academic performance. These doubts echo Lord Swann's (1985) comment: '. . . there is now a good deal of evidence that low self-esteem among minority children, is not the widespread phenomenon that might be expected and has often been supposed' (p. 8).

The 'Paradox of Asian Performance' noted by Swann (*ibid.*, p. 9) was also discovered by our research, but in contrast to the reported inability of his Committee to find an explanation, our report has suggested (with hopefully minimal colonial presumption) that at least the manifest successes of Indo-Asians and ethnic Chinese in Australia may be due to what we term the 'ethnic success ethic'. This is discussed in more detail below, but raises another question: is Britain the exception to what we claim could be a widespread phenomenon and, if so, why? Are the answers to be found in the different dynamics of the British scenario that involves race relations embedded in intractable historical factors that may be lacking in Australia?

Swann makes the suggestion, which we have met so often as to suggest that it is almost ideologically obligatory, that a great deal of ethnic groups' disadvantage in Britain is due to socioeconomic factors and implies that this is virtually a universal correlation. How was it then that our research for the Human Rights Commission found clear evidence which adds to the steadily mounting body of findings in Australia, United States and Canada that some ethnic groups—in our case notably Greeks, Italians, Yugoslavs, Chinese and some Indo-Asians—achieve academic and socioeconomic success out of all proportion to their numbers in the society despite coming from lower socioeconomic backgrounds?

The 'Hidden Agenda' in Lord Swann's Paper

Other reflections have been prompted by reading between the lines of Lord Swann's comments—their 'hidden agenda' or ability to hint at a Pandora's box sitting in the wings of the ethnic and race relations stage. The 'box' (Swann, 1985) was his Committee's proposal to mount 'a major research project, in the hope that it might throw more light on the factors in school, in the community and in the home, that led to the success or failure of ethnic minority pupils' (pp. 8–9). Surely this was a laudable aim? Surely all persons of goodwill would welcome such an investigation for, after all, would they not want to see harmony prevail in Britain and what could they fear when all is said and done? Knowing how things really operate in the disorderly world we inhabit it comes as no surprise to learn that 'the project aroused hostility in various circles, and it had to be abandoned'.

Our sense of *déjà vu* is at its strongest here. Wasn't this the fate of several Schools Council research reports or surveys in the 1970s? Wasn't it the teachers' unions which embargoed the publication of the findings (see discussion in Bullivant, 1981a, pp. 26–28; Dorn and Troyna, 1982)? Has anyone really asked why we seem compelled to ignore the lessons of history and appear to believe naively that teaching is an apolitical 'calling' still carried out by professionals? The Brent LEA experience in Britain during 1985/86 illustrated that teachers' unions can resist such demands to hold an independent investigation into the schooling of black students in local schools, and shows that the situation has changed little during the intervening period.

But this British episode it not unique. As we indicate below, Australian teacher unions are now threatening the continued existence and operation of the non-government or private, independent schools, many of which cater for the academic aspirations of children from ethnic groups. Some of the unions' motives may be due to declining numbers of pupils entering the government or state schools and the threat to teachers' jobs this poses. However, at least one (albeit right-wing) newspaper columnist (Keegan, 1987), whose views are given below, has suggested other hegemonic reasons, and has painted a scenario in the state of New South Wales that is Orwellian in the extreme.

In the case of the Swann enquiry the matter appears to have been more complex, as the 'various circles' included some black community groups spokespersons for the National Anti-racist Movement in Education (NAME) and equal opportunity advisers (Troyna, 1986). Such a situation suggests that complex factors producing the underachievement of black and other minority groups in Britain were not being addressed. 'From this perspective it is difficult to dispute NAME's insistence that Swann should have commissioned research to consider "some of the major factors which impinge on success or failure in schools"....Only research could identify how far each of these embrace racist impulses, intent, practices or consequences' (*ibid.*, 177).

The Australian Research Challenge to the Conventional Wisdom

Since the end of the Second World War and the influx of immigrant children into Australian schools, it has been assumed that the majority of them have been disadvantaged academically. This picture of immigrant education virtually attained the status of eternal truth, and stimulated numerous remedial and compensatory programs and their supporting institutional agencies (Bullivant, 1981a, Chapter 7). A little-challenged corollary of the conventional wisdom has been the assumption that Anglo-Australian children — the yardstick for measuring ethnics' success — have been higher achievers than their ethnic peers. So the picture has remained until very recently.

However, the findings of several research studies have shown that numbers of second-generation children from some ethnic groups are outperforming Anglo-Australian children academically, are gaining a disproportionate share of tertiary education places, and have greater motivation and aspirations to achieve. Comparable data from overseas studies summarized by Sowell (1986) among others suggest that this phenomenon is not unique to Australia and should be regarded as an inherent feature of some immigrants' life situations. Our research for the Human Rights Commission is another contribution to a growing corpus of findings which suggest that some ethnic groups are able to resist the force of ethnocultural hegemony imposed by the dominant 'Staatsvolk' of the society in which they are living.

Theoretical Base of the Research Design

Aims of the Research

Our research design adopted an approach paradigm which from the outset did not assume that ethnic students were being successful. In fact, the project was commissioned and funded by the Human Rights Commission to establish whether prejudice and discrimination, due to social class, ethnic, racial and gender differences, were disadvantaging the career decisions of students at the senior level of schooling in seven Melbourne high schools.

To focus on this possibility, three broad sources of prejudice and discrimination were hypothesized: (a) those originating from within the schools, i.e. systemic factors; (b) those resulting from interactions between students; and (c) those originating from the wider school context and community. We selected the last two years of students' school careers when they are making plans about further study or employment, as the paradigm period when prejudice and discrimination might be expected to be present and have most effect as the outcome of attempts by Anglo-Australians to minimize the successes of those from ethnic backgrounds.

Theoretically the research took its direction from a modification of the well-known social and cultural reproduction theories of Bernstein (1971), Bourdieu (1973), Bourdieu and Passeron (1977) and others. They have proposed that the domination over power and economic resources by the ruling classes in society is reproduced through schooling and the curriculum to favour children from similar classes. This thesis has been used mainly to focus on differences in a class-stratified society.

In a complex pluralist society, other grounds such as cultural, racial, ethnic and gender bases of discrimination can be incorporated into a theoretical model. The one developed here takes its direction from 'realistic group-conflict theory' (Le Vine and Campbell, 1972, pp. 29–42) and a modification of Banton's (1983) 'rational choice theory'. Our view stresses the central force of ethnocultural hegemony under conditions of multi-faceted pluralism, in which groups and individuals strive to maximize their life satisfaction and advantages *vis-à-vis* other individuals and groups by various strategies of 'social closure' (Weber, 1968); Parkin, 1974; Bullivant, 1984). As Parkin has put it

> By social closure Weber means the process by which social collectivities seek to maximize rewards by restricting access to rewards and opportunities to a limited circle of eligibles. This entails the singling out of certain identifiable social or physical attributes as the justificatory basis for exclusion. Weber suggests that virtually any group attribute — race, language, social origin, descent — may be seized upon provided it can be used for 'the monopolization of specific, usually economic opportunities... its purpose is always the closure of social and economic opportunities to outsiders'. (p. 3)

Groups and individuals employ distinguishing characteristics of race, gender, social class, ethnicity and culture as symbolic boundary markers for purposes of exclusion and inclusion to protect their socioeconomic and political interests. Their adoption of such boundary markers varies historically and according to the prevailing political, social and economic situation. Each boundary marker assumes saliency only when a group becomes aware of its need to promote social closure. For example, racial differences may be ignored in a multiracial society as long as all its constituent groups maintain relative parity. When this breaks down, a group wishing to establish economic or political dominance can seize upon 'race' (phenotypical differences) as a convenient boundary marker to symbolize the exclusion of those who should not obtain a commensurate share of the economic resources claimed by the dominants. In other words race awareness must be a necessary condition for racialism to occur.

Attempts at social closure by the dominant group in a society can be resisted by reciprocal strategies of inclusion and exclusion, which are employed by subordinated groups or conceivably even individuals. Such collective types of *reciprocal social closure* involve the use of 'solidarism' to usurp a share of the dominant group's socioeconomic resources and rewards. 'Solidaristic efforts are always directed at the usurpation of resources in the sense that claims to rewards, if successful, will normally result in some diminution of the share accruing to superordinate groups' (*ibid.*, p. 10).

Both social closure and usurpation are enacted by institutional agencies, i.e. organized groups carrying out particular institutional functions (Theodorson and Theodorson, 1970, p. 207). For example, schools are institutional agencies carrying out the functions of education, which is part of the wider institution of enculturation, i.e. cultural transmission. To operate effectively institutional agencies are programmed by the relevant parts of the culture or sub-culture of the society or a sub-group of it which they represent. Thus state or government schools attempt to transmit as representative a selection of the common culture as possible. An ethnic or socioeconomic sub-group within the society may not agree with what is being transmitted and will establish its own institutional agency such as an ethnic or private school. This can be interpreted as a kind of usurpation or solidaristic attempt to resist dominance by the mainstream school system.

The 'black voluntary school movement' in Britain has been interpreted in this light by Chevannes and Reeves (1987):

> The success of the voluntary black school lies in its ability to generate a strong group solidarity based on common experiences of being black in a white society, perceived by teachers, parents, and students alike as hostile and unfriendly. The school constitutes a black environment, insulating, protecting and supporting the individual against the unpredictability of white behaviour and the constant difficulty of interpreting outcomes in a context of widespread white prejudice and discrimination. (p. 151)

Ethnic schools have become a major feature in Australia and those affiliated to some ethnic groups, particularly the Jewish community (Bullivant, 1978b and 1982), have been relatively successful in enabling children from their ethnic constituencies to master the curriculum necessary both for success at the Higher School Certificate (HSC) examination and to maintain elements of their ethnic cultures. However, they form part of the general independent school system that has grown very rapidly in recent years partly due to declining standards in the state system, but is now threatened by general opposition from militant left-wing trade unions.

The latest in a number of measures to this effect is a television campaign commissioned by the Australian Teachers' Federation and aimed at bolstering the image of the state schools and implicitly denigrating the work of independent schools. However, legislation before the New South Wales Parliament in 1987 went even further, and anyone familiar with the authoritarian nature of the former Labor government's political control in that State would not find its draconian terms at all surprising. In the words of Dr N.K. Weeks, a historian at the University of Sydney, cited verbatim by Keegan (1987):

'The means chosen to prevent loss of State influence are massive increases in the power of the State in education. The Bills, in the Upper House, give the State control over "courses of instruction, patterns of study, educational facilities and other prescribed matters" in private schools.

Anybody who defies the regulation procedures faces jail or fines; inspectors can enter any building suspected to be a school, seize materials, take photographs and compel a person to give personal details.

With the aid of a search warrant they can do the same with a private home. The Bills seek to bar appeals to the courts against school registration decisions. An appeal tribunal is made the final court of appeal and the minister for education appoints the appeal tribunal. It can be stacked'. (p. 29)

If passed into law, one of the major effects of the proposed legislation would have been to prevent the 'development of alternative curricula and credentials in the private system'. These are anathema to the left-wing supporters of the egalitarian ideology that is so prevalent in the general ethos of Australia. However, in a period of serious economic difficulties — becoming 'a banana republic' and 'going down the tubes' in one politician's memorable phrase — successful ethnic groups may be perceived as an economic threat to Anglo-Australian workers (however inefficient and pampered) and more hegemonic measures may have been deemed necessary to curb their successes.

The Swann Committee also debated the issue of 'separate schools'. As the following comment from the Runnymede Trust (1985) appears to suggest, by presuming to speak on behalf of pupils, parents and communities, its considerations were not devoid of hegemonic implications:

Creating an artificially separate situation in which children are taught exclusively by teachers from the same ethnic group is not desirable from the point of view of the children, the minority community or society as a whole. Separate schools cannot therefore be supported on these grounds. The only way of ensuring that minority communities are able both to retain their religious, cultural and linguistic heritages, and to be accorded full equality, is within the broader pluralist context for which the [Swann] report argues. Separate schools could well fail to tackle many of the underlying concerns of the communities and might also exacerbate the very feelings of rejection which they were seeking to overcome. (p. 19)

Once again we note the almost ritual reference to 'equality' in the above, but must strongly question the logic behind its use. The origins of ethnocultural hegemony illustrated by or implied in the foregoing examples can often be traced historically, but the question of the fundamental reasons why they occur can only be conjectured (for example, van den Berghe, 1978; Bullivant, 1981b). Competition and conflict are universal phenomena in all sexually reproducing species. Humankind is no exception to this rule; to maintain otherwise is to deny the major evolutionary forces that have made it into the most successful (and predatory) species on earth. The processes of social closure and usurpation are ways in which competition and conflict are effected. Others are force and naked aggression. Altruism is a relatively rare phenomenon but even that can be explained in sociobiological terms (Dawkins, 1976). Might not all attempts to redress inequality be chimerical and doomed to failure in the final analysis?

Perspectives on Occupational Socialization

Our research focused on what we termed 'occupational socialization', i.e. that phase within the wider process of socialization, in which a young person is specifically concerned with preparing for and planning a future career scenario, in the sense of 'an account or synopsis of a projected course of action' (Webster's New Collegiate Dictionary). For research purposes we assumed that the processes involved could be interpreted from a synthesis of two theoretical perspectives, the structural-functional and the phenomenological.

From the structural-functional or systemic perspective our analysis was mainly concerned with the structures, processes and practices that were taken for granted as 'givens', somehow external to and influencing or constraining the career scenarios of students. To obtain information about these we focused mainly on the institutional agencies and activities of the school and its curriculum. Other agencies were the family, peer group, government bodies such as careers advice centres, and employers.

The second perspective was based on taking a symbolic interactionist view of behaviour. Students construct their social realities and views of the world, by interpreting and manipulating information feedback from the environments and numerous sociocultural contexts with which they interact. One important context is provided by the school and its classrooms; other contexts are the agencies mentioned in the previous paragraph.

The process of occupational socialization is essentially a synthesis combined effects of external structures, over which students have little if any control, with their own idiosyncratic interpretations of reality. In our view this dual process is fundamental to forming career scenarios. It enables a student to reflect on his/her life possibilities, form job aspirations or more realistic expectations and interpret all the constraints on likely futures, while not neglecting to take into account the fact that all this has to take place within some non-negotiable structures and systemic constraints.

Factors Affecting Occupational Socialization

The Curriculum

Central to understanding the operation of schooling and ethnocultural hegemony is the curriculum. This can be thought of as the set of knowledge, ideas and experiences resulting from ideologically influenced and value-laden processes of selection from a social group's public stock of current knowledge, ideas and experiences (i.e. its culture), their organization into sub-sets (syllabuses and units) and necessary logistical backup facilities, transmission to clients (students, pupils) in teaching-learning interface settings, and periodic evaluation, which provides feedback into previous processes.

The inclusion of experiences draws attention to the fact that the curriculum contains more than knowledge and ideas. Equally, it needs to be stressed that all of the processes are not necessarily confined to what takes place within the school campus. Important learning occurs on school excursions and visits. These are not extra-curricular activities as is often assumed; rather they are extra-mural and have an important contribution to make to the total learning experiences open to children. For example, one of those available for senior students is work experience programs of various sorts, that operate within the community where the school is located. Our research revealed that they provide opportunities for employers to exercise discrimination against students.

Related Features

Three related features of the model need to be stressed. Firstly, the curriculum should partly be, but quite often is not, a response to clients', i.e. students' and parents', wants. More often it reflects teachers' and other educationists' idiosyncratic interpretations of these needs and wants, and can therefore be subject to their unconscious and even deliberate bias. This can occur especially if some teachers and educationists place some of their clients into a category which is considered to be undeserving of a full share of the knowledge, ideas and experiences that constitute the curriculum.

Secondly, in the kinds of open education systems usual in Western societies, all the four processes of the curriculum are not only subject to the influences of value judgments and ideologies that are held by teachers and educationists within a school, but they are also influenced by the ideologies of external systems. Examples of the latter are subject associations and official government and semi-government organizations and, as we have shown, teachers' unions.

Such situations provide opportunities for many bodies and individuals to exercise ethnocultural hegemony through the curriculum. For example, if they hold value judgments and ideologies based on racist and ethnocentric assumptions, they can influence the selection, organization, transmission and evaluation processes in a way that discriminates against the rights of children from ethnocultural minorities.

Thirdly, the process of selection must preserve the balance between instrumental knowledge and conceptions and expressive knowledge and conceptions (more fully discussed in Bullivant, 1981b, Chapter 2). This also provides opportunities for educators to be biased towards some children and favour others. For example, a curriculum that is unduly weighted with a selection of the expressive aspects from the ethnic group's cultural stock and stresses ethnic life styles may not provide students with sufficient instrumental survival knowledge to compete for life chances when they leave school. Thus equipping children with a surfeit, say, of ethnic community languages, history and music in an attempt to improve their cultural awareness, may be of far less survival value in the final analysis than mathematics, skills in using computers, and accountancy. This is not to say that ethnic community languages and heritages are not intrinsically valuable, but they may have less pragmatic value for a person's survival in a society dominated by English.

Fourthly, the processes of evaluation and assessment also provide ways of controlling the futures of students. Many professional careers are gained by passing examinations in competition for places at universities or colleges of further education. School staff are in a position to control how fast or easily students are allowed to attain these qualifications. For example, Cecile Wright (1987) has shown how procedures used in two British case study schools to allocate students to the 'O' level or CSE courses at the beginning of their fourth year discriminated against Afro-Caribbean students. 'Figures show that the proportion of Afro-Caribbean students entered for, and thus gaining 'O' levels, was dramatically lower than for the Asian and white students' (p. 123).

A corollary concerns the subjects needed to successfully negotiate examination hurdles on the way to final examinations. Some subjects are prerequisites and may have to be provided in the curriculum, despite the inherent attractiveness of subjects with less survival value. For example, an ethnic community language may be on the list of examinable subjects, and may even have high expressive value but not be useful for obtaining a job or gaining university selection. Only high achievement in high status subjects, such as sciences, mathematics, biology, accountancy, economics will achieve this. Channelling children away from these into other, lower-status subjects may do them a disservice in the survival race.

The Sample and Research Methodology

Following exploratory research in a pilot school, our main research was carried out in a non-random (quota) sample of seven other high schools within the Melbourne metropolitan area. They were selected to match the characteristics of the cells in a two by three matrix based on the concept of ethclass (Gordon, 1964), i.e. a combination of socioeconomic status (SES) in three sub-divisions, and high/low ethnicity as defined by the Victorian Education Department Annual School Census. In this children are counted as ethnics if they were either born overseas in a non-English-speaking country or have one parent who was born in such a country. A supplementary measure used by some schools is the language other than English spoken in the home (see Bullivant, 1986b, for more details).

Two days of intensive condensed fieldwork were spent in each school using naturalistic or neo-ethnographic methodology (Bullivant, 1978a and 1978b) and a questionnaire developed in the pilot school. In all some 200 students in grades 11 and 12 (approximate ages 16–17 years) were interviewed in small groups and some sixty staff most closely connected with students' careers planning were spoken to individually and at length. Most interviews with staff and students were tape-recorded and later transcribed to be reproduced verbatim in the final report.

We obviously cannot claim that this sample is in any way representative and generalizable to the wider school system. However, since the publication of our report supportive feedback has been received from teachers within Victoria who were not associated with the research and was also apparent in the reactions of some ethnic communities, radio and television commentary and debates in the daily press. Informal interviews conducted in other schools by mass media representatives in Victoria and Western Australia to produce follow-up feature programs also substantiated the major findings of our research.

Whether they have been positive or negative all the reactions have indicated unequivocally that the research has brought into the public arena of concern issues that are critical to Australia's future and probably have relevance for other pluralist societies. It is the latter aspect that provides the comparative focus for reacting to the Swann Report.

Unexpected Findings in the Curricula of the Schools

The theoretical design of the research assumed that the schools would function as vehicles for the operation of ethnocultural hegemony or sociocultural reproduction by the dominant Anglo-Australian staff in matters relating to careers planning and related academic attainment. In effect this would constitute a form of social closure that would favour Anglo-Australian students and disadvantage those from recent immigrant non-English-speaking (NES) backgrounds, whether Asian and Indo-Asian or those second-generation students from earlier waves of immigration such as Greeks, Italians, Yugoslavs and similar groups. In fact the reverse was the case.

Selection of Curriculum

The Higher School Certificate (HSC) and its academically oriented group 1 subjects dominated currriculum selection in all schools and attempts to introduce the more liberal group 2 subjects were strongly resisted by students and parents from all ethnic backgrounds. They clearly demanded the group 1 subjects that would provide a route to tertiary education and professional career opportunities. The most demanding in this respect were Greeks, Italians, Yugoslavs and Asian students.

Only in one inner-city school was an alternative curriculum selection offered. This comprised subjects for the Schools' Year Twelve and Tertiary Entrance Certificate (STC). These are much more 'liberal' in emphasis and provide a broader vocationally-oriented education. Both HSC and STC are terminal qualifications. Both are accepted by the great majority of tertiary institutions for entry purposes, although Monash and Melbourne universities do not recognize STC. Some NES students claimed that this hampered their future career plans, and to that extent they were disadvantaged. However, this situation applied to all students regardless of ethnic background, and was out of the school's control. The likelihood of it being some kind of ethnocultural reproduction could not be sustained.

In all schools the curriculum selection was made after maximum opportunities had been given to students to make known their needs and subject requirements either through their respective Student Representative Councils or by the thorough subject selection procedures at the end of years 10 (for year 11) and 11 (for year 12). 'Blocking' was used in the construction of timetables to maximize students' choices. Staff claimed to be highly responsive to students' needs, and there was little evidence from data to suggest otherwise.

In fact, in the inner-city high school, located in a depressed socioeconomic area where one might have expected ethnocultural hegemony to operate, the structure of the curriculum at year 12, and particularly the inclusion of sciences and mathematics, owed their establishment and continuation to the decision of staff back in the late 1970s not to drop these subjects. They took it mainly on ideological grounds that even students from lower SES backgrounds should be given a chance to go on to HSC and tertiary entrance if they wished. The decision also acceded to the demands of students and their parents from NES and Indo-Asian backgrounds for high-prestige mathematics and science subjects, which they considered would open the door to university entrance and professional careers.

In all the schools it was this ubiquitous pattern of catering for ethnic students' demands that made it extremely difficult to establish a case for ethnocultural hegemony in curriculum selection which worked against the interests of those from NES and Indo-Asian backgrounds, and in favour of Anglo-Australian students. The reverse was more likely. Those who stood to gain from the selection of HSC group 1 subjects were the students who had high career aspirations, were academically motivated and aimed towards tertiary education and professional careers. Evidence suggested that these tended to come from some NES (particularly Greek and Italian), and Asian (particularly Chinese) backgrounds, together with some middle- to high-SES Anglo-Australian students and their parents.

Whether this will continue in Victoria is extremely debatable. A new Victorian Certificate of Education (VCE) is due to be introduced in all schools to replace the HSC. One of the grounds for this innovation is claimed to be that it will increase the 'educational equality' of all students. As we pointed out above, this is a logically dubious proposition and may actually disadvantage NES students by lessening the academic emphasis they so clearly demand. By insisting that all students do compulsory components which need facility with English, new courses could also discriminate against those who are weak in this subject.

One of those which has been strongly criticized, on this and ideological grounds, is Australian Studies. This will be broadly based on history, social studies and the 'study of work', all areas in which non-English-speaking (NES) students' limitations could be inhibiting. Teachers of English as a second language are also concerned that the compulsory sections in the VCE will reduce the time NES students have to improve their English language skills. At present the HSC allows NES students to present for a special English examination in year 12.

It would be theoretically tempting, but too facile, to interpret such imminent changes as deliberate attempts at ethnocultural reproduction or hegemony on the part of the Victorian state education system. The recent unhappy history of the system has seen a succession of changes to school organization and curricula on an often *ad hoc* basis. Many of them have been attempts to counter declining educational standards and dwindling student numbers due to demographic changes in the overall population, and have resulted in the wholesale amalgamation or closure of schools. Other changes have been more ideologically motivated and justified by using social class analysis with Marxist overtones, carried out either by left-wing teachers' unions or by influential radicals with proven left-wing track records in educational reform.

One result of their efforts has been to accelerate the exodus of students from state schools to the independent, non-government schools where discipline, academic standards and examination results are perceived by parents to be superior. However, it is evident that even these schools will not be untouched by the provisions of the new VCE. It is a matter for growing concern that the independent schools' attempts to encourage meritocratic excellence will be thwarted by state control over assessment procedures and a possible reduction in the say the universities will have over academic standards.

Concurrent with what is happening in the wider Australian context, as we have seen, it is particularly worrying that the power of left-wing unions to curb the expansion of private schools is gathering momentum. Victorian teacher unions are having marked success in a campaign of opposition to the development of new and existing private schools (Maslen, 1987, p. 6). Admittedly this will disadvantage all their students, but many students from NES and Asian backgrounds could be more disadvantaged in comparison with their Anglo-Australian peers.

However, as matters stood at the time of our research, those in the seven state schools we studied who were most likely to be disadvantaged were *inter alia* Anglo-Australian students from lower-SES backgrounds, along with students from NES and Asian backgrounds who did not aspire to tertiary education. Evidence suggested that the numbers of the latter dropped off in senior levels due to them leaving the school by year level 10, to seek alternative education. Whether they were disadvantaged, or would have transferred due to perceived lack of ability or preference for such education anyway, is a moot point. From the data it was clear that not all students aspired to careers needing HSC or university qualifications, and it could have been those students who had chosen other options.

Rejection of Multicultural Education

In every school, there was very limited provision of multicultural education, supporting Cahill's (1984) findings regarding the generally low support for multicultural education in Australia as a whole. What there was appeared to be tokenistic, stressing ethnic life-style matters such as national festivals, foods, dances and dress. Bastille Day featured strongly in those schools that taught French. In one school the demands from the Greek community to have its national day recognized led to so much opposition from other ethnic groups that the whole matter became very divisive and the principal banned all public recognition of ethnic national days apart from Australia Day when the Australian flag was flown. It is illuminating to note that this tokenistic kind of emphasis was criticized by the Swann Committee.

In two of the schools, staff were antagonistic towards multicultural education and even some ethnic teacher aides questioned its usefulness. In no school was there any 'politicized multicultural education' of the kind proposed by this writer (Bullivant, 1986a) to improve ethnic life chances. Moreover, nothing of this kind was demanded by students and parents from ethnic backgrounds, and in the opinion of some staff would have been rejected anyway had it been offered.

Brian M. Bullivant

Evaluation for Entry into HSC — A Potential Filtering System

As suggested above, one possible way of controlling the life chances of students is to prevent their promotion into the higher year levels, which are the gateways to tertiary academic futures and the professions. All schools operated systems of evaluation by term examinations for controlling entry into the year 11 and 12 HSC group 1 streams. In general, students must have passed the stipulated number of subjects at the year 11 level, especially in the prerequisites laid down for the HSC examination. Lack of them could effectively act as a barrier to going on to some subjects, thus limiting the career options available.

In all schools, the year 11 and 12 coordinators, assisted by the careers teacher and others called in if necessary, were in a position to exercise a channelling role in deciding who went on to HSC. They had the overall effect of operating a *filtering system*, through which students had to pass towards their chosen careers. Conceivably the discussions about each student's 'promotability' that occurred at the end of each year provided one opportunity for exercising control over the aspirations of those who wanted to proceed to university and on into the professions. However, the 'filter papers' or examinations — to pursue the metaphor — were built into the system through the prerequisites set down for HSC, and were thus largely outside the control of the schools and applied across the board for all students regardless of ethnicity.

However, the possibility still existed within schools for the promotion system to be used to discriminate against students, but we found no evidence of this. The severity with which the system was applied did vary from school to school. For example, in one we were informed rather cryptically that 'we take the selection for year 12 as an opportunity to weed out those who are not suited to HSC. . .they go on to Technical and Further Education (TAFE) Colleges'. However there was no evidence to suggest that any particular ethnic group was picked on for this weeding out procedure.

Indeed, in the inner-city high school bureaucratic policy worked in favour of students from ethnic backgrounds. The staff sometimes felt that a student should not attempt HSC and advised against it. In theory this was one way by which a student's ambitions could be curtailed. In practice, however, students could get around this barrier provided they could establish a case and had the prerequisites, even though some staff felt that their unrealistic aspirations worked against them. Those students who wanted to do mathematics and sciences were especially favoured, as their ambitions were backed by a directive from the Regional Director of Education that no students were to be excluded if they wanted to do these subjects. From the evidence such students were more likely to be from NES and Asian backgrounds, so it was difficult to conclude that they were being discriminated against, compared with Anglo-Australian students. Prima facie it would appear that as much as possible was being done in that school to cater for their career ambitions.

It would have taken extremely fine-grained research well outside the scope of the study to establish if discrimination through the evaluation procedures was being practised in subtle ways in any of the schools. Even if such research had been feasible, it would have been difficult to establish whether illegitimate discrimination was present. This applied particularly to Indo-Asian students, for whom it was not always easy to recommend promotion into the HSC year. They often had difficulties with English, which could hamper their progress, even though their standards in other subjects such as mathematics and sciences were satisfactory.

In such a situation, the English as a Second Language (ESL) coordinator was in the position of having a major say in a student's promotion. Of necessity, in what she perceived to be the best interest of the student, she could recommend that he or she not be promoted. *De facto* legitimate discrimination may have resulted in such cases, but may not have been perceived as such by those who failed to gain promotion. Only one isolated example of this was found. It concerned a Cambodian student who considered that he had been kept down and not promoted because of discrimination rather than because the ESL teacher felt that his English was not up to scratch.

There may well have been similar cases in other schools but we were not able to elicit information about them, and their complexity admits of no simple solution. The pronounced academic motivation and drive to work hard of Indo-Asian and ethnic Chinese students, probably stimulated by the Confucian ethic, has the corollary that it necessitates a high degree of dedication that many Anglo-Australians just cannot understand. Some teachers may thus fail to empathize with such drive and also not understand the considerable loss of face for these students when high goals are not achieved. Lacking such deep understanding, Anglo staff might be excused for adopting policies towards Asian students, which may be completely rational and even non-discriminatory, but are nonetheless culturally insensitive.

Organization of Careers Advice — The Referral System

In all schools, the personnel involved with providing careers advice and guidance were the careers teacher, year 11 and 12 level coordinators and, for students from NES and Indo-Asian backgrounds, the ESL teachers. In addition there were impersonal, written sources of information such as career guides, brochures and other material. However, it was the careers teacher (almost always a female) in each school who played the major role in careers education because the organization of the curriculum made it virtually mandatory for all students to be referred to her. This was due to Victorian Education Department regulations stemming from a High Court decision in 1984 forbidding staff other than the careers teacher from giving advice on careers to avoid the possibility of litigation from parents if the advice proved to be wrong. In effect the careers advice 'buck' stopped at the careers teacher's desk.

The operation of this 'referral system' placed considerable importance on her skills, sensitivity and understanding of students' needs. We found no firm evidence, either written or verbal, to suggest that students from NES and Asian backgrounds claimed that there were prejudice and discrimination in her help and advice. It was evident that some of the deficiencies in the careers advice system that students mentioned could have been due to the careers teacher not having enough time to carry out her work. This could not be blamed on the school, however, but again must be laid at the door of secondary teachers' unions. In the Victorian Educational Department the careers teacher is not allowed to be full time, but must teach at least five periods in a normal school subject, typically English or history in the schools we studied. We were told that this was one of the job specifications 'negotiated' (usually a pseudonym for being pressured) by teacher unions out of the Department some years ago.

However, despite the referral system there was evidence that senior staff took advantage of informal situations such as school camps or educational excursions to chat to students and give them careers advice. Paradoxically such opportunities were frequently denied to some students from traditional NES backgrounds because they were not allowed by their parents to go on school camps. Obviously this could not be attributed to discrimination on the part of the staff, as it was a parental decision whether or not their children, girls especially, should participate in extra-mural activities.

In principle, there was the strong possibility that the careers teacher might have been less sensitive to the needs of NES and Asian than Anglo-Australian students in every school. All the careers teachers were Anglo-Australians, and made no mention of being able to speak either a European or Asian language. Research by Davis (1986) has shown this to be the case in the great majority of schools throughout Australia. This situation has prompted her to comment:

> Unfortunately... this lack of language skills also reflects a lack of real familiarity with non-Anglo cultures... Schools seem to acknowledge that there are special needs but, whether because of a lack of appropriate material resources or a lack of staff expertise, little is being done. The picture is all too bleak. (pp.49 and 83–4)

The Role of the ESL Teachers

The special responsibilities of the ESL teachers in all but one school where there were few NES students brought them closer to NES and Indo-Asian students to a degree that may not have been the case with other staff. We found no evidence to suggest that the ESL teachers were lacking in sensitivity towards the aspirations of students from NES and Indo-Asian backgrounds. ESL teachers told us that they did give advice on careers, even if this contravened departmental regulations. It is difficult to see how they could avoid doing so if they were concerned to equip young NES and Indo-Asian students with more than the bare essentials of language skills.

Transmission of the Curriculum

The classroom teaching-learning interface is one of the main arenas where prejudice and discrimination can operate, but we found little evidence from students' comments to suggest that they experienced them from staff. There were some comments from girls from Greek backgrounds that some Greek male staff were chauvinists and there was an incident in one school where a group of Greek and Italian girls felt that an Anglo member of staff had unfairly asked them to stop making a noise during their lunch hour so that Asian students could use the computer room in peace and quiet.

We expected to find students using the term 'racist' about members of staff in all schools, but this did not occur. It was used by students from all backgrounds about employers in the community, and by some few students from NES and Asian backgrounds about Anglo-Australians in general. But this was the limit of perceptions of so-called 'racism'.

In particular, we found very little evidence that staff were prejudiced against Asian students. The converse appeared to be the case. They considered them to be exemplary students, quiet, diligent and highly motivated, and valued their presence in class more than any other groups of students. The only contrary opinion we heard was during an informal discussion in the staffroom at the pilot school, when a female member of staff commented half in joke that Asian students were so successful that 'very soon Australia will find itself taken over and run by Asians'.

The perceptions of staff in all but one of the schools about male students from some non-Asian NES backgrounds focused on their high aspirations, macho attitudes and sexist comments about girls. Most comments on these features were adverse, but whether this would lead to systematic discrimination is debatable. However, as a corollary, the frequency of the remarks we heard constituted a strong stereotype which may have had several effects. Firstly, it may have caused some staff to treat the aspirations of students from NES backgrounds less seriously than they warranted, because 'everybody knows' that their ambitions are too high. Secondly, macho behaviour may have produced a labelling effect which made staff assume that all students from NES backgrounds treated girls in a disparaging way, whereas there would obviously have been exceptions in any representative group.

Staff did not appear to discriminate deliberately against Anglo-Australian students and we expected that this would be the case in line with the logic of cultural reproduction theory. However, we were surprised at the degree to which Anglo-Australian students even from higher SES backgrounds invited *discrimination by default* against themselves. It was clear that there was a group of senior Anglo-Australian students, who by their own admission 'mucked around' in class, attempted to challenge teachers' authority, made sexist comments about girls and generally did not work as hard as students fron NES or Asian backgrounds. This contrast was invariably drawn by teachers in every school with significant numbers of ethnic students and we were left in no doubt about their preferences for the hardworking Asian students.

Interethnic Prejudice and Discrimination

The incidence of interethnic prejudice and tensions was rarely obvious to the external observer. However, we were frequently told that interethnic tensions existed outside in the community and could lead to violence between members of ethnic groups, which was then brought into the schools. 'When Greeks and Turks get together it's a real ding-dong' we were told in one school. Internal 'territorial' ambitions by some ethnic groups to control particularly favoured playing spaces on the campus of the inner-city school could trigger off serious tensions and ugly violence and some of the students we talked to also commented on this aspect of their lives.

Unexpected findings in Patterns of Prejudice between Students

We were told about many cases of *negative prejudice* leading to overt acts of illegitimate discrimination on the part of students towards their peers in both schools: verbal abuse, name calling, violence between ethnic groups. Whether these kinds of discrimination affected students' ability to plan and work towards career scenarios is debatable. On the one hand, as the old adage has it: 'Sticks and stones may break my bones, but names will never hurt me'. In other words, adopting Rose's (1974) term, some students may have been 'prejudiced nondiscriminators'. On the other hand Troyna has commented (personal communication) that the climate of racial abuse in a school is likely to undermine the security of the ethnic student and negatively affect his/her performance and general disposition to work.

Despite this caution, it must be observed that the case that such prejudice did lead to discrimination which in turn would affect students' academic attainment or aspirations rests on a very tenuous set of causal assumptions. It must first be established that prejudice does adversely affect a person's perceptions of his/her own worth, i.e. self-esteem, as is often claimed in the conventional wisdom and ideology of ethnic equality. Discounting for sake of argument the possibility that this may be a relatively minor issue compared with what fear of abuse, lack of security and being a target for harassment may do to a student's stability, it does not necessarily follow that academic achievement will fall as a result of lowered self-esteem. Even Coopersmith, one of the architects of self-esteem theory (1975), has acknowledged the tenuousness of the relationship between self-esteem and academic performance. The likelihood that poor self-esteem will adversely affect career aspirations is similarly debatable.

The most unexpected comments we heard concerned the depth of the prejudice and discrimination between students of different ethnic backgrounds, which quickly made it clear that prejudice was not the sole preserve of Anglo-Australian students. The very dark-skinned student who called a boy from India a 'black bastard' despite the fact that he had a lighter skin, and Greeks calling Italian students 'peasants' were surprising incidents because it might have been assumed that those from ethnic backgrounds were 'comrades in adversity' and united against the Anglos. This was far from the case and casts doubt on our theory of inevitable Anglo-Australian ethnocultural hegemony. In fact the most racist comments about Indo-Asian and Asian students we tape-recorded came from a group of students of long-settled parents from British and Northern European backgrounds.

Prejudice in Work Experience

All groups of students claimed that they had experienced prejudice and discrimination in the workplace, during work experience programs and part-time employment. As a result of this some students claimed to have been put off their career plans and disadvantaged. One or two examples suggested that Asians experienced prejudice and discrimination that amounted to outright racism. The discrimination students experienced was not confined to those from Asian or NES backgrounds and again dispelled the conventional view that racism and prejudice are Anglo-Australian prerogatives. In areas of high ethnic concentration Anglo-Australian students felt that they were disadvantaged and cited examples of discrimination from ethnic employers.

The Effect of Socioeconomic Status

There was some evidence that the disadvantages some students claimed they experienced may not have been solely a function of ethnic and cultural differences, but that these factors were augmented or even exceeded by SES differences. This complicating factor operated especially in the case of some students from lower to lower-middle SES homes. Regardless of ethnic background, they tended to be more apathetic, less confident of their career plans and did not aspire so highly as students across all ethnic groups from middle- to upper-SES backgrounds. We cannot make generalizations from the limited data, but one tentative conclusion is that under certain circumstances SES factors in the schools may have 'washed out' ethnicity and cultural differences as a correlation of either actual or perceived disadvantage.

However, there were important exceptions to this such as Vietnamese in lower-socioeconomic areas of first settlement, who move out as quickly as they can and have upwardly socially mobile aspirations. Cultural factors may be more important in this case and lend some support to Sturman's (1985) opinion, based on a comprehensive review of research studies of immigrants' levels of achievement in Australia: 'As was the case with educational aspirations, occupational aspirations were less closely linked to socioeconomic status for ethnic groups than other groups in the Australian population' (p. 76).

Challenging Conventional Assumptions about Sexism

The relationships between boys and girls that indicated sexist prejudice showed several patterns. In general sexism occurred more within ethnic groups (intraethnic) than between groups (interethnic). However, it would be oversimplistic invariably to label every incident as discrimination.

The Basic Pattern

General sexism in the school and classroom undoubtedly existed to judge from comments across all ethnic groups. It was more prevalent in junior grades, but tended to diminish in the senior classes where common concern to prepare for the HSC examination may have reduced its impact. However, sexist prejudice by name calling and macho behaviour is one thing, but discrimination that affects planning career scenarios is another. Apart from some relatively isolated examples, there was little to suggest that girls felt so put down that their career planning suffered. No comments to this effect appeared in answers to the questionnaire. Considerable evidence was available that boys were sexist during mixed sport and PE, but to claim that this could affect career scenarios would be stretching things too far.

Sexism within Ethnic Groups — Culturally Legitimate Discrimination?

When analyzing sexism that affects girls from ethnic backgrounds it is important to recall the two kinds of discrimination that have been used above. One is legitimate, being an accepted part of a society's institutional structures, such as the different ranks in an army. The other is illegitimate discrimination. 'Whether or not discrimination is considered illegitimate depends on societal values' (Theodorson and Theodorson, 1970, p. 116).

To an external observer from a society with a different culture and different values some of the apparent discrimination seen in the sample schools could well be interpreted as sexist prejudice. Such incidents as macho arrogance from Greek boys when putting Greek girls down in class could be seen in this light. However, some of the comments of Greek and Italian girls showed clearly that they did not feel put down by the sexist, macho behaviour of boys from the same ethnic backgrounds. Such girls claimed to be 'used to it', and even responded by 'rubbishing' the boys. Some girls' comments also suggested that boys' sexist remarks stimulated them to try even harder, 'just to show them'.

Taking a cultural relativist view of such incidents, it is possible to maintain that within an ethnic group there may be what can be termed *culturally legitimate discrimination*. This may have been behind what occurred during our discussions with male and female Vietnamese students, especially at the pilot school. The senior boys — virtually young men in some cases — were apparently in a position of some authority, and gave curt orders in Vietnamese to the girls who obviously deferred to them. It is possible that this style of relationship was a function of their relatively recent arrival in Australia, whereas those who had been in the country longer may have had a less obvious pattern of deference. The point at issue, however, is that this too could have been another form of apparent discrimination that is culturally sanctioned. To interpret it as discrimination in the illegitimate sense of sexism could have been an oversimplification.

We did find examples that indicated more extreme examples of sexist discrimination which are harder to condone. One concerned a Turkish girl, who was badly beaten up by her brother outside one of the schools because he had seen her talking to boys. It is possible to take the position that if this kind of sibling control over a sister's sexual integrity is customary in Turkish culture, then once again it may be insensitive to label it as sexist discrimination.

However, there are some cultural practices that have been universally condemned at no less a level than the United Nations, and in Western societies such behaviour is hard to condone. When faced with it a teacher can be trapped by cultural relativism and placed in the dilemma of not wanting to interfere in a matter that may be culturally sanctioned. Alternatively he can make an *assumption of normative equivalence* and choose to interfere, with possibly unfortunate results. Normative equivalence — an extension of Wolfe's (1985) concept of moral equivalence — assumes that persons from another sociocultural group share one's own norms, sanctions, values and world view, and can therefore be judged by the same standards as are applied to one's own people.

This is a real dilemma for teachers as Troyna and Carrington (1987) have shown. They cite Lynch's (1983, p. 17) observation as one possible solution (Troyna and Carrington, 1987, p. 63): '...whereas schools ought to foster "a critical-rational acceptance of cultural diversity and the creative affirmation of individual and group differences within a common humanity", not all cultural beliefs and values are of equal worth'. Whether this provides adequate guidelines for teachers is debatable as the problem of deciding on what constitutes 'equal worth' is still not resolved.

This places those from all the helping professions in a quandary in places like Melbourne where there are still many ethnic groups which follow traditional cultural lifestyles. In our research comments suggesting the existence of *fossilized cultures* within some NES families cropped up several times. These are cultural practices that have been 'frozen' as they were in countries of origin when the families concerned originally emigrated some thirty years ago. Their continued existence and manifestly detrimental effects especially on girls cast considerable doubt on official government policies wedded to the doctrine of cultural relativism that encourage their maintenance.

By the same token it should not be assumed that all the girls from NES backgrounds passively accepted the culturally legitimate discrimination they experienced within their families. They were quite prepared to speak out against it, and some have managed to break away and get into professional careers and tertiary education. On the other hand we heard of several girls from Greek, Italian, Yugoslav and similar backgrounds whose aspirations were discouraged by their parents in favour of their brothers, who were invariably spoken of as being 'spoiled'.

Sex Discrimination in the Workplace

There was little doubt that girls were discriminated against in the workplace on the basis of their gender. Comments about barriers to getting into some jobs came from Anglo-Australian, NES and Asian girls, so it was difficult to sustain a case for discrimination against girls from specific ethnic groups. Against this it should be noted that in some jobs their gender was a positive attribute. An attractive girl manning a checkout counter in the foodstore was apparently considered to be preferable to a boy, especially if she could speak one of the ethnic languages used in the surrounding area. This generated some adverse comments from boys, and in several instances they obviously had stereotyped views about girls' employment. However, as we have noted above in other contexts, whether this generated the level of prejudice and discrimination that worked against NES and Indo-Asian girls' career scenarios is debatable.

Lack of Provisions to Combat Interethnic and Sexist Prejudice

There appeared to be no systematic attempts in any of the schools to use culture maintenance programs based on culture contact theory to reduce interethnic tensions. In any case their effectiveness is highly questionable (for example, Amir, 1969; Blanc, 1984; Bochner, 1982; Horowitz, 1980). Evidence from Canada and the United States discussed elsewhere (Bullivant, 1981a; see also Sowell, 1986) suggests that interest in language and cultural maintenance surfaces in the adult and established migrant generation once it has overcome economic difficulties. With those concerns settled, it can begin to concentrate on a revival of ethnicity and culture that have been neglected in the struggle for survival.

There was no indication from students that they were concerned about the lack of anti-sexist education. Several staff, including the careers teachers in three schools, considered that its effectiveness was debatable. Not surprisingly some opposition from boys to courses of anti-sexist education was found, and even some staff were of the opinion that such courses may be counterproductive.

As one Greek boy commented: 'I think that equal opportunity is pushed onto us too much, because now I'm sort of scared to speak up. I think that a male could do the job better than girls, but we're scared of a backlash from the chicks.'

More surprising was the comment of the young female careers teacher, a strong advocate of women's liberation, in the inner city school.

> I think that a lot of things we have tried to do to encourage girls into non-traditional lines of work don't succeed... and doesn't seem to be very effective... we must get to the parents. They are the ones to be addressed and maybe that means advertising in the ethnic papers and things like that.... I think that getting to the girls themselves is not the right kind of thing, because there has been a lot of that sort of semi-feminist stuff around for a good five or six years now, and I don't see it is effective.

Towards a Model of Ethnic Aspirations and Motivation

It was abundantly clear that our hypotheses about the existence of inevitable Anglo-Australian ethnocultural hegemony in the seven schools could not be sustained. Probably the most convincing evidence for this was the many students from NES and Asian backgrounds we were told about who had done very well academically, gained tertiary entrance, were dux of school, or attained comparable types of success even in the schools located in lower SES areas where one might have expected that social class barriers would have worked against them. Against all our expectations and commitment to the logic of cultural reproduction theory for the purposes of the research, it was obvious that very many students from non-Anglo backgrounds were not being disadvantaged and were doing better than Anglos.

Other research evidence is now available to clinch this case. It suggests that the conventional picture of the inevitably 'disadvantaged migrant' must be abandoned. On the basis of his comprehensive research review, Sturman (1985) has concluded:

> In summary, with respect to the educational experiences of immigrant Australians, although there is a lack of data relating to certain aspects of disadvantage, in connection with educational outcomes (participation and performance) there is no indication that the immigrant groups are disadvantaged in Australian society. (p. 83)

Burke and Davis (1986) have demonstrated from detailed statistical analysis that greater proportions of second generation students from NES and Asian backgrounds are gaining tertiary education places than are Anglo-Australian students. The numbers of Greek students have shown a dramatic increase, and those from Italian backgrounds have also increased. Birrell and

Seitz (1986) used first-year enrolment figures from Monash University — one of the universities to which many students in our research aspired — to show that the proportion of students from Italian, Greek and Asian backgrounds has increased over the last ten years, while the proportion of students from Anglo-Australian backgrounds has decreased.

Of equal importance was the fact that significant numbers of these first-year NES and Asian students were upwardly socially mobile, coming from lower-SES homes, while the majority of students from Anglo-Australian backgrounds came from middle- to upper-middle-SES homes. In other words, many first-year students from NES and Asian backgrounds had 'made it' against all cultural and socioeconomic odds.

> The magnitude of the migrant achievement can be appreciated when we compare the occupational background of Monash students' families. Whereas hardly any Australians were from blue collar families, the majority of Greek and Italian students came from this background. (*ibid.*, p. 24)

Research by Clifton and Williams (1986) and Williams (1987) based on Australia-wide evaluative studies of educational attainment has shown a comparable picture. Mistilis (1986) has used 1981 Census data to demonstrate a form of SES 'gradient', similar to the one proposed below, with Asians, Greeks, Italians, Yugoslavs among other ethnic groups occupying disproportionate percentages of high-status occupations compared with Anglo-Australians.

Despite the above claims of ethnic success, it is necessary to be aware of several qualifications to this favourable picture. Jakubowicz and Castles (1986) give a number of logical deficiencies and statistical anomalies in the causal path analysis employed by the majority of the above studies. When they are taken into account the picture is not as favourable as it appears. For example, although Birrell and Seitz give data that show the relatively high numbers of second generation migrants in high-status occupations, they omit to give figures for the large numbers of those who are unemployed. The rapid trajectory of immigrants' upward social mobility is similarly suspect. As Jakubowicz and Castles comment:

> The conclusions that have been drawn by analysts fascinated by the success of ethnics, has (sic) served to disguise a number of important features of these trajectories. Inside ethnic communities the range of experience is vast and cannot be ascribed to ethnicity in any useful way. Moreover, the failure of the education system to address the learning needs of working class children, a significant component of whom are of ethnic origin, is a more pervasive problem that cannot be swept away by simply labelling the issue as 'mythical' or the problem (whatever it is) as 'solved'. (*ibid.*, p. 11)

The positive views of ethnic success must also be qualified by acknowledging that it entails often hidden costs. For example, research by Tanna (1985) in the United Kingdom showed that Asians may achieve on a par with Anglos, but only because they invest more time into their formal schooling (see also Troyna, 1986).

The Swann Committee was also aware of the risks of stereotyping some ethnic groups as being invariably successful and the Runnymede Trust (1985) has commented on the Chinese in particular:

> Teachers should be wary of accepting their overall perception of Chinese pupils as being hard workers and high achievers, as they may well underestimate or overlook educational difficulties. The stereotype of high achiever is as dangerous as that of the low achiever and strengthens the view put forward of the need to regard all pupils on their own merits as individuals with differing needs and problems. (p. 27)

An Aspiration — Motivation Gradient

With these reservations in mind, we can still systematize the implications of our own research in what we have termed the aspiration-motivation gradient, which extends the findings of earlier studies such as those by Taft (1975). However, it must be stressed that adopting blanket terms, such as 'NES', 'Asian', 'Anglo-Australian', carries with it many dangers of oversimplifying matters and even of creating new stereotypes. These groups are not homogeneous, and contain within them many variations: bright and achievement-oriented Anglo-Australian students with high aspirations from lower-SES homes,and dull uncaring NES or Asian students with low aspirations from middle- to upper-middle-SES homes.

At the risk of such oversimplification, our model suggests that the levels of students' aspirations and motivation to achieve them form a gradient. At the top are significant numbers of Asian students, especially Chinese from well-established homes, although later arrivals such as some Indo-Chinese and ethnic Chinese from Indo-China have very high aspirations and motivation. As Nguyen and Cahill (1986) have pointed out: '...[Vietnamese] children usually study very hard. As a result, most students who are backed by strong motivation from their families perform well at school and some of them become outstanding students' (p. 68).

Data did not include students from Jewish backgrounds, but many of these would be included in the top positions on the gradient. Most Anglo-Australian students from middle- to high-SES homes are close to this top group. A few rank at the top with the Asian students. Next, and somewhat lower in the gradient, as far as aspirations and motivations are concerned, are students from NES backgrounds, especially Greeks, Yugoslavs and Italians. Lower again on the gradient are other ethnic groups and significant numbers of Anglo-Australian students, especially those from middle-to-low SES areas, together with many who are from Northern European and British origins.

This aspiration-motivation gradient does not fully represent the complexity of the way those from ethnic backgrounds see their futures in a society that is characterized by multifaceted pluralism. However, we cannot ignore the consistency with which the factors constituting the gradient were emphasized by staff and substantially confirmed by discussions with students. Rather, we wish to extend them by suggesting that a significant number of second generation students in some ethnic groups have higher achievable aspirations and motivations than many Anglo-Australian students, and are no longer the disadvantaged in schools as has been conventionally assumed. In essence they are motivated by what we term the *ethnic success ethic*.

In contrast it is highly probable that significant numbers of Anglo-Australian students are at risk of becoming a new category, namely, the *self-deprived*, in the sense of inhibiting their own life possibilities and career scenarios. In essence these are motivated by a *shirk-work ethic* associated with the *self-deprivation syndrome*. From teachers' comments and even some Anglo students' own admissions, we can conclude that the 'syndrome' is partly due to their own lackadaisical attitudes towards the value of education and disinclination to work hard to achieve their goals. It also appears to be due to lack of parental encouragement and drive, which in contrast are so apparent among parents from NES and Asian backgrounds.

It would further appear from our research evidence that a number of British migrant-settler and Anglo-Australian parents and students, particularly from lower SES areas, choose to shift the blame for their own inadequacies on to those from NES and particularly Asian backgrounds — the classical scapegoating strategy. It even extends to criticizing Asian students for having 'brains' and working too hard. Another tendency commented on by staff was for Anglo-Australian and former British parents to take a militant quasi-trade-union attitude towards what the schools were trying to do for their children, and making invalid claims that Asians were being given preferential treatment. It may not be stretching matters too far to suggest that most of these aspects form part of a general and regrettable Anglo-Australian value system.

Ironically, it may also be the case that such attitudes about education and the value of hard work are 'catching' and that even the aspirations of Chinese students may be at risk of being affected by the length of stay in Australia as a doctoral study by Helen Chan (1987) at Monash University suggests. She studied the effects of length of stay in Australia and weakening maintenance of Chinese cultural values on educational aspirations and achievement. Her research showed that length of exposure to Australian values and loss of Chinese cultural values, especially those concerning education, did indeed have a deleterious effect on aspirations, motivation and achievement.

Challenging Conventional Wisdom about Ethnic Disadvantage

The models of the aspiration-motivation gradient and self-deprivation syndrome present an interpretation of findings that are at variance with the assumptions concerning ubiquitous ethnic disadvantage, which have long influenced much of the thinking and utopian ideologies about pluralist education in English-speaking Western societies. A contrary picture is now emerging and finds support in the United States and Canada: the conventional wisdom that students from NES and Asian backgrounds *must* be disadvantaged is no longer tenable and should be abandoned. Many second-generation and even some first-generation ethnic students are resisting the forces of ethnocultural reproduction and are achieving better than their Anglo peers, even though they may have to invest more time and energy into schoolwork to achieve their goals. Only they can say whether the gains are worth the costs.

This has an important corollary. Most English-speaking societies are said by educationists to be 'multicultural', and if multiculturalism means anything it is that the contributions of all ethnic groups within a pluralist society should be equally valued, including their high academic aspirations and upward socioeconomic mobility, regardless of whether this risks usurping a fairer share of economic and social rewards from the dominant groups.

It is in the national interest that the ethnic success ethic be encouraged and dominant Anglo attempts to impose social closure against ethnics curbed so important have 'brains' and hard work become for national survival on the world scene. Solving this pluralist dilemma has yet to be achieved and is something that a committee such as that chaired by Lord Swann might address.

Acknowledgment

I am grateful for Barry Troyna's constructive comments on an earlier draft of this chapter. It draws heavily on the original Report (Bullivant, 1986b) and subsequent publications (e.g. Bullivant, 1987).

References

AMIR, Y. (1969) 'Contact hypothesis in ethnic relations', *Psychological Bulletin*, 71, 5, pp. 319–42.

ARDREY, R. (1970) *The Social Contract: A Personal Inquiry into the Evolutionary Sources of Order and Disorder*, London, Collins.

BANTON, M. (1983) *Racial and Ethnic Competition*, Cambridge, Cambridge University Press.

BERNSTEIN, B. (1971) 'On the classification and framing of educational knowledge' in YOUNG, M.F.D. *Knowledge and Control: New Directions for the Sociology of Education*, London, Collier-Macmillan.

BIRRELL, R. and SEITZ, A. (1986) 'The ethnic problem in education: The emergence and definition of an issue', paper presented to the Ethnicity and Multiculturalism 1986 National Research Conference, Australian Institute of Multicultural Affairs. 14–16 May, unpublished, Melbourne.

BLANC, M. (1984) 'Social sciences for a multicultural society', *Multicultural Teaching to Combat Racism in School and Community*, 2, 2, pp. 36–8.

BOCHNER, S. (1982) *Culture in Contact*, London, Pergamon.

BOURDIEU, P. (1973) 'Cultural reproduction and social reproduction' in BROWN, R. (Ed) *Knowledge, Education and Social Change,* London, Tavistock.

BOURDIEU, P. and PASSERON, J.-C. (1977) *Reproduction in Education, Society and Culture,* (trans R. Nice) London, Sage.

BULLIVANT, B.M. (1978a) 'Towards a neo-ethnographic methodology for small-group research', *Australian and New Zealand Journal of Sociology,* 14, 3, pp. 239–49.

BULLIVANT, B.M. (1978b) *The Way of Tradition: Life in an Orthodox Jewish School,* Melbourne, Australian Council for Educational Research.

BULLIVANT, B.M. (1981a) *The Pluralist Dilemma in Education: Six Case Studies,* Sydney, George Allen & Unwin.

BULLIVANT, B.M. (1981b) *Race, Ethnicity and Curriculum,* Melbourne, Macmillan.

BULLIVANT, B.M. (1982) 'Are ethnic schools the solution to ethnic children's accommodation to Australian society?', *Journal of Intercultural Studies,* 3, 2, pp. 17–35.

BULLIVANT, B.M. (1984) *Pluralism: Cultural Maintenance and Evolution.* Clevedon, Multilingual Matters.

BULLIVANT, B.M. (1986a) 'Towards radical multiculturalism: Resolving tensions in curriculum and educational planning' in MODGIL, S. *et al.* (Eds) *Multicultural Education: The Interminable Debate,* Lewes, Falmer Press.

BULLIVANT, B.M. (1986b) *Getting a Fair Go, Case Studies of Occupational Socialization and Perceptions of Discrimination in a Sample of Seven Melbourne High Schools,* Canberra, Human Rights Commission.

BULLIVANT, B.M. (1987) *The Ethnic Encounter in the Secondary School: Ethnocultural Reproduction and Resistance; Theory and Case Studies,* Lewes, Falmer Press.

BURKE, G. and DAVIS, D. (1986) 'Ethnic groups and post-compulsory education' in AUSTRALIAN INSTITUTE OF MULTICULTURAL AFFAIRS (Ed) *Migrants, Labour Markets and Training Programs: Studies of the Migrant Youth Workforce,* Melbourne, AIMA.

CAHILL, D. and REVIEW TEAM OF THE LANGUAGE AND LITERACY CENTRE, PHILLIP INSTITUTE OF TECHNOLOGY (1984) *Review of the Commonwealth Multicultural Education Program,* report to the Commonwealth Schools Commission, Vol. 1, Canberra, Commonwealth Schools Commission.

CHAN, H. (1987) 'The adaptation and achievement of Chinese students in Victoria', unpublished PHD thesis, Melbourne, Monash University.

CHEVANNES, M. and REEVES, F. (1987) 'The black voluntary school movement: Definition, context and prospects' in TROYNA, B. *Racial Inequality in Education,* London, Tavistock.

CLIFTON, R.A. and WILLIAMS, T.H. (1986) 'Ethnic differences in the academic attainment process in Australia', paper presented to the Ethnicity and Multiculturalism 1986 Research Conference, Australian Institute of Multicultural Affairs. 14–16 May, unpublished, Melbourne.

COOPERSMITH, S. (1975) 'Self-concept, race and education' in VERMA, G.K. and BAGLEY, C. (Eds) *Race and Education Across Cultures,* London, Heinemann.

DAVIS, D.F. (1986) 'Careers education: Cinderella of schooling' in AUSTRALIAN INSTITUTE OF MULTICULTURAL AFFAIRS (Ed) *Migrants, Labour Markets and Training Programs: Studies of the Migrant Youth Workforce,* Melbourne, AIMA.

DAWKINS, R. (1976) *The Selfish Gene,* Oxford, Oxford University Press.

DEPARTMENT OF EDUCATION AND SCIENCE (1985) *Education for All: Report of the Committee of Enquiry into the Education of Children from Ethnic Minority Groups* (The Swann Report), Cmnd. 9453, London, HMSO.

DORN, A. and TROYNA, B. (1982) 'Multiracial education and the politics of decision making', *Oxford Review of Education,* 8, 2, pp. 175–85.

GORDON, M.M. (1964) *Assimilation in American Life: The Role of Race, Religion and National Origins,* New York, Oxford University Press.

HALSEY, A.H. (1972) *Educational Priority: E.P.A. Problems and Policies,* London, HMSO.

HOROWITZ, T. (1980) 'Integration and the social gap', *Jerusalem Quarterly,* 15, pp. 133–44.

JAKUBOWICZ, A. and CASTLES, S. (1986) 'The inherent subjectivity of the apparently objective in research on ethnicity and class', *Journal of Intercultural Studies,* 7, 3, pp. 5–25.

KEEGAN, D. (1987) 'Decline in schools—a lesson for politicians', *The Weekend Australian,* 25–26 August, p. 29.

LE VINE, R.A. and CAMPBELL, D.T. (1972) *Ethnocentrism: Theories of Conflict, Ethnic Attitudes and Group Behaviour,* New York, Wiley.

LYNCH, J. (1983) *The Multicultural Curriculum,* London, Batsford.

MASLEN, G. (1987) 'Teachers' bid on funds successful', *The Age,* 8 August, p. 6.

MISTILIS, N. (1986) 'Destroying myths: Second-generation Australians' educational achievements', paper presented to Work-in-Progress Seminar, 30 June, Melbourne, Centre for Migrant and Intercultural Studies, Monash University.

NGUYEN, X.T. and CAHILL, D. (Eds) (1986) *Understanding Vietnamese Refugees in Australia,* Community Studies Occasional Paper 1/86, Coburg, Phillip Institute of Technology, School of Community Studies.

PARKIN, F. (Ed) (1974) *The Social Analysis of Class Structure,* London, Tavistock.

ROSE, P.I. (1974) *They and We: Racial and Ethnic Relations in the United States,* (2nd edn), New York, Random House.

RUNNYMEDE TRUST (1985) *Education for All: A Summary of the Swann Report on the Education of the Ethnic Minority Children,* London, Runnymede Trust.

SOWELL, T. (1986) *Education Assumptions Versus History: Collected Papers,* Stanford, CA, Hoover Institution Press.

STURMAN, A. (1985) *Immigrant Australians and Education: A Review of Research,* Melbourne, ACER.

SWANN, Lord (1985) *Education for All: A Brief Guide to the Main Issues of the Report,* London, HMSO.

TAFT, R. (1975) 'The aspirations of secondary school children of immigrant families in Victoria', *Education News,* 15, 1, pp. 38–41.

TANNA, K. (1985) 'Opening the black box', *Times Educational Supplement,* 20 September, p. 27.

THEODORSON, G.A. and THEODORSON, A.G. (1970) *A Modern Dictionary of Sociology,* London, Methuen.

TROYNA, B. (1984) 'Multicultural education: Emancipation or containment?' in BARTON, L. and WALKER, S. (Eds) *Social Crisis and Educational Research,* Beckenham, Croom Helm.

TROYNA, B. (1986) ' "Swann's song": The origins, ideology and implications of Education for All', *Journal of Educational Policy,* 1, 2, pp. 171–81.

TROYNA, B. and CARRINGTON, B. (1987) 'Anti-sexist/anti-racist education—false dilemma: A reply to Walkling and Branningan', *Journal of Moral Education,* 16, 1, pp.60–5.

VAN DEN BERGHE, P.L. (1978) 'Race and ethnicity: A sociobiological perspective', *Ethnic and Racial Studies,* 1, 4, pp. 401–11.

WEBER, M. (1968) *Economy and Society,* (Ed. G. Roth and C. Wittich), New York, Bedminster Press.

WILLIAMS, T. (1987) *Participation in Education,* ACER Research Monograph No. 30, Melbourne, Australian Council for Educational Research.

WOLFE, T. (1985) 'Are the USA and the USSR morally equivalent?', *Quadrant,* October, pp. 10–18.

WRIGHT, C. (1987) 'Black students—White teachers' in TROYNA, B. (Ed) *Racial Inequality in Education,* London, Tavistock.

Chapter 6

Education for All: A Canadian Dimension

Christopher Bagley

Introduction

That education in modern society should be for all people, regardless of age, sex, social class, religion, ethnicity or other status seems to be a fundamental principle of social justice. Yet education's development to encompass all people has been a slow one, and is still not complete. Moreover, the extension of education to wider classes of people seems to have been justified not on liberal principle, but on grounds of economic advantage or of political expediency. Although the Education Act of 1870 was a piece of reform with major implications for the extension of at least primary education to all children, for Britain and her colonies in the Second World (but certainly not in the Third World), the Act seems to have been justified on grounds of efficiency, control and order (Morton, 1938).

The simple idea of universal education ('education for all') begs a number of questions. What kinds of education should be made available to all classes of people? Will universal access to 'primary' or first-level education (at least until the legal age for leaving school) be sufficient to serve principles of efficiency, order or social justice? Or should universal education include easy or universal access to college, university and professional education? Should we include adult education, or lifelong education within any principle of universality? Yet more contentious is the issue of selection and 'ability' in the transfer from one sector of education to another. While in Canada transfer from elementary to high school education is assumed to be independent of any assessment of ability or achievement, this principle seems to be still not universally accepted in Britain, where principles of elitism still have sway in many educational debates.

Should education for 'all' include the profoundly disabled, as the advocates of 'normalization' have argued (Wolfensberger, 1972)? And should education for all include equality of achievement as well as equality of access (Crosland, 1974)? This last point is extremely important: many of those writing from a broadly liberal position argue that removing structural barriers to access is all that is really required for equality in education. Universities in Britain for example, will admit any student with excellent 'advanced level' examination results, regardless of age, sex, ethnicity, religion or disability. Yet we know that the pressures which prevent many young people from realizing their talents and achieving the requisite 'advanced level' passes are numerous, and exist in forces both within and beyond the school.[1] Innate ability may have some bearing too, although the available evidence leads us to hold an agnostic position on the IQ question (Schiff and Lewontin, 1987).

The best we can say is that the assumption of equality of intelligence between all groups at the outset is the best way of ensuring that members of those groups achieve at a high level, or at a level which is compatible with their interests and motivations (Bagley, 1982). The 'strong' position on equality in education urges that teaching should be organized so as to maximize the possibilities for educational outcome for each student, regardless of ability. For example, the long-term evaluations of the Head Start programs begun in the United States in the 1960s have shown, in apparent fulfilment of this principle, that intensive and individualized effort for 'disadvantaged' pre-schoolers can be highly effective (Breedlove and Schweinart, 1982).

We can now offer a model of 'education for all' which seems to fulfil a number of desirable educational goals. Such education:

1 Accepts all members of society, regardless of origin, sex or status, at all levels and types of education, throughout the lifespan.
2 Attempts, through special or individualized programs in each educational setting, to give students abilities and skills which can maximize their final achievement in each stage or type of education.
3 Transmits to students skills and talents which can maximize their effective employment and social participation.
4 Attends to the cultural, religious and linguistic needs of particular groups, through heritage education programs.
5 Attends to the needs of the major culture for a balanced and harmonious society based on principles of equality, harmony and cooperation, through programs of intercultural education compatible with both the needs of a complex, multicultural or plural society, and the needs for cultural, religious and linguistic integrity on the part of various groups within society.
6 Develops programs of lifelong education in which older students can increase knowledge and skills, at all stages of their career, and after retirement.
7 Ultimately, education shall become a social force which binds the members of a society together in cooperative bonds, but also fosters the individuality, culture and personal talents of each member of society in ways which maximize self-development.[2]

Christopher Bagley

Education in Canada and Britain: Some Comparisons

I shall argue that Canada, by default rather than by design, has been more successful in achieving these goals of 'education for all' than has Britain. This idea of an excellent education system outlined above has evolved through my experience of Canadian society in the past seven years, which stands in marked contrast to an experience of the British educational system, as pupil, student, and university teacher over a thirty-year period.

First of all, salient dimensions of Canadian society must be sketched, particularly those surrounding multiculturalism and ethnic and linguistic division and integration. Canadian society has been characterized in the classic study by Porter (1965) as a mosaic, made up of groups defined by cross-cutting tangents of class, ethnicity, region, religion and language. The divisions of language are most obvious, while those of class, economy and wealth are remarkable if not for their absence, at least for their lack of meaning for the average Canadian. There is distinct lack of public consciousness about problems of economic inequality and exploitation, and Canadian students in classes on social welfare and social policy often find the idea of 'social class' curious, irrelevant and even repugnant, an alien import from Europe. In Marxian terms, the class divisions in Canadian society (which certainly do exist, as Porter has shown) remain 'unmasked'. The ideology that personal effort is the harbinger of security and wealth prevails across the land, almost without challenge. Canada has never had a federal socialist government, and in only three of the ten provinces has a socialist government of any colour been elected for any period. Indeed, such socialism has usually been the political expression of farmers' cooperatives in the Prairie region, in which individual entrepreneurs cooperated in the provision of an economic superstructure, but still maintained personal land holdings and fierce personal independence.

At the ethnic and cultural levels the hegemony of the Anglo-Saxon, Protestant settlers, the sons and daughters of empire, has always been challenged by a large settler population of Scottish and Irish Catholics, and then by increasingly large numbers of German, Ukranian, Italian and Dutch settlers and, after 1970, large numbers of immigrants from the Caribbean and Asia. The most powerful challenge to the established order was, however, from the large French-speaking minority who, after the convolutions of social order in the 1960s and 1970s became fully integrated into corridors of influence and power in Ontario and Quebec. It is now impossible to make one's way in federal government hierarchies without being bilingual, and the two official languages, French and English, have constitutional and legal parity. Since virtually all Francophones also speak English, while only a small minority of Anglophones speak French, effective power in the federal civil service has moved into the hands of the most prevalent bilingual group. Recognizing that bilingual effectiveness is a key to professional advancement, immersion schools (in which the language of instruction from Grade 1 is French) have become popular even in the traditionally Francophobic Prairie regions: here about

10 per cent of all English-speaking children are enrolled in immersion programs, which give effective fluency in French by the time the student is in Grade 10 (Parliament, 1986b; Lapkin *et al.*, 1983). Though we have no direct evidence, it is possible that the parents of children in bilingual programs are also those most ambitious for their children, and those who are most dissatisfied with the easy pace of education which characterizes Canadian life.

Canada has seen remarkable social changes in the past two decades, changes which demonstrate the flexibility of response to changing demographic, economic and culture pressures — a flexibility which seems lacking in British society. These changes have included an abandonment of an immigration policy which until the 1960s gave preference to white British immigrants. The revision of this policy, giving way to a a new bias in the admission of immigrants, had important symbolic significance since it represented the beginning of an important era of social change. The new bias in immigration policy is in the careful screening for admission of individuals who can assist economic development: applicants are selected according to youth and health, education, professional experience and personal wealth.

The 'entrepreneur' class of immigrant is particularly symbolic: anyone who will import to Canada a quarter of a million dollars or more, and demonstrates the capacity or desire to engage in successful business practice will be accepted for entry (Lapkin *et al.*, 1983). Implicit in this policy is the minimization of social service costs, as well as the maximization of economic development. The policy is discriminatory of course, to the degree that it excludes poor, uneducated individuals, or those with any health problems. There is an important rider to this qualification: Canada puts significant emphasis on family reunion following immigration, and will allow the entry of an individual's children under 21 and parents over 60. New rules introduced in 1987 will also allow the immigration of an individual's children over 21, adult brothers and sisters, and nephews and nieces, provided that the sponsor agrees to meet all social service costs for the new immigrant for a ten-year period. The rationale underlying this new policy is the problem of population growth (births are now falling below replacement level, a change with negative economic implications), and the perceived possibilities for family business enterprise.

Canada's official policy of multiculturalism which aims to integrate and support the many different ethnic and cultural groups who make up Canada's mosaic of population, stands in marked contrast to that of Britain. The policy is generously funded and vigorously promoted by a powerful government department, and the premises of the program — the support of the separate cultural and linguistic identity of different ethnic groups, including recent immigrants — is supported by all major parties, and by all provincial governments. Multiculturalism's critics are rarely heard in the public arena: they consist mainly of radicals who argue that the policy is one of obfuscation through which the true inequalities and divisions of society are masked (see Moodley, 1981 and 1983; Lambert *et al.*, 1986; and Mazurek, 1987). Groups attending to ethnic issues will, the argument goes, be diverted from examining issues of class and ethnic exploitation. It is also argued that multiculturalism is a sop to the many 'third language' groups (particularly Ukranians, Italians and Germans) who have to cope with two official languages, but who resist having to learn French, particularly in Quebec where all new immigrants are required to attend French-medium schools.

What is also striking about multicultural policy in Canada is the degree to which most of the designated ethnic groups seem to be apathetic about retention of cultural identity. The federal government has identified some eighty official ethnic groups, and for each identified group generous funding is available, particularly for educational purposes involving language and cultural maintenance. Funding is also offered for university chairs devoted to the study of the history and culture of any of the eighty ethnic groups. But to date only half a dozen such chairs have been created, since the agreement and sponsorship of the official group representing any ethnic group is required. It appears, paradoxically, that the government is aggressively pushing funds upon officially defined ethnic groups, many of whom have only limited interest in cultural retention (Bagley, 1984a).

Hubert Campfens, a Dutch sociologist living in Canada, has undertaken a systematic comparison of multicultural policies in the Netherlands and Canada. Campfens concludes from his analysis that:

> Canadian policy introduced in 1971...is an explicit commitment to multiculturalism within the framework of Canada's bilingualism and biculturalism, and has permitted many immigrant groups and their descendants to maintain a high degree of cultural and institutional pluralism...Unlike the new procedures introduced in 1967 in Canada which began to relate immigration to labour market needs and favour entry of those who scored highly in a number of criteria that would facilitate their adaptation to Canadian life, the Netherlands could not exercise much control over the intake of subjects from its former colonies, many of whom were 'unschooled' and economically disadvantaged...This explains in part the emergence in the Netherlands of specific group-related policies and programs, in contrast to the more general policy on immigrants and ethno-cultural groups developed in Canada. They also explain the growing preoccupation among Dutch authorities with socio-economic measures to improve the disadvantaged position of migrants as individuals in Dutch society and the secondary interest shown in the cultural identity issues...in contrast to Canada's greater concern with multiculturalism and pluralist approaches to problem-solving...The most surprising finding is the limited part Dutch national government has played in assisting in the integration of migrants in spite of the country's tradition of strong central government, in comparison with Canada's tradition of a strong

and active private sector yet where senior levels of government have assumed a significant role in this area. (Campfens, 1980)

Some parallels can also be drawn between the Dutch and British situations (see Bagley, 1973 and 1983). Britain, like the Netherlands, faces the structural problems of a declining capitalist economy, in which workers recruited from the former colonies seem to be forming a traditional 'reserve army' of labour. While children of immigrant groups often have high levels of motivation to complete school and examinations, their career aspirations are frequently checked by structural employment, as the Yorkshire research by Verma (1983) has shown. 'Education for all' can be meaningless unless it is linked to an obvious career strategy, or at least to a curriculum which prepares students for creative use of leisure, and self-sufficient economic roles. There is little evidence that the curriculum of the average secondary school in Britain has achieved this. The result, especially for black students in Britain, is a degree of profound alienation which negates any concept of universality in education (Bagley, 1982). No systematic evidence exists of such profound alienation amongst the children of black and Asian immigrants to Canada. A prosperous, black middle class has a visible profile, however, and such role models of success and prosperity seem to offer role models for young people: though discrimination against minorities does persist in Canada, its nature and extent appear to be considerably less than discrimination in the United Kingdom (Bagley, 1985a).

It can be argued that this apparent lack of discrimination against black people in Canada reflects an immigration policy which has selected individuals on the basis of potential for economic success. But the evidence on racial discrimination in Britain suggests that blocks to advancement are greatest against those minority groups who have the highest levels of aspiration (Brown, 1984). On the basis of the United Kingdom evidence on discrimination, we suspect that severe strains would be experienced if a well-educated and highly aspirant group of blacks were to emerge in Britain. Britain can accommodate black people to a certain extent, provided that they do not advance in any numbers past the blue collar stage (Bagley and Verma, 1979). Discrimination provides its own socialization, and the ambition of many young blacks in Britain, both within the educational system and beyond, has been effectively thwarted and turned to alienation, anger, rebellion and despair.[3]

In this respect, Elizabeth Thomas-Hope's comparative study of Britain, Canada and the United States is instructive and important (Thomas-Hope, 1982).

She compared the adjustment and satisfaction with achieving the goals of migration between broadly similar groups of Caribbean migrants to Britain, Canada and the United States. She interviewed several hundred Caribbean respondents in London and other centres in the UK; in New York, Hartford and Boston in the US; and in Toronto and Hamilton in Canada. The West Indians studied were established settlers in the three countries, who had migrated in the early and mid-1960s, in an era when British colonial immigrants to North America were regarded, by default, as British. Canada had not at this time begun to rationalize or humanize her immigration policies.

The three groups of Caribbean immigrants were broadly comparable in terms of age, sex and educational qualifications prior to leaving the Caribbean (most respondents were from Jamaica). The goals of migration for these West Indian immigrants were straightforward: to advance occupationally and materially, and to achieve educationally both for themselves and their children. The subjects were questioned by the researchers about their satisfaction with achieving the goals of their migration. Nearly half of the Caribbean immigrants to Britain expressed dissatisfaction with the achievement of such goals, and over a third were 'very dissatisfied'. However, only 14 per cent of migrants to the United States, and 20 per cent of those migrating to Canada expressed any kind of dissatisfaction.

Parallel to this, the majority of the West Indian sample in Britain hoped some day to return permanently to the Caribbean, compared with a minority of those who had migrated to North America. There was a close coincidence between failing to reach goals and wanting to return in the migrants to Britain; but the potential returners from North America were, by contrast, those who had achieved most. In fact, commuting between Kingston, Jamaica and New York or Toronto every week is a distinct possibility for the very successful.

In Toronto there is a constant coming and going between the metropolis and the islands: children may spend the summer with granny in the Caribbean, or granny comes to Canada for the summer. Despite, or because of, this frequency of cultural contact with the country of origin, West Indians in Canada seem conspicuous by their adaptation to the mainstream of society, and there is a solid, black bourgeoisie in most cities of Eastern Canada. In Western Canada in particular, blacks are likely to be found in the elite groups of doctors, lawyers and professional engineers, a group who have engaged in secondary migration from Eastern Canada.

In the United States, West Indian immigrants have been dubbed 'black Jews' because of their aspiration and drive: in New York they form one-eighth of the city's black population, but one-third of New York's black professionals (Lowenthal, 1967). Children of West Indian immigrants to the States are usually absorbed in the black bourgeoisie, and the alienation experienced by second generation blacks in Britain is rare. Blacks in Canada, according to Thomas-Hope, occupy an intermediate position, since there is no long-established tradition of a black middle class in Canada. However, blacks in Canada have been allowed, in a social structure which rewards effort, achievement and enterprise with relatively little regard for ethnic origins to achieve the original goals of their migration. The same cannot be said of Britain, in which the structural barriers to advancement by black people have been profound (Bagley and Verma, 1979). In this sense, Britain's educational system has failed in providing 'education for all' (an education linked through principles of social justice to occupational advancement and reward) in relation to all citizens; and Canada has been relatively successful.

In the remainder of this chapter this theme is elaborated drawing on a number of empirical, cross-cultural studies we have undertaken.

Cognitive Style in West Indian Children in Canada and Britain

For some years we have been pursuing a program of cross-cultural research on cognitive style in ten-year-olds from England, India, Japan, Jamaica and Canada (Bagley and Verma, 1983). This research, besides comparing perceptual and cognitive style in indigenous children, has examined changes in cognitive style in children who are first or second generation migrants, and who came (or whose parents came) from India, Jamaica or Japan and who are now settled in England or Canada.

One of the findings of this research has been the remarkable skill in perceptual disembedding possessed by Japanese children, both before and after migration (Bagley *et al.*, 1983). We found, however, that the longer Japanese children had lived in Britain or Canada, the more likely it was that their ability to perceive figures in a complex background (the skill of field independence or perceptual disembedding) the more likely it was that their cognitive style became similar to that of the mainstream or indigenous group. In the case of the Japanese children, they increasingly lost their superior skills in certain perceptual tasks the longer they had been in Canada or Britain. Consistent with hypothesis, the acculturation process was faster in Canada than in Britain.

We also studied children in a rural area of Jamaica who had not migrated; and children from parents from the same social strata in this rural area who had migrated to England and Canada, respectively. Both groups of migrant children improved their perceptual disembedding skills in the metropolitan cultures, but those who had migrated to Toronto did so at a significantly faster rate than did children who had migrated to London (Bagley, 1985b). Although we had no direct measure, we assumed that the more rapid absorption of Jamaican children into Canadian society would reflect the degree to which the migrant children were motivated to absorb the general folkways, tenets, norms, values and styles of interaction which the major culture represents. Canada, being a more open society and more receptive to immigrants than Britain, promotes such absorption at a faster rate (just as it promoted Japanese children's acculturation at a seemingly faster rate). It takes a newly migrant Jamaican child about the same time to learn to ice-skate as it does to become cognitively field independent at the level of the average Canadian child. Spending summer holidays in Jamaica did not seem to impair the acquisition of these essential skills for surviving in Canadian culture.

The principle of education for all should in our judgment include fostering the rapid development of mainstream cultural styles and norms, with a parallel support for retention of important traditional values, languages and religious customs. The evidence we have on changes in cognitive style in young migrants, is that Canadian society with its easy-going system of universalistic values fostering individual development within a free-enterprise social structure, seems to facilitate rapid psychological entry into Canadian society. Although the 'cultural context of thinking' for young migrants in Britain is also the mainstream culture, the influence of that mainstream is more complex (Bagley and Verma, 1979). Although migrants eventually absorb these mainstream values, the rewards for doing so are not automatic. The British educational system is, according to our analysis, ambiguous about the acceptance of minority aspirations. The result, for a number of minority groups, can be a state of profound alienation, the antithesis of the principle of 'education for all'.[4]

Evaluation of Colour and Ethnicity in Young Children in Canada and England

In parallel to cross-cultural work on cognitive style in 10-year-olds, we have for some years been collecting data on the Pre-School Racial Attitudes Measure (PRAM), and the linked Colour Meanings Test (CMT) devised by Williams and Morland (Bagley and Young, 1979 and 1988; Young and Bagley, 1982). We have recently replicated and extended this work with samples of 4- and 5-year-olds in England, Canada, Jamaica and Ghana. Our samples have included white, indigenous children in Britain; black, indigenous children in Ghana; and both black (Ghanaian and Jamaican) and white (European) children in Canada, as well as children of West Indian and West African black settlers in Britain (Bagley and Young, 1987). The purpose of this research has been to explore the degree to which ethnic groups with differing migrant and minority group status, perceived and evaluated the skin colour of individuals like themselves and their parents, as well as the skin colour of members of the dominant or majority ethnic group.

The results of this first comparison, carried out in the late 1970s, indicated that young children in rural Jamaica evaluated black skin colour in particularly negative terms. Black West Indian children in England had more favourable ethnic self-perception, despite being a minority group in a racist social structure (Bagley and Young, 1979).

We found, however, in work in the early 1980s that black children in Canada had more positive ethnic self-concepts than did their counterparts in the United Kingdom. Since parents of the two groups of children had migrated from the same areas of rural Jamaica, we concluded that it was aspects of Canadian social structure which could account for these differences (Bagley and Young, 1987). While these interesting results cannot show a direct link between educational inputs and a positive evaluation of ethnicity, we do argue that general structural values in Canada inform a more tolerant climate in which individual groups can both participate freely at all levels of the general society, at the same time retaining aspects of cultural identity (Bagley, 1985a). These values influence the educational system, which is geared in a rather tolerant and relaxed way, to meeting the psychological and social needs of diverse groups, educated in a common setting.

Achievement and Self-Esteem: A Transatlantic Comparison

The European observer of the Canadian (and North American) educational scene is immediately impressed by its emphasis on social participation, social development and self-esteem enhancement, and by its apparent lack of concentration on the achievement of academic goals. The university teacher used to the British system, is impressed with the wide range of ability amongst his students, especially at the junior levels. While some students are intellectually self-sufficient or indeed extremely able, a greater number have difficulties with spelling, punctuation, grammar, and the organization of ideas.

The language called 'English' in Canada is a creolized version of the mother tongue (just as French has been creolized in Quebec). This has a number of distinct advantages, not least for the many Canadians whose first language is not English. Learning this language is, for the many immigrants, a relatively easy task. The scholastic attainment required of students at all levels of the educational system seems, in a parallel fashion, to be geared towards the goal of integration of all, regardless of their initial ability. Elitism and the definition of scholastic elites through the identification of academic 'excellence' is definitely discouraged in the Canadian educational system.

There is a parallel emphasis in the ideologies of the culture on the irrelevance of ethnicity and social class as factors in education, and in social and occupational achievement. It is important for the culture and its social system, however, that recent immigrants (who in some parts of urban Ontario constitute some 40 per cent of the population) rapidly acquire the social, interpersonal and linguistic skills which will enable them to participate in the culture with maximum efficiency. The educational system is, of course, an important institution in this respect. Each of the ten Canadian provinces sets its own formal goals by which the educational system should be evaluated. But common to all provinces is an emphasis on social goals (maximizing effective social participation) together with support for the student's self-esteem, from the earliest stages of schooling.

The high school diploma is granted almost automatically to all those students (the large majority) who remain at school until the age of 18 (grade 12 or 13, according to province). This diploma will automatically earn the student admission to a variety of further and higher educational courses, although a 65 per cent passing average is usually required for admission to university. A high school diploma at this level is about equivalent to a reasonable set of passes in the General Certificate of Secondary Education. The first two years of university in the Canadian system will give the student the equivalent of two or three 'A' level passes. About a third of the students do not proceed beyond the first two years of university or college. In 1984, 18 per cent of the age group 18–24 had completed the requirements for a university degree, a proportion which is some three times that in the United Kingdom (Parliament, 1986a).

Even the attempt to acquire a university degree is democratized. 'Part university' is an honourable statement of achievement in higher education, and the majority of the degrees completed are by English standards, 'ordinary' or 'pass' degrees. Only a minority pass at the honours level. In the social sciences and education most 'doctoral' theses would be of an MPhil standard in Britain. There seems, however, to be a greater range of individual ability than in Britain, and some Canadian doctoral theses are of the highest quality. Usually less than a year is allowed for data collection and writing of a doctoral thesis within a 'doctoral program', and three years can be spent on course work which is remedial in nature, bringing the Canadian student up to the level of a British master's degree in the relevant discipline.

The high school, college and university system in Canada is comprehensive in nature, accepting students who pass rather minimal hurdles. The system is inclusive rather than exclusive, offering 'education for all', rather than for a highly selected elite. This is done at the expense of 'quality for all'. Teachers in schools and colleges have to be capable of teaching students of a much wider ability range than would be the case in the British system. There is pressure, moreover, on the teacher not to devalue his students, not to separate sheep from goats.

It seems, then, that there are advantages and disadvantages of both the Canadian and the British systems. Our personal preference is for the Canadian system: there is less demeaning or negative pressure, less elitism, less snobbery and class consciousness, less inequality, less stratification by status and ethnicity. And in the final analysis we can find no evidence that Canada (and the United States too) is any less efficient than Britain in producing an energetic and well-qualified labour force which contributes to national productivity and economic growth. Indeed, a strong case for the greater economic and technological efficiency of Canada can be made.

Overt class consciousness and class division is seemingly absent in Canada; but in Britain it is still pervasive, and seems to inhibit rational economic management and policy. In Marxian terms, however, Canada has excluded the real proletariat by immigration procedures which admit only the young, the well-qualified and the healthy, and those who are particularly disposed to work in a free enterprise system (Bagley, 1985a). Only the original inhabitants, the so-called Indians, represent a totally oppressed and alienated class, subject to a vigorously racist policy (Morse, 1984).

In Britain, in extensive work using self-esteem measures, we found that a persistent and pervasive correlate of poor self-esteem was low scholastic achievement, together with placement in a lower stream or set (Bagley *et al.*, 1979). It was clear from our research that the social organization of schools had an implicit or indirect influence on self-esteem, to the extent that students felt that they were failing or underperforming scholastically. By contrast,

Canadian schools have an explicit, direct goal of encouraging or enhancing pupil self-esteem.

We expected, then, that Canadian students would have higher self-esteem but lower achievement levels, while British students would have higher achievement and, if not lower self-esteem, at least levels of self-esteem which reflected to a certain extent their levels of achievement.

We have been able to explore these hypotheses with Canadian and British students aged 12–14 (attending junior high school), using the Canadian Test of Basic Skills (Birch, 1972; King, 1981) and the Coopersmith Self-Esteem Inventory (Coopersmith, 1967). The self-esteem measure is a 23-item version of the original measure (Bagley and Evan-Wong, 1976), and has been previously validated in large samples in England and Canada (Verma and Bagley, 1982). The Canadian Test of Basic Skills is a Canadianized version of the Iowa Test of Basic Skills. In this study we have utilized the parts of the test measuring vocabulary, reading comprehension and English language skills.

The Canadian students were all attending non-denominational schools in the city of Calgary, a large metropolis in Western Canada. The English students attended secondary schools in the London area. Testing was carried out in 1983, and it could be that recent educational reforms in Britain including the introduction of new forms of examination at the secondary stage (for example, the GCSE) will make British education more open and accessible, without the rigid and demeaning divisions which have existed for many decades.

Table 6.1 indicates that in all comparisons, the English students do significantly better than their Canadian counterparts at all ages on the test of English language skills. The differences became larger in each age comparison, ranging from a difference of nearly one standard deviation at age 12 to 1.3 standard deviations by age 14. Our presumptions about the academic demands made by the two systems seem to be borne out by these results. It should be cautioned, however, that our samples are relatively small, and the schools studied were selected on the basis of their interest in the research, rather than on a random basis. The five Canadian schools cooperating all expected, in fact, that their students would do well in comparison with English students.

The self-esteem comparisons (Table 6.2) show less clear-cut results. Only the comparisons of the grade 6 children (and of all grades combined) indicated clear support for the initial hypothesis: the Canadian 12-year-olds have significantly better self-esteem than do the English 12-year-olds. Comparisons of the other two age groupings show differences in the expected direction, but not at an acceptable level of significance.

A secondary hypothesis was that poorer self-esteem and lower scores on the test measuring English language and verbal reasoning abilities would only reach significance in the English sample. Table 6.3 indicates partial support for this idea. There is a moderate but highly significant correlation for the English male school students between poorer self-esteem, and poorer English

Christopher Bagley

Table 6.1. *Comparisons of Scores of Canadian and English Students on the Canadian Test of Basic Skills in English Language Skills*

	Canadian	**English**	**Value of T**	**Significance**
Grade 6				
Mean age	12.3	12.6	—	—
English test score,				
standardized (SD)	102.7 (18.41)	114.2 (16.86)	9.81	<0.000
Percent male	52%	47%	—	—
N	206	227		
Grade 7				
Mean age	13.6	13.5	—	—
English test score,				
standardized (SD)	103.9 (18.31)	119.1 (16.46)	8.40	<0.000
N	188	180		
Percent male	50%	55%	—	—
Grade 8				
Mean age	14.5	14.3	—	—
English test score,				
standardized (SD)	104.8 (17.78)	127.8 (15.70)	5.7	<0.000
N	40	32		
Percent male	50%	59%	—	—

Table 6.2. *Comparisons of Scores of Canadian and English Students on the Coopersmith Self-Esteem Inventory (Short Form)*

	Canadian	**English**	**Value of T**	**Significance**
Grade 6				
SEI score (SD)	14.41 (8.13)	16.37 (8.40)	2.54	<0.01>0.001
N	220	240		
Grade 7				
SEI score (SD)	13.23 (8.21)	14.52 (7.58)	1.62	<0.10>0.05
N	200	193		
Grade 8	12.40 (8.08)	13.91 (7.68)	0.86	<0.25>0.10
N	44	36		
All three grades	13.76 (8.75)	15.33 (8.47)	2.73	<0.01>0.001
N	464	409		

Note: The higher the SE1 score, the poorer the self-esteem

Table 6.3. *Correlations Between Self-Esteem Scores and a Test of Verbal Ability in Canadian and British Students*

| | English | | Canadian | |
	Male	Female	Male	Female
Grades 6, 7, and 8				
Correlation	−0.29**	−0.20**	−0.16*	0.06
N	284	276	288	256

Notes: **Indicates significance at the 1 per cent level. *Indicates significance at the 5 per cent level. Since a high score on the Self-Esteem Inventory indicates poor self-esteem, negative correlations in the above table indicate a link between poorer verbal ability and poorer self-esteem.

language ability. The significance of the correlation is also apparent for the English school girls. A smaller, but nevertheless significant, correlation was obtained for the younger Canadian males, but not for the females.

We conclude from the psychometric data that Canadian students do indeed have poorer skills in the formal manipulation and understanding of the English language than do their English counterparts of similar age. In qualification of this conclusion we should point out that social class and ethnicity were not controlled for directly. Indeed, the Calgary School Board would not allow us to ask questions about ethnicity or class origins, arguing that such an enquiry would offend the privacy of students and their families. Canadian academic studies looking at class and ethnic variables in relation to achievement or adjustment are rare—a reflection of the low saliency which these variables have in Canadian society.

We do know, however, that the four schools involved in the Canadian study drew their students from largely white, middle class areas. In contrast, the English schools served diverse social areas, in terms of class and ethnicity. In a separate analysis of the English data we found that ethnicity and self-esteem were not linked, a finding which supports recent British and European research (Verma and Bagley, 1982; Brock, 1987). The apparent social and ethnic difference between the Canadian and English samples should, if anything, have depressed the academic achievement scores of the English subjects, who actually have much higher academic achievement scores.

Conclusions

We have argued in this chapter that the principles of 'education for all' are better established in Canada than in Britain. There is an important qualification to this argument, namely the failure of Canadian society to either incorporate aboriginal people into mainstream institutions with equity, or to support the aspirations of Native people within a pluralist framework. Aboriginal people in Canada are an extremely disadvantaged and discriminated against group. Their traditional lands have been confiscated by force, fraud or deceit with minimal, if any, compensation. Disease and death rates at all ages are very high, and housing conditions extremely poor (Bagley, 1984b). Educational provision and achievement are extremely low (Kirkness, 1981), and on most parameters Native people in Canada fare no better than many people in Third World countries (CJPH, 1982). The irony of this is that the land and resources confiscated from aboriginal people have formed the basis of the economic expansion which has made Canada one of the world's richest nations.

Native people have been excluded from the generous multicultural framework established by the Secretary of State for other ethnic groups in Canada. The Department of Indian Affairs, which 'administers' the so-called Indian people, steadfastly refuses to recognize the aspirations of the different linguistic and ethnic groups amongst aboriginal people for separate identity and nationhood. In terms of the social psychology of prejudice (Bagley *et al.*, 1979), the case of Canada demonstrates the principle that tolerance for some ethnic groups is based on the rigid oppression of a stigmatized group whose traditional lifestyle makes them unsuitable for incorporation into a capitalistic framework of development.

We have argued that ethnicity and class are variables which have low salience in Canadian society, and that the values supporting tolerance for most immigrant groups are implicit or low-key. A concomitant of this is that analytical or sociological studies of class and ethnicity in Canadian society are quite rare. We assume, for example, from indirect, rather than direct, evidence that discrimination against black people is relatively rare, and the 'situation testing' familiar in the United Kingdom (Brown, 1984) has not been attempted in Canada. However, one formal study of discrimination against black people in Toronto indicates that such discrimination *does* exist, albeit on a lesser scale than in Britain.

Recent studies by David Livingstoke and his colleagues at the Ontario Institute for Studies in Education (Livingstone, 1987) have been unusual in focusing on the class and ethnic origins of students moving between various stages of secondary education and into the university and college sector. A sample of public opinion indicated that 69 per cent of Ontario residents believed that all students had equal opportunities in the school system, regardless of economic or social origin. The reality, Livingstone and his colleagues suggest, is that 46 per cent of students with parents in lower blue collar jobs completed a high school diploma enabling them to enter tertiary education, compared with 88 per cent of students with parents in upper middle class occupations. About 10 per cent of all students from lower blue collar backgrounds graduate after four years of university education, compared with 33 per cent of all students with parents with professional jobs. Black students tend, in terms of their class origins, to overachieve but to the extent that their parents are in blue collar jobs, they are not properly represented in the university sector.

How do these findings compare with the contemporary situation in the

United Kingdom? We have no direct data which would enable us to make valid comparisons. We would suggest however that although 'education for all' is still not a proper reality in Canada, nevertheless things are *relatively* better in Canada.

A second critique that may be advanced against the idea that the Canadian education system fulfils some of the criteria of 'education for all', concerns the issue of quantity versus quality. Even though much larger numbers enter the tertiary stage of education in North America, is the quality of that education so poor that the exercise is hardly worthwhile? A critique of American higher education by the Association of American Colleges (AAC, 1985) entered a blistering critique of tertiary education, arguing that much that was offered was 'virtually meaningless'. The report identifies the failure of many American graduates to write clearly or grammatically, their inability to engage in abstract thinking and logical analysis, and their lack of appreciation of historical, international and multicultural issues affecting all Americans.

In a recent polemic, Allan Bloom (1987) subtitled his book 'how higher education has failed democracy and impoverished the souls of today's students'. His main critique centres on the dominance of instrumental values in American universities, and a concentration on vocational goals at the expense of a broad, liberal education. It may be that Bloom's critique can apply to all western universities: certainly, the contractions and strains imposed by the policy in recent years on British higher education would seem to be a fit subject for Bloom's critique.

The failure of quality in Canadian education has recently been underlined by a national study of literacy (Calamai, 1987). This indicated that 14 per cent of Canadian adults were 'functionally illiterate' in English according to the test used. The test consisted of the ability to answer multiple choice questions identifying characters, sequences and events in a newspaper story; writing a simple precis; and reading and understanding a request to find an appropriate number from the *Yellow Pages* directory. Having a high school certificate was no guarantee against 'illiteracy' — 13 per cent of high school and 8 per cent of college 'graduates' (with at least two years of college education), failed the test of basic literacy. The survey attributes the greatest responsibility for these problems to the failure of the educational system at all levels to give appropriate instruction in English language. French speakers for whom English was a second language were somewhat *less* illiterate; and first generation immigrants were significantly over-achieving on the literacy test, compared with non-migrants.

Recent data from the International Educational Achievement study of mathematics and science (IAEEA, 1987) indicates the overall superiority of British over North American students. The British students scored at least a standard deviation higher than US students of similar age on standardized tests of chemistry, biology and physics. In fact, British students had on average the highest scores in these three subjects in comparison with students from the US, Japan, Sweden and Israel. The average second year science student (aged 18 or 19) at an average US college scored 44 per cent on the physics test, compared with an average of 58 per cent on the same test for 16-year-old English students preparing for the then GCE or CSE in physics.

Canada was not included in the initial report on these international comparisons; but there is some informal evidence that Canadian educational standards are somewhat higher than those in the United States. For example, Canadian high school students seem particularly successful in the College Admission Test, in winning scholarships to prestigious American universities.

Our original point was that Canadian education attempts to be inclusive, offering a version of an 'education for all' which can maximize pupil self-concept, by minimizing the exclusions and invidious comparisons that concentrating on high educational standards seems to involve.

There is little doubt, from the evidence, that Canadian society and its educational system are kinder to immigrants ('new Canadians' as they are termed) than is British society, and to this extent is more likely to meet the goals of 'education for all'.

This is paralleled by political developments in Canada aimed at incorporating multiculturalism, along with bilingualism, as a basic political right (CEC, 1987). 'Multiculturalism' is also a political process, a rallying cry for political change in an optimistic culture in which it is assumed that things can only improve. In a decade the situation regarding minorities, education and scholastic and educational achievement will almost certainly have improved in Canada. We cannot be so optimistic with regard to Britain.

The best that we can conclude for the present is that Canadian education is good in parts, with both positive and negative aspects. The problem of quality is probably not as severe as it is in the United States, and in Canada some university administrations have taken positive steps to broaden university education and improve its quality, including compulsory literacy tests and remedial education for all university students, and two years of liberal education in arts and science before entering an honours or professional school.

Summary

The idea of 'education for all' has been extended, and considered as a metaphor for evaluating society, and the degree to which it affords all citizens and all minority groups an equitable access to educational development, cultural participation and economic advancement.

English and Canadian educational systems have been compared and evaluated, according to the degree to which they have contributed to these ideal goals for education. We suggested after considering evidence from some cross-cultural psychological studies, that while education in Britain is of an intrinsically high quality so far as the academic achievement of a selected minority is concerned, its rigid elitism fails to meet adequately the affective and other goals of education, including the enabling of new migrants to participate in the culture with equity. Canadian education, by contrast, is more inclusive and allows a much fuller and more rapid access and participation by minority groups. The emphasis on affective rather than cognitive goals in education is reflected in somewhat higher levels of self-esteem in Canadian students.

Canadian education has problems, however, particularly in relation to its failure to achieve reasonably high academic standards for any or all groups in society. This is a problem shared with educational systems in the United States. Another profound problem of Canadian education has been its failure to address the educational and other needs of aboriginal peoples.

Canadian education has, however, largely by default rather than by design, provided a system which is highly accessible to minority groups with differing linguistic, ethnic and cultural backgrounds. While some barriers of class and race still prevail in the provision of access to life chances in Canadian society, these are of a different order and intensity from those which prevail in Britain.

Notes

1 Many studies and reports in Britain, ranging from the Robbins Report in the early 1960s to the Swann Report in the 1980s have provided evidence on this point.
2 This is, of course, a pluralist or liberal model of education, and assumes that education shall assist in the task of overcoming structural barriers to educational entry, based on economic and class forces. A socialist model of 'education for all' might be quite different from this.
3 See the commentary and prescription concerning these issues in the editorial introductions to Verma and Bagley (1975, 1982 and 1984); and Bagley and Verma (1983).
4 The Swann Committee Report speaks of a 'sense of despair and frustration' engendered by the structural barriers and blocks to the aspirations of immigrant communities (p. 21). Those aspirations are characterized in the Report:

> Those immigrants who came for economic betterment and to enhance the prospects for their children, came on the understanding that they had every right to come to this country and, once they and their families were established here, they would not only be entitled to full equality of opportunity in terms of having jobs and education...but would also be in a position to seek changes in existing systems and procedures where these took no account of their presence here. (pp. 19–20)

References

AAC (1985) *Integrity in the College Curriculum*, Washington, DC, Association of American Colleges.
BAGLEY, C. (1973) *The Dutch Plural Society: A Comparative Study of Race Relations*, London, Oxford University Press.
BAGLEY, C. (1982) 'Achievement, behaviour disorder and social circumstances in West Indian children and other ethnic groups' in VERMA, G. and BAGLEY, C. (Eds) *Self-Concept, Achievement and Multicultural Education*, London, Macmillan.

BAGLEY, C. (1983) 'Dutch social structure and the alienation of black youth' in BAGLEY, C. and VERMA, G. (Eds) *Multicultural Childhood: Education, Ethnicity and Cognitive Styles*, Aldershot, Gower Press.

BAGLEY, C. (1984a) 'Education, ethnicity and racism: A European-Canadian perspective', *Currents: Readings in Race Relations*, Fall, pp. 8–12.

BAGLEY, C. (1984b) 'The state of the world's children', *Canadian Children*. 9, pp. 1–5.

BAGLEY, C. (1985a) 'Education and ethnicity: A European-Canadian comparison' in MODGIL, S. *et al.* (Eds) *Multicultural Education: The Interminable Debate*, Lewes, Falmer Press.

BAGLEY, C. (1985b) 'Field dependence and verbal reasoning in Blackfoot, Japanese and Anglo-Celtish children in Canada' in DIAZ-GUERRO, R. (Ed) *Crosscultural and National Studies in Social Psychology*, Amsterdam, Elsevier.

BAGLEY. C. and EVAN-WONG, L. (1976) 'Neuroticism and extraversion in responses to Coopersmith's self-esteem inventory'. *Psychological Reports*, 36, pp. 253–4.

BAGLEY, C., IWAWAKI, S. and YOUNG, L. (1983) 'Japanese children: Group oriented but not field-dependent?' in BAGLEY, C. and VERMA, G. (Eds) *Multicultural Childhood*, Aldershot, Gower Press.

BAGLEY, C. and VERMA, G. (1979) *Racial Prejudice, the Individual and Society*, Farnborough, Saxon House.

BAGLEY, C. and VERMA, G. *et al* (1979) *Personalities, Self-esteem, and Prejudice*, Farnborough, Saxon House.

BAGLEY, C. and VERMA, G. (Eds) (1983) *Multicultural Childhood: Education, Ethnicity and Cognitive Styles*, Aldershot, Gower Press.

BAGLEY, C. and YOUNG, L. (1979) 'A comparative study of cognitive style and socialization in 10-year-olds in England and Jamaica'. *New Community*, 8, pp. 37–50.

BAGLEY, C. and YOUNG, L. (1988) 'Evaluation of color and ethnicity in young children in Jamaica, Ghana and England', *International Journal of Intercultural Relations*, 12, pp. 45–60.

BIRCH, L. (1972) 'Review of Canadian tests of basic skills' in BUROS, O. (Ed) *Seventh Mental Measurements Yearbook*, Vol. 1, Highland Park, NJ, Gryphon Press, pp. 15–16.

BLOOM, A. (1987) *The Closing of the American Mind: How Higher Education has Failed Democracy and Impoverished the Souls of Today's Students*, New York, General Books.

BREEDLOVE, C. and SCHWEINART, L. (1982) *The Cost-Effectiveness of High Quality Early Childhood Programs*, Ypsilanti, MI, Centre for Public Policies for Young Children.

BROCK, C. (1987) *The Caribbean in Europe: Aspects of the West Indian Experience in Britain, France and the Netherlands*, London, Frank Cass.

BROWN, C. (1984) *Black and White in Britain: The Third PSI Survey*, London, Heinemann for the Policy Studies Institute.

BURKE, A. (1986) 'Immigration', *Canadian Social Trends*, autumn, pp. 23–7.

CALAMAI, P. (1987) *The Canadian Literacy Survey*, Toronto, Southam Press.

CAMPFENS, H. (1980) *The Integration of Ethno-Cultural Minorities in the Netherlands and Canada*, The Hague, Ministry of Cultural Affairs.

CEC (1987) *Multiculturalism and the Meech Lake Accord*, Toronto, Canadian Ethnocultural Council.

CJPH (1982) 'Editorial: Health of Native Canadians — its relevance to world health' *Canadian Journal of Public Health*, 73, pp. 297–8.

COOPERSMITH, S. (1967) *The Antecedents of Self-Esteem*, San Francisco, CA, Freeman.

CROSLAND, A. (1974) *Socialism and Education*, London, Penguin Books.

IAEEA (1987) *Science Achievement: International Comparisons*, New York, Columbia University Teachers College for the IAEEA.

KING, E. (1981) *Canadian Test of Basic Skills*, Toronto, Nelson.

KIRKNESS, V. (1981) 'The education of Canadian Indian children', *Child Welfare*, 60, pp. 447–54.

LAMBERT, R., BROWN, S., CURTIS, J. and KAY, B. (1986) 'Canadians' beliefs about differences between social classes', *Canadian Journal of Sociology*, 11, pp. 379–90.

LAPKIN, S., SWAIN, M. and ARGUE, V. (1983) *French Immersion: The Trial Balloon That Flew*, Toronto, Ontario Institute for Studies in Education.

LIVINGSTONE, D. (1987) *Critical Pedagogy and Cultural Power*, Toronto, Ontario Institute for Studies in Education.

LOWENTHAL, D. (1967) 'Race and color in the West Indies', *Daedalus*, spring, pp. 580–626.

MAZUREK, K. (1987) 'Multiculturalism, education and the ideology of the meritocracy' in WOTHERSPORN, T. (Ed) *The Political Economy of Canadian Schooling*, Toronto, Methuen.

MOODLEY, K. (1981) 'Canadian ethnicity in comparative perspective' in DAHLIE, J. and FERNANDO, T. (Eds) *Ethnicity, Power and Politics in Canada*, Toronto, Methuen.

MOODLEY, K. (1983) 'Canadian multiculturalism as ideology', *Ethnic and Racial Studies*, 6, pp. 1–12.

MORSE, B. (1984) 'Native Indian and Metis children in Canada: Victims of the child welfare system' in VERMA, G. and BAGLEY, C. (Eds) *Race Relations and Cultural Differences*, London, Croom Helm.

MORTON, A. (1938) *A People's History of England*, London, Gollancz.

PARLIAMENT, J. (1986a) 'Education in Canada: Selected highlights', *Canadian Social Trends*, autumn, pp. 15–21.

PARLIAMENT, J. (1986b) 'French immersion', *Canadian Social Trends*, autumn, 14.

PORTER, J. (1965) *The Vertical Mosaic*, Toronto, University of Toronto Press.

REITZ, G. (1981) *Ethnic Inequality and Segregation in Jobs*, Toronto, Centre for Urban and Community Studies.

SCHIFF, M. and LEWONTIN, R. (1987) *Education and Class: The Irrelevance of IQ Genetic Studies*, London, Oxford University Press.

THOMAS-HOPE, E.(1982) 'Identity and adaptation of migrants from the English-speaking Caribbean in Britain and North America' in VERMA, G. and BAGLEY, C. (Eds) *Self-Concept, Achievement and Multicultural Education*, London, Macmillan.

VERMA, G. (1983) 'Consciousness, disadvantage and opportunity: The struggle for South Asian youth in British society' in BAGLEY, C. and VERMA, G. (Eds) *Multicultural Childhood*, Aldershot, Gower Press.

VERMA, G. and BAGLEY, C. (Eds) (1975) *Race and Education Across Cultures*, London, Heinemann.

VERMA, G. and BAGLEY, C. (Eds) (1979) *Race, Education and Identity*, London, Macmillan.

VERMA, G. and BAGLEY, C. (Eds) (1982) *Self-Concept, Achievement and Multicultural Education*, London, Macmillan.

VERMA, G. and BAGLEY, C. (Eds) (1984) *Race Relations and Cultural Differences*, London, Croom Helm.

WOLFENSBERGER, W. (1972) *Normalization Policies*, Toronto, National Institute for Mental Retardation.

YOUNG, L. and BAGLEY, C. (1982) 'Identity, self-esteem and evaluation of colour and ethnicity in young children in Jamaica and London' in VERMA, G. and BAGLEY, C. (Eds) *Self-Concept, Achievement and Multicultural Education*, London, Macmillan.

Chapter 7

International Interdependence: Swann's Contribution*

James Lynch

Multiculturalism: An International Phenomenon

In the various Western democracies, the debate about the principles, practice and promise of multicultural education has tended to be conducted on a largely exclusive national or regional basis. One of the major contributions of the Swann Report in England (DES, 1985) is the way in which it incorporates the global dimension into our understanding of multicultural education. It is emphatic that:

> In our view an education which seek only to emphasize and enhance the ethnic group identity of a child, at the expense of developing both a national identity and indeed an international global perspective, cannot be regarded as in any sense multicultural. (p. 322)

The Report argues unequivocally that, 'A good education must reflect the diversity of British society and indeed of the contemporary world' (p. 318). The Report advocates an education for all '. . . essentially synonymous with a good and relevant education for a life in the modern world' (*ibid*), and it castigates the inaccurate, outdated and stereotyped views on the Third World frequently projected by schools (p. 234). The argument is that our cultural, political, environmental and economic interconnections on 'space capsule earth' are such that any overall educational philosophy that does not include those dimensions accurately and fairly portrayed is inevitably incomplete, narrow, parochial, and, therefore, inappropriate to a multicultural society.

True, the Report does not elaborate the further and compelling argument for a global approach, namely the view that the struggle for human justice and against prejudice and discrimination cannot be restricted to national boundaries, nor can the identification of what is 'moral' behaviour in a multicultural society be left to merely national ethics. Rather, it must be susceptible to the widest possible discourse in a context of maximum possible freedom of expression, against a background of certain commonly accepted

*This chapter is based on a paper given in Bristol in April 1986.

human values: human rights. For, as Greenbaum (1974) proposed a number of years ago, with the decline of former national ideals in Western democracies, an important source of the new core ideals is to be found in oppressed groups, not only in the 'home base' society, but also in the developing countries of the Third World. Such groups, which have experienced victimization and opposition at first hand, may not only provide Western nations with a new and broader social conscience, but also an enrichment of their national ideals and their moral values.

Implicit in this latter point (and the Swann Report) is the need for a new perception by Western nations of the North–South divide and the relationships among developed and developing countries. In the context of my own past experience in the developing nations of Asia and Africa, working for United Nations agencies, this perception will demand a new effort on the part of educationists in East and West to identify with the cultural and economic circumstances of exploited nations: the abandonment of the conviction of cultural hegemony and learning, in order to achieve what Freire (1970) calls 'conscientization', in a concerted effort to reverse the consequences of standing on the shoulders of developing nations for the maintenance of our irresponsible consumerism. How far we are from achieving such a moral responsibility in our dealings with developing countries may be gauged in the Report of the Brandt Commission (1983) and the Independent Commission on International Development Issues (1980). In this latter report Willy Brandt expanded on the theme of the role of education in fostering a better knowledge of international, and not least North–South, affairs, widening horizons, fostering a concern for the fate of other nations and for problems of common interest. Edward Heath, in an article in the *Times Educational Supplement* (1980) of the time emphasized the Commission's feeling that schools should pay more attention to international problems, so that young people may see more clearly the dangers they face, their own responsibilities and the opportunities of cooperation — globally and regionally as well as within their own neighbourhood.

I want to prepare for that theme by offering one or two preliminary reflections about the nature of global ethnic and cultural diversity, and the way in which attempts have been made to conceptualize and implement responses to it. Cultural diversity — that is, the presence of a number of different cultural, linguistic, ethnic, credal, or racial groups — has a very long history, and it is a commonplace in the modern world. Because the specific cultural biography and profile of different regions and districts within nations and across them internationally varies considerably, I want to offer a commentary on the development of cultural pluralism and to introduce some of the theoretical responses to that pluralism. I want to refer to examples of major international instruments and declarations that are of direct relevance to the development and implementation of multicultural education with a global perspective by teachers who are committed to combating prejudice and discrimination in all its various forms, such as racism, sexism and credism; and who are committed to achieving greater respect for persons, both nationally and internationally.

Cultural Diversity and Western Democratic Societies

Cultural diversity has been a fact of life in the countries of East and West, North and South for many centuries. Ancient communities on the Australian continent, on the Indian sub-continent, and in North and South America and Africa have been culturally heterogeneous from time immemorial. Notwithstanding a similar scenario in Europe, contemporary recognition of linguistic, cultural and religious diversity in Western societies in Europe is more recent. By the nineteenth century, the era of nationalism and cultural pluralism in Europe was already very marked in terms of differences in the religious, linguistic and ethnic backgrounds of its inhabitants. With the establishment of nation-states in Europe, however, came a new, wider role for education, as political cohesion was sought through educational and broader social policies. Whether in France, Great Britain or Imperial Germany, immense efforts were made to acculturate divergent and often conquered groups into the dominant culture and language.

In spite of these efforts, the European nation-states always retained within their political boundaries very substantial ethnic minorities whose cultures varied significantly from that of the dominant state. Even the post-World War I settlements, which attempted to establish culturally homogeneous nation-states, did not eliminate that cultural diversity and in some cases only served to accentuate it. Both new nations such as Yugoslavia and older, truncated ones, such as Austria, retained substantial cultural minorities within their boundaries; while the border settlements between such countries as Germany, on the one hand, and France, Denmark and Belgium, on the other, resulted in increased cultural diversity. In some cases, as with the Danes in Germany and the Germans in Denmark, the legal, political and educational status of those minorities was internationally secured (Lynch, 1986a).

Post-World War II Developments

It was not until the end of World War II that three major factors came together to motivate educational policy makers and educators to consider how education might respond to newer perceptions of cultural diversity. These three factors were:

(i) the post-1945 economic expansion which demanded a large additional labour force, where recruitment was achieved by mass immigration;
(ii) growing concern for human rights stemming from the atrocities of World War II and vitalized by new national and international organizations like

the United Nations and its agencies such as UNESCO;

(iii) the resultant emergence of ethnic revitalization movements (Banks, 1986a) which responded also to the disparity between the declared values of democratic societies toward their minorities and the realities of the operation of those societies.

These factors were closely followed by a fourth which was to revolutionize the relationships of rich and poor, North and South, developed and developing countries: the wind of change which brought decolonization to the countries of Asia and Africa.

Such factors were to transform perceptions of the cultural composition of Western society and of the role of education and the school. They led to educational strategies with labels such as 'intergroup', 'intercultural', 'multicultural', 'multiethnic', or 'multiracial' education; 'education in a multicultural society', 'education for prejudice reduction', and, more recently, 'anti-racist education'. These were complemented by world studies, global and development education and education for human rights. Not all the terms had in common an acceptance of permanent cultural pluralism and a rejection of assimilationist or separatist policies. Some were more radical than others; some less tolerant, some more. Some accepted democratic values as their motivation and aim; others did not. Indeed, in the same period, there has been only a gradual movement toward policies aimed at democratic inclusion and cultural pluralism, consistent with democratic values; rather than all-out integration, separation, or assimilation, which were the goals of the earlier responses to cultural diversity. Thus, while more recent developments in the field of multicultural education may have received their spur from the arrival of newer ethnic minorities in societies as diverse and separated as Australia, Canada, the United Kingdom, and France, this is by no means the only motivator of that educational strategy, nor the only major limit of its concerns.

Older established and indigenous ethnic, racial, religious, and other cultural minorities have contributed over centuries to cultural diversity in the United States, Canada, the United Kingdom, Australia, and other Western democracies, as well as in other new nations in Africa and elsewhere. Not all culturally pluralist societies have sought to mirror that diversity in education and not all societies are committed to democratic cultural pluralism. Only a few have sought to implement policies of multicultural education consistent with democratic ideals. None has yet fully succeeded, and most face a glaring gap between their declared democratic ideals and the reality and experience of victimized groups — especially visible minorities.

The Goals of Multicultural Education

I have argued elsewhere (Lynch, 1983, 1986a and 1987), that if education for cultural pluralism is to be effective, it must address not only the special needs of minorities but also the education of majorities in terms of their values and the way they relate to minorities. It must aim to facilitate the inclusion of minorities in the benefits of living in a free and democratic society, as well as to support their right to cultural diversity within an agreed legal framework. It must engage them in creative discourse to define and implement the common core values of the nation-state. For all these goals, the normative reeducation of the majority must form a priority of multicultural policies, so that minorities will be able to achieve access to educational and broader social equality as full members of the society, while their right is respected to retain their own legitimate and distinctive cultures, within the context of the 'national political covenant'. That covenant implies, in democratic societies, the acceptance of common shared values such as the commitment to justice and human rights, as well as a commitment to improvement by persuasion rather than by violence, not solely within their own nation state, but internationally as well.

The major goals of multicultural education may accordingly be defined as addressing:

   (i) the creative enhancement of cultural diversity and not solely the maintenance of existing cultures;
  (ii) the achievement of equality of educational opportunity for all regardless of sex, race, creed, ethnic background, class, etc.; and
 (iii) the propagation of a sense of shared values, rights and access to political power and economic satisfaction.

The goals may be summarized as pluralism, equality and cohesion (PEC) and they represent goals which democratic societies should hold not only for themselves but also for others.

Countries have reacted differently to the demands inherent in cultural diversity. Watson (1979), for example, differentiates among the countries that have adopted policies of multicultural education as:

   (i) those having deep-rooted racial and cultural diversity such as the Soviet Union;
  (ii) those having a cultural mix resulting largely from colonialization, as recipients or donors, such as France, Fiji, Malaysia and Holland; and
 (iii) those having become multicultural mainly as a result of voluntary immigration.

While his categorization invites further refinement, it also serves to alert us to the 'pluralism or pluralisms' inherent in cultural diversity, seen internationally, and to the wide range of dimensions that contribute to such diversity in different countries and thus to the avoidance of facile attempts at cultural transfer. This does not, of course, mean that we cannot learn from one another. Quite the reverse.

Migration and Cultural Diversity

Migration has contributed substantially to the mosaic of modern Western democratic societies as well as those in the socialist countries and the Third World. Castles (1984), for example, identified five major patterns of post-war migration into Western European countries:

(i) the return migration of settlers from former colonies such as the *pieds noirs* from Algeria and the Dutch from Indonesia;
(ii) immigration of ethnically distinct citizens of colonies and former colonies;
(iii) labour migration of mainly manual workers from areas such as the Mediterranean;
(iv) migration of skilled employed between highly developed countries; and
(v) the entry of foreign refugees seeking political asylum.

In all Western countries, immigration regulations and legislation have become more stringent over the past fifteen or twenty years, the only exceptions now being migrations of a *consequential, adoptive,* or *refugee* kind. As we are all aware, in view of the recent press given to asylum-seekers in Western Europe, the definition of this latter category is subject to an ever-tightening restriction.

Differing patterns of migration combined with the differing political structure, cultural context, historical development and administrative organization in various countries have led to different views of, and responses to, cultural pluralism and particularly to the identification of the needs of newly-arrived cultural groups. The educational and social responses of countries are therefore often distinctly different from each other. Several authors have tried to conceptualize this interaction of challenge and response. Wirth (1976), for example, sees ethnic minorities responding to the surrounding society in one of four ways:

(i) assimilation — a complete abandonment of their cultural differences and absorption into the dominant culture;
(ii) pluralism — the acceptance and tolerance of their differences by dominant and majority communities;
(iii) secession or complete independence;
(iv) militancy in an attempt to take power from a dominant or majority group.

Alternative options have been advocated, but within a democratic society where change is achieved by persuasion and discourse, some form of cultural pluralism is the most likely to be adopted since the only real alternative is the use of coercion, which is incongruent with the underlying values of these societies.

Gordon (1975) has identified two major forms of cultural pluralism: liberal and corporate. In the first form, difference is tolerated but not officially recognized, for example, by the allocation of supportive resources. In the second form, there is explicit recognition of ethnic groups as a basis for the allocation of social and political power and access to economic rewards and resources. Bullivant (1984) has recently extended this proposition, arguing that ethnic minorities need to establish separate structures and institutions in order to survive.

Most Western societies, however, have hardly begun to involve minorities in the process of the discourse, essential to the definition of shared values, against which political and narrower educational judgments can be made. Until they do, international instruments, agreements, and interlearning constitute some of the few marker posts for moral behaviour in a multicultural society.

Ethnic Revitalization Movements

A more recent conceptualization of the process of challenge and response, which has given birth to multicultural education, is offered by Banks (1986a) as part of what he describes as the emergence of *ethnic revitalization movements*. He envisages four major phases in educational support for equality on the part of currently victimized racial and cultural minorities. In the first phase, characterized by colonialism, imperialism, victimization and marginalization, democratic societies attempt to close the gap between their democratic ideals and their social realities, sometimes by coercive or assimilationist methods. This only serves to raise expectations and demands on the part of victimized groups and leads inevitably to the next phase. This phase is characterized by ethnic polarization and a quest for identity by victimized ethnic groups whose educational underachievement has not been considered by majority communities in terms of racism, credism or sexism.

The third phase to emerge is characterized by discourse between minority and dominant ethnic groups, and an increasing number of coalitions, which reduces ethnic polarization and facilitates the search for multi-causal explanations of the problems suffered by victimized groups. Minorities having achieved the legitimization of racism as one accepted cause of their problems, cooperate in the quest for further explanations and strategies to tackle their problems. A final phase sees the implementation of reforms proposed during the earlier phases, which gradually become 'institutionalized orthodoxies' and thus pave the way for the emergence of new ethnic revitalization movements to overturn that orthodoxy, but based this time on the acceptance of discourse as the means to such resolution.

Banks envisages a crucial role for education to facilitate the movement of society and individuals through these four phases, and to assist individual students to develop healthier identification with their *cultural groups*, which he sees as essential to healthy identification at national and global levels. To facilitate the development of the appropriate attitudes, knowledge, and skills, this first stage of identification with one's own cultural group is thus indispensable, because it promotes healthy attitudes within *the nation-state* and *the global community*. This identification with one's ethnic, national and international self-concept is seen by Banks as an essential goal of any realistic multicultural education.

Bank's conceptualization calls to mind the statement in the Swann Report (DES, 1985) that:

> A good education must in our view give every youngster the knowledge, understanding, and skills to function effectively as an *individual*, as a *citizen* in a wider national society, and in the interdependent *world community* of which he is also a member. (my emphasis, p. 319)

Banks' work is thus important for the way in which it offers a conceptualization, on a developmental basis, of the relationship between three levels of multicultural education: *community, national,* and *global*. But it is also important for its central focus on the legitimization of race and racism as an explicator of the problems of disadvantaged visible minorities, this being a prerequisite to the development of more sophisticated multi-factor explanations and responses on the part of education to the needs of all citizens.

Educational Responses

The responses of Western nations to the process of ethnic revitalization, as reflected in their educational policies and in the behaviour of their majority communities, as well as their financial relationships with developing countries, have been essentially defensive, restrictive, selfish and exclusive, as they have sought to defend their cultural and social hegemony and to marginalize the impact of minority cultures and groups (where they have recognized them at all). Only in very recent times have there been isolated attempts to engage ethnic minorities in potent and equal discourse as a means of resolving conflicting interests. As new economic crises have accentuated the vicious cycle of economic exclusion and cultural marginalization in which many members of ethnic minority communities are trapped, however, the alienation of those communities has increased, leading to crises in social cohesion, political disruption, and urban unrest in several countries. A similar process internationally has led to mass starvation, deforestation, environmental pollution, insuperable debt and increased poverty in developing nations.

The refusal of majority communities to accept the elimination of racism as a part of their agenda for educational policy and practice and as an item for vigorous social and political action has led to increasing alienation on the part of many ethnic minority individuals and a polarization within democratic societies between their declared and operative values. A legitimation crisis has thus developed, which can only be resolved by intensified discourse and cooperative political action. By and large, this has not yet happened, as dominant groups have routinely developed new ideologies in their efforts to legitimate the status quo. It is in this context of inaction that the issue of race has been seen in several European countries, including the United Kingdom, as the major focus for societal and educational strategies, both nationally and

James Lynch

internationally. Such strategies are currently labelled *anti-racist*. This, in turn, had led to the rejection by many members of minorities of broader strategies aimed at increasing equality, and to a reappraisal of the aims and concerns of multicultural education, in particular the sharpness of its focus on issues of race, sex, and class (Bottomley and Lepervanche, 1984) and on international interdependence.

The Central Role of Discourse

Democratic societies need to engage in meaningful discourse with their minorities and to seek to come to terms with those minorities' perceptions of their own reality in order to better understand their own relationships with developing countries. The only alternative recourse would be to coercion and that would be fruitless for it would vitiate the very values that democratic societies declare they esteem. Cultural diversity, then, must be made creative in school and society by weaving together the interrelated principles of freedom, discourse and rationality (Lynch, 1986b). As absolute standards governing the behaviour of individuals and groups decline and legal measures alone are insufficient to regulate all aspects of life, national and international, the need is accentuated for new shared values, norms, and mores to be generated by discourse. That discourse, if it is to be real, needs to be structurally inclusive of all cultural groups and to be conducted on a rational basis in the context of maximum freedom—i.e. without compulsion or coercion. (Rational discourse is required to set negotiated bounds or the consequence is license, anarchy and disintegration.) Without freedom, rationality in discourse may be slanted to the rationality of only one group, which will inhibit the discourse necessary for mutuality—i.e., common determination and acceptance of negotiated and agreed values as a basis for social and political cohesion. But where are the pathfinders for such values?

Some International Dimensions of Multicultural Education

Until racism as a legitimized explanation of the problems of victimized groups in most Western societies has been more widely accepted, tensions and conflicts will be endemic to democratic society and in their relationships with developing countries. Thus, consideration of the two educational goals of *social cohesion* and *cultural diversity* and their relevance for international relations has been deferred. Of the major factors proposed as leading to multicultural education policy and practice in culturally plural societies, I now intend to consider in further detail the second: concern with human rights after World War II. Human rights instruments set an indispensable context to the aspirations of ethnic minorities in Western societies to overcome victimization, and may direct educational policy and practice toward the goal of greater justice, which is rightly demanded by anti-racist theorists. Fundamental also to the study of cultural diversity is that democratic societies, whatever their own legislation in response to cultural pluralism, should recognize that there are overarching values at the core of democratic cultural pluralism and related educational practice — the pathfinders previously referred to — for their relationships with developing countries.

Human Rights Instruments

By 1983 there were over fifty international declarations, covenants and agreements concerning human rights (United Nations, 1978 and 1983). While not all these had been agreed, signed, or, indeed, ratified after signature by all nations, these international instruments set the baseline for democratic societies, their relationships with their minorities and the nations of 'the South':

- the United Nations Declaration on Human Rights (1948);
- the European Convention on Human Rights (dating from 1950);
- the Convention on Consent to Marriage, Minimum Age for Marriage, and Registration of Marriages (1962);
- the International Convention on the Elimination of all Forms of Racial Discrimination (1965), together with the United Nations' General Assembly Declaration (1965);
- the International Covenant on Civil Rights (1966), and the UNESCO Declaration on Race and Racial Prejudice (1978); and
- the Convention on the Elimination of all Forms of Discrimination against Women (1979).

The Universal Declaration declares in Article (ii):

> Everyone is entitled to all rights and freedoms set forth in this declaration without distinction of any kind, such as race, colour, sex, language, religion, political or other origin, national or social origin, property, birth or other status.

Similarly, the Convention on Consent to Marriage, Minimum Age for Marriage, and Registration of Marriages states:

> No marriage shall be legally entered into without full and free consent of both parties, such consent to be expressed by them in person after due publicity.

The subsequent General Assembly resolution added further:

> Member States shall legislate action to specify a minimum age for marriage which in any case shall not be less than 15 years of age.

The United Nations' Declaration on the Elimination of all Forms of Racial

Discrimination was signed in 1963 and had (by April 1984) been ratified by 123 nations. It states:

> Discrimination between human beings on the grounds of race, colour or ethnic origins is an offence to human dignity and shall be condemned.

and further:

> Particular efforts shall be made to prevent discrimination based on race, colour or ethnic origin especially in the field of civil rights, access to citizenship, education, religion, employment, occupation and housing.

This latter convention has been endorsed and updated by the UNESCO Declaration on Race and Racial Prejudice (UNESCO, 1978) which was adopted and proclaimed by the General Conference of UNESCO at its 24th Session on 27 November 1978. It states:

> Any distinction, exclusion, restriction or preference based on race, colour, ethnic or national origin or religious intolerance motivated by racist considerations which destroys or compromises the sovereign equality of states and the rights of people to self determination, or which limits in an arbitrary or discriminatory manner the right of every human being and group to full development is incompatible with the requirements of the international order which is just and guarantees respect for human rights.

On the twenty-fifth aniversary of the Universal Declaration of Human Rights, the United Nations convened in New York a Special General Assembly on 10 December 1973, which officially launched the decade of action to combat racism and racial discrimination.

Thus, racial prejudice and discrimination are not just morally wrong, or solely illegal in terms of national legislation, nor do they only offend local school board or state policy — rather they are declared to be outlawed, an offence against humanity as codified in international moral instruments. Such instruments and their declarations provide an indispensable ethical baseline for democratic cultural pluralism.

Regional Agreements

Regional agreements have also been concluded under the auspices of such organizations as the Council of Europe and the European Economic Community. The European Convention, for example, signed on 4 November 1950, and enforced from September 1953, the Second Protocol to that Convention, which confers on the European Court of Human Rights its competence to give advisory opinions. This protocol has been increasingly utilized by citizens of the various nation-states in Europe, not the least from the United Kingdom which does not have a Bill of Rights of its own; and whose citizens see their rights constrained or threatened by the state. Indeed the United Kingdom has been found 'in error' in more cases than has any other state in Europe.

The Council of Europe's work in the field of human rights education in schools also dates from the late 1970s and has been addressed as a specific objective of the Council's second medium-term plan and in its declaration of 14 May 1981. The European Economic Community has also played a role in establishing the social, political, and educational rights of migrant workers and their children, notably in the Directive on Mother-Tongue Instruction (July 1977). This directive has been neglected by a number of European nations, according to a recent EEC report, although it is mandatory and there is the stipulation that nation-states must give account of their progress toward the stated common goals. The directive also sets an indispensable wider and regional context within which those wishing to implement policies of multicultural education may see their own tasks.

The United States and Canada as Examples

In the United States, developments in multiethnic education grew out of the potent Civil Rights Movement which emerged in the 1960s as a result of legislation dismantling segregation. Spurred by riots in the mid and late 1960s, a series of federal and state initiatives was enacted to enforce civil rights legislation. The Civil Rights Act of 1984 forbade discrimination on the basis of race, colour, religion or national origins in American public accommodations and education, in federally assisted programs, and in most areas of private employment. It marked the official start of the movement and the acceptance of race and racism as legitimized explanations of the problems of victimized ethnic minority groups. Judgments in the United States federal and district courts have played an important role in the shaping of educational policy, and educators have faced a wide array of imperatives on how to achieve their goals (Banks, 1986b).

In Canada, the Province of Ontario passed the Racial Discrimination Act as early as 1944, four years before the United Nations Declaration on Human Rights. The Bill of Rights was passed for all of Canada in 1960. During a period of violence and unrest in the 1950s and early 1960s, other provinces responded, establishing human rights commissions, and the Royal Commission on Bilingualism and Biculturalism was set up, which had the specific task of reconciling the maintenance of two basic (European) cultures in Canadian society. However, it was mainly as part of the process of the patriation of the Canadian Constitution that the Canadian Charter of Rights and Freedom was established for all citizens. Human rights commissions, such as the one proclaimed as law on 15 June 1982 for the Province of Ontario with explicit

Human Rights Codes, now exist at the federal level and in all Canadian provinces. From the early 1980s, massive resources were allocated to race relations; in 1982 a race relations unit was established to improve understanding among Canadians of different racial background. This led to the establishment, in 1983, of a special parliamentary committee on the participation of visible minorities in Canadian education, which reported to Parliament in 1984 with the urgent call for 'Equality Now', the title of its report. Much still remains to be done to realize the ideals (Moodley, 1986) but Canada has models, approaches, structures, and ideals from which others may learn after critical appraisal.

Looked at critically, the American legislation and the Canadian Human Rights Codes and Commissions indicate gaps in the provisions of other Western societies: the lack of commitment to grant all citizens a baseline bill of democratic freedoms and rights, enforceable by law without a lengthy and costly process, for those wishing to seek rectification of the infringement of their human rights; a much tighter national legislation and normative framework, and so forth. The experience of democratic societies in North America might be described as giving an endoscopic view of the cracks in the internal structure of other Western democratic societies; perhaps the effect could be mutual with developing nations.

Conclusion

To conclude, let me reiterate briefly what I said at the beginning of this chapter: multicultural education without international dimensions is incomplete and therefore impoverished. As the Swann Report asserts, 'The role of education cannot be expected to reinforce the values, beliefs and cultural identity which each child brings to school. . .' (DES, 1985, p. 321). We are interdependent with others, we have common problems, struggles, and destinies; as educationists committed to multicultural education, our basic ethic requires an international dimension — and, in what the North-South Report (1980) called 'the race between education and catastrophe', we cannot remain neutral. The Swann Report has provided a tiny spur to us all to develop a national curriculum, which is less ethnocentric and selfish, more world-open and focused on human interdependence and co-responsibility. In that respect the Swann Report is indeed a landmark in pluralism — a tiny first step for mankind in response to an ever more urgent problem.

References

BANKS, J.A. (1986a) 'Multicultural education: Development, paradigms and goals' in BANKS, J.A. and LYNCH, J. (Eds) *Multicultural Education in Western Societies*, Eastbourne, Holt, Rinehart and Winston.

BANKS, J.A. (1986b) 'Race, ethnicity and schooling in the United States: Past, present and future' in BANKS, J.A. and LYNCH, J. (Eds) *Multicultural Education in Western Societies*, Eastbourne, Holt, Rinehart and Winston.

BANKS, J.A. and LYNCH, J. (Eds) (1986) *Multicultural Education in Western Societies*, Eastbourne, Holt, Rinehart and Winston.

BOTTOMLEY, G. and LEPERVANCHE, M.M. (Eds) (1984) *Ethnicity, Class and Gender in Australia*, Sydney, Allen and Unwin.

BRANDT COMMISSION (1983) *Common Crisis*, (North-South in Cooperation for World Recovery), London, Pan Books.

BULLIVANT, B.M. (1984) *Pluralism, Cultural Maintenance and Evolution*, Clevedon, Multilingual Matters Ltd.

CASTLES, S. *et al.* (1984) *Here for Good: Western Europe's New Ethnic Minorities*, London, Pluto Press.

DEPARTMENT OF EDUCATION AND SCIENCE (1985) *Education for All: Report of the Committee of Enquiry into the Education of Children from Ethnic Minority Groups* (The Swann Report), Cmnd. 9453, London, HMSO.

FREIRE, P. (1970) *Pedagogy of the Oppressed*, New York, Seabury Press.

GORDON, M.M. (1975) 'Towards a theory of ethnic group relations' in GLAZER, N. and MOYNIHAN, D. (Eds) *Ethnicity: Theory and Experience*, Cambridge, MA, Harvard University Press.

GREENBAUM, W. (1974) 'America in search of a new ideal: An essay on the rise of pluralism', *Harvard Educational Review*, 44, 3, pp. 411–40.

HEATH, E. (1980) 'Windows on the world', *Times Educational Supplement*, 21 November, p. 4.

INDEPENDENT COMMISSION ON INTERNATIONAL DEVELOPMENT ISSUES, (1980) *North-South: A Programme for Survival*, London, Pan Books.

LYNCH, J. (1989) *Multicultural Education: A Global Approach*, Lewes, Falmer Press.

LYNCH, J. (1983) *The Multicultural Curriculum*, London, Batsford.

LYNCH, J. (1986a) 'Multicultural education in Western Europe' in BANKS, J.A. and LYNCH, J. (Eds) *Multicultural Education in Western Societies*, Eastbourne, Holt, Rinehart and Winston.

LYNCH, J. (1986b) *Multicultural Education: Policy and Practice*, London, Routledge.

LYNCH, J. (1987) *Prejudice Reduction and the Schools*, London, Cassell.

MOODLEY, K. (1986) 'Canadian multicultural education: Promises and practices' in BANKS, J.A. and LYNCH, J. (Eds) *Multicultural Education in Western Societies*, Eastbourne, Holt, Rinehart and Winston.

UNESCO GENERAL CONFERENCE (1978) *Declaration on Race and Racial Prejudice*, Paris, UNESCO.

UNITED NATIONS (1978) *Human Rights: A Compilation of International Instruments*, New York, United Nations.

UNITED NATIONS (1983) *Human Rights: International Instruments, Signatures, Ratifications, Accessions etc.*, New York, United Nations, 1 September.

WATSON, K. (1979) 'Education policies in multicultural societies', *Comparative Education*, 18, pp. 17–31.

WIRTH, P.M. (1976) 'Ethnic minorities and school policy in European democracies: Theory and case studies', paper presented at the annual meeting of the American Political Science Association, Chicago, September.

Chapter 8

Teacher Education in a Multicultural Society*

Maurice Craft

Context

During the 1980s a series of massive changes in British education has been introduced by government, affecting all areas of provision and practice. Significant among these are changes in the initial and in-service training of teachers. The Swann Report (DES, 1985), a major review of education in a multicultural society, appeared in 1985 after a six-year sifting of evidence, and it too included a substantial section on teacher education. This has sought to convey the central, strategic significance of equipping all new and practising teachers — 'the key figures in the education process' — with an informed awareness of what teaching in a multicultural society involves.

This is not a new situation. The need has been regularly highlighted for some twenty years, and there has been hardly a government report or other major enquiry into immigration, race relations or ethnic minority children which has not made reference to teacher education. One of the more recent was in the Scarman Report on The Brixton Disorders, which asserted:

> There is a clear need for improved training of teachers in the particular needs, the cultural background, and the expectations of minority group children and parents. (Home Office, 1981, para. 6.20)

But as long ago as 1969, the Select Committee on Race Relations and Immigration observed:

> We would like to see every college of education in the country teaching its students something about race relations, and the problems of immigrants. To say that there is no need to educate all students about such matters because, as one college has said, 'very few of our students go into schools where they are likely to meet mixed classes', is to miss the point. Teachers should be equipped to prepare all their children for life in a multicultural society. (para. 214)

This was an important statement because it pointed up the two broad objectives of a multicultural approach in teacher education to be found in most writing on the subject: first, preparing students to cope effectively with the particular

*An earlier version of this chapter was published by the University of Nottingham in 1986.

needs of minority group children; and second, to help student teachers to acquaint *all* the children in their future classes with the realities of a culturally plural society. This second, broader objective seems to have been overlooked by Lord Scarman, as though there is only one party to social conflict rather than several, but it was fundamental to Swann whose Report is called *Education for All.*

These two quotations will suffice, for a fuller documentation can be found elsewhere, (Craft, 1981; Watson, 1984). But perhaps two points might be emphasized. First, that we are not discussing a passing fashion, a new bandwagon; the need has been recognized for quite some time. Second, that we are not simply talking about equipping teachers to cope more effectively with the particular needs of minority children. We are also — and more importantly — considering ways of enabling teachers to convey to *all* children a more intelligent appreciation of the diversity of our society. We are not alone in this in the UK. On the continent, the foreign migrant worker population is now in the region of 15,000,000, comprising some 14 per cent of the Swiss labour force, 9 per cent of the French and 7 per cent of the German (Banks and Lynch, 1986; Castles *et al.*, 1984). Linguistic and cultural diversity is a reality in most countries, and whether we regard this as an enrichment to be maximized (as we should) or as a potential source of conflict or even violence (and it sometimes is), we can hardly ignore the heavy responsibility which lies with teacher education. In the United States, teacher educators have similarly become more sensitive to this responsibility. In 1980, the American Association of Colleges for Teacher Education published detailed strategies for implementing a multicultural perspective, and in Australia a national review of such strategies has been carried out (Lynch, 1985; Suzuki, 1984; Washburn, 1982).

As the Swann Report indicates, a number of initial teacher training (ITT) institutions have for some years offered a multicultural element by means of special *options* in the BEd or PGCE; some specialized Diploma and MEd courses exist; and there has been a growing number of relevant in-service (INSET) short courses offered by LEAs and ITT institutions over the years. But these reach mainly the committed. A second approach is to include an element in the ITT *core course*, which ensures that all students gain some exposure to the issues. But this can only be of limited duration, and some have argued that it risks trivialization and that it is preferable to train specialists in greater depth (Latham, 1982). Thirdly, there is '*permeation*' where everything which is taught in ITT and INSET reflects the multicultural context of the world outside schools. This does not necessarily require additional time, but rather a modified perspective, 'another screen or lens through which to operationalize [or] interpret... generic and theoretical concepts and principles of pedagogy' (Gay, 1983). It may simply involve a wider range of exemplification: in making reference, say, to age or gender or social class variations in learning, one might also indicate *ethnic* variations. Permeated syllabuses are gradually being developed, and this is returned to in more detail later. Meanwhile, the advantage of options and core studies is that a single lecturer or LEA adviser can make a beginning, and this itself can provide the basis of some staff development as other colleagues are drawn in.

Since the publication in 1981 of four major reports on multicultural education (DES, 1981; Eggleston *et al.*, 1981; House of Commons, 1981; Schools Council, 1981), several of them including particularly pointed references to the tardy response of ITT and INSET to the needs of a culturally plural society, and particularly since the Swann Report, there have been numerous developments affecting teacher educators. A large number of LEAs, for example, have published policy statements on multicultural education; many have made specialist appointments to their in-service advisory staffs, as has the DES which now has some twenty-six members of HM Inspectorate with specialist concerns in this field. All ITT courses submitted to the CNAA for validation or renewal are now expected to demonstrate some awareness of the multicultural dimension, in accordance with the Council's national guidelines on this matter which were published in 1984. The Universities Council for the Education of Teachers (UCET) published similar guidelines in 1985. All initial teacher-training courses on *both* sides of the binary line are now submitted to the national Council for the Accreditation of Teacher Education (CATE), whose stated criteria include the requirement that:

> Students should be prepared... to teach the full range of pupils whom they are likely to encounter in an ordinary school, with their diversity of ability, behaviour, social background and ethnic and cultural origins. They will need to learn how to respond flexibly to such diversity and to guard against preconceptions based on the race or sex of pupils. (DES, 1984b, annex, para. 11)

In the United States, such a requirement was enacted by the National Council for the Accreditation of Teacher Education in 1977, in order 'to help institutions and individuals become more responsive to the human condition, cultural integrity, and cultural pluralism in society', and it stated that 'multicultural education should receive attention in courses, seminars, directed readings, laboratory and clinical experiences, practicum and other types of field experiences', (NCATE, 1977). As to in-service teacher training in Britain, education for a multiethnic society has until very recently been included in the list of national priorities.

There have also been significant changes in the public examination system. The GCSE general criteria include a section entitled 'Recognition of cultural diversity', which states:

> In devising syllabuses and setting question papers, examining groups should bear in mind the linguistic and cultural diversity of society. The value to all candidates of incorporating material which reflects this diversity should be recognized.

The School Examinations and Assessment Council (SEAC) and the examinations boards have responsibility for ensuring that the new GCSE syllabuses and examinations meet this multicultural criterion. It is, therefore, essential that all secondary teachers are adequately prepared by teacher educators for this task.

Strategies

So much for context. What then should teacher educators be expected to do, given the now much greater recognition of cultural diversity in our national life? This section will look briefly at three major aspects of strategy: first, those involved in preparing students to meet the particular needs of minority children; secondly, strategies concerned with the needs of all children in a plural society; and thirdly, those focused upon intercultural relations.

The Particular Needs of Ethnic Minority Children

What are these particular needs, now that there are far fewer immigrants and that the great majority of minority children have been born here? English as a second language is far less important, but large numbers of children are still entering school having spoken little English at home (even though born here), and are growing up with varied degrees of bilingualism. The capacity for code-switching within two or three languages, with parents, peers and teachers, is a considerable source of national strength. As the former Secretary of State observed, 'Linguistic minorities need not be seen as having a problem — lack of practice in English — but as having an asset, a skill in language' (DES, 1984a). At the same time, there are many pupils who require English language support across the curriculum at both primary and secondary levels in order to ensure full equality of opportunity, for Standard English is the language of school and of the world of work. In 1982, a national survey in teacher education found that some three-quarters of ITT institutions in England and Wales sought to convey to all students, through core courses, an awareness of dialect and language differences, and a 'repertoire' approach to language learning in schools. However, only half included any work on the existence and main characteristics of minority community languages in Britain or included reference to current professional discussion of mother tongue teaching, bilingualism, etc.; and less than one-third claimed to convey a minimal competence to offer language support across the curriculum in linguistically diverse schools (Craft and Atkins, 1983). There are evidently many opportunities here for ITT specialists in language development and linguistics.

Going a little further, providing some teaching through the mother tongue at infant and junior levels, and offering community languages in the modern languages curriculum of the secondary school are now encouraged in a number of LEAs. But preparation for all these roles in ITT and INSET is probably still limited. As indicated above, in 1982, a number of institutions claimed to convey an awareness of the existence and main characteristics of ethnic minority community languages in Britain, and to consider the issues of mother tongue teaching, bilingualism, etc, with their students. But far fewer said they offered any specific techniques for teaching in multilingual classrooms (the acquisition of some basic vocabulary, for example); and no more than one or two ITT institutions said they offered any preparation for student teachers who wished to teach Asian languages or Italian to 'O' and 'A' level (*ibid.*). At that time, there was *no* provision in modern Greek, Turkish or in any Asian language and only a little in Spanish or Italian, compared with the far more widespread provision in French or German. The situation in ITT-based in-service work appeared to be little better, although the EEC-funded Linguistic Diversity Project at the University of Nottingham is one of a number of subsequent INSET initiatives.

And yet the 1987 ILEA Language Census identified *172* spoken languages in London schools, with 23 per cent of the school population (i.e. 64,987 children) using a language other than or in addition to English at home (ILEA, 1987a). A 1983 survey by the Brent LEA reported in the same vein: of 35,051 pupils surveyed in 103 of the Authority's 104 schools, 35 per cent speak a language other than English, and while Gujarati and Urdu predominate, more than twenty different languages are in existence (Brent LEA, 1983a). The University of London Linguistic Minorities Project has similarly identified nine languages in Coventry, ten in Peterborough, and eleven in Bradford (LMP, 1983). In fact, 'the majority of LEAs now have a multilingual school population', according to a national survey by the former Schools Council, carried out in 1983, and at least one-half of all LEAs in England and Wales have a *minimum* of one primary school with over 10 per cent of pupils who are bilingual (Tansley and Craft, 1984). This survey also reported the growing provision by LEAs for community languages teaching in mainstream primary schools, which is likely to increase the demand for suitably qualified teachers.

As to the particular language needs of children of West Indian origin, it is possible that rather more ITT institutions offer relevant language work, for as indicated above issues relating to accent, dialect, and language repertoire are very widely claimed to be part of the normal, core language work in ITT. But we do not actually know how many BEd or PGCE students consider bidialectalism, and the classroom discussion (and classroom use) of Creole dialects. This is probably unlikely to be widespread (see also Houlton, 1986, on all these issues).

A further element of the strategy of preparing ITT students to meet the particular needs of ethnic minority students are those less tangible aspects of professional skill which are associated with problems of *identity*, the intergenerational stress experienced by minority children growing up in the two often contrasting cultures of home and school. As Wilce (1984) reported:

> The majority of teenage Asian girls are the British-born offspring of first generation immigrants. As such they can walk a tight-rope existence — the normal tensions of adolescence stretched to breaking

point by the differing expectations of home, school and themselves...Most girls adapt to their two worlds with admirable skill—often by keeping home and school as separate as possible...Changing from school uniform to Shalwar Kamiz (the traditional dress of the Punjab), from English to Punjabi, and noisy self-expression to a more subdued form of behaviour, are all part of the daily routine.

This is the culture clash which may be experienced by Asian children, and especially girls, born in British industrial cities into families from more rural, hierarchical, and sexist environments; a culture clash additionally involving the interface of religious and secular perspectives, and which ought not to be underestimated.

Clearly, it is important to avoid sweeping generalizations. Culture clash may also occur in many other ethnic minority groups, and is far from unknown among working-class children of the majority culture. Furthermore, the Asian community is heterogeneous in the extreme, and it includes many highly Westernized families. But the often quite sharp differences in perspective between adolescents and their parents which is such a well-recognized feature of all rapidly-changing societies will obviously be heightened for those children whose parents are from overseas—whether from Cyprus, Italy, the West Indies, the Indian sub-continent, or elsewhere. This is a particular need so far little recognized in ITT or INSET; and it has implications for classroom teaching skills, for pastoral care and counselling, and for home–school relations, all of which one would expect to be reflected in core courses in educational theory and professional studies.

A third area of particular need must be the continuing underachievement of children in Bangladeshi, Turkish and West Indian origin, the latter being a special concern of the Rampton Committee (DES, 1981), and which has attracted further attention in the Swann Report and in more recent studies (ILEA, 1987b; Kelly, 1987). By no means all West Indian children are underachievers; but even those who do well may sometimes prefer to move into further education and the labour market, rather than take the sixth form route into higher education (Craft and Craft, 1983). For the majority, a fuller understanding by their teachers of school values, ethos and teacher expectation effects (Figueroa, 1984), of research into family values and self-esteem, of dialect issues and the questions of identity touched on above, should all be engendered in initial and in-service teacher education. On none of these variables, however, is there anything like a clear indication of cause and effect, and students should be sensitized to the range of possible factors. There are no simple answers (see also Tomlinson, 1986).

The Needs of All Children

A second aspect of strategy for initial and in-service teacher education highlighted by the Swann Report relates to the needs of *all* children growing up in a culturally plural society. It may, of course, be argued that our minority population only amounts to around 5-6 per cent in all, including the Irish (about 700,000), Asians, West Indians, Jews, Germans, Italians, Poles, Cypriots and Spanish, and smaller groups from elsewhere in the Mediterranean, Africa and the Far East. The total may stabilize at around 10 per cent by the end of the century (Coleman, 1982; Runnymede Trust, 1980), a far smaller proportion than, say, that of Australia where some 25 per cent of the population were born abroad. On the other hand, our ethnic minority citizens are likely to be encountered everywhere in Britain, and particularly in the conurbations where their proportions are often much higher (perhaps 50 per cent of the total population in some electoral wards in Greater London, for example). And as the ethnic minorities are a young population, their children form more than 5-6 per cent of the total *child* population.

It therefore follows that if schoolchildren from the majority culture are to be made aware of the nature and extent of ethnic minority groups in modern Britain (many of whose members were born here), their *teachers* need to be adequately informed. Then again, demographic information is one thing. But some understanding of the concept of culture, of the intrinsic value of all cultures, and of the diverse origins of most cultures — an attitudinal dimension — is also involved here. Few have expressed this concern more effectively than Ralph Linton in his classic, *The Study of Man*, published fifty years ago. The following well-known passage is a commentary upon what we take to be our own distinctive, unique, homogeneous national culture:

> Our solid American citizen awakens in a bed built on a pattern which originated in the Near East but which was modified in Northern Europe before it was transmitted to America. He throws back covers made from cotton, domesticated in India, or linen, domesticated in the Near East,...or silk, the use of which was discovered in China. All of these materials have been spun and woven by processes invented in the Near East. He slips into his moccasins, invented by the Indians of the Eastern woodlands, and goes to the bathroom, whose fixtures are a mixture of European and American inventions, both of recent date. He takes off his pajamas, a garment invented in India, and washes with soap invented by the ancient Gauls. He then shaves, a masochistic rite which seems to have been derived from either Sumer or ancient Egypt. (Linton, 1936)

Linton continues in this vein, describing the diverse origins of each garment donned. He continues,

> On his way to breakfast he stops to buy a paper, paying for it with coins, an ancient Lydian invention. At the restaurant a whole new series of borrowed elements confronts him. His plate is made of a form of pottery invented in China. His knife is of steel, an alloy first made in southern India, his fork a medieval Italian invention, and his spoon a derivative of a Roman original. (*ibid.*)

Linton then describes the varied origins of each part of the American's breakfast, and he concludes as follows:

> When our friend has finished eating he settles back to smoke, an American Indian habit, consuming a plant domesticated in Brazil in either a pipe, derived from the Indians of Virginia, or a cigarette, derived from Mexico. If he is hardy enough he may even attempt a cigar, transmitted to us from the Antilles by way of Spain. While smoking he reads the news of the day, imprinted in characters invented by the ancient Semites upon a material invented in China by a process invented in Germany. As he absorbs the accounts of foreign troubles he will, if he is a good conservative citizen, thank a Hebrew deity in an Indo-European language that he is 100 per cent American. (*ibid.*)

This passage is all about the *diffusion* of cultural elements from one society to another; and it would seem to be painfully self-evident that if schools are to make a real contribution to social harmony and to equality of opportunity in society at large, *all* children — and therefore all teachers — need a far more sophisticated grasp of the diverse origins of the majority culture, and of the regional, religious, social class and other variations within it. The aim should be the achievement of a less judgmental and less ethnocentric approach among teachers. As Fisher and Hicks (1985) indicate, for example, everyday words such as pyjamas or shampoo are of Indian origin; telephone or cycle are Greek; piano or corridor Italian; and boss or hiccup, Dutch. The English language itself is, of course, drawn from other European languages, just as the grand public architecture of London, Liverpool or Leeds is based on that of ancient Rome and Athens.

In ITT, as indicated earlier, this may mean the insertion of special *options*, or of multicultural elements in the educational theory or professional studies *core*. It is difficult to see how material of this kind could be avoided in a core strand in the sociology of education; and it is there, in language work, in any discussion of what is 'deficient' or 'different'. But as the Swann Report indicates, it should also mean the *permeation*, through all that is taught, of a multicultural sensitivity, both in ITT and INSET, including both pedagogy and main subject content. In BEd science and mathematics main courses, and BEd and PGCE methods courses, for example, one might expect the diverse origins of scientific and mathematical discovery to be made more explicit. Our numerals themselves originated in India, and comprise only one of many systems of computation. Biology, in particular, in considering diverse dietary patterns and diet-linked diseases, race and genetics, differential fertility and mortality, or childbirth and child care, readily lends itself. In history, the varied origins of the British people, their language and culture, and their continuous economic and political interactions with overseas territories as a trading and imperial nation present many opportunities for broader comment and interpretation. A Eurocentric view appears to imply that North America, Africa or Australia were empty continents awaiting 'discovery' and settlement. In literature and the arts, some appreciation of the huge variety of these forms of experience may be conveyed through the inclusion of examples of minority group literature, drama, art and music; and they may, of course, be used as a powerful means of extending knowledge of other peoples, their perceptions and preoccupations. The visual arts have always provided a means of considering the social and cultural context — in religious art, for example. Music and dance may have a similar value, apart from naturally extending aural skills, and competence in performing and composing. Naturally, we are not here considering matters of content alone, but also of *process*. Collaborative learning techniques whereby children work in small groups using selected resourced materials have always complemented more formal classroom methods, and they may have a particular potential in multiethnic schools where pupils' intercultural experience may thus be more effectively disseminated.

Some school curriculum areas lend themselves to permeation more readily than others: religious education in many LEAs already includes an introduction to world religions (and the variations within them), and is traditionally the focus for the discussion of moral issues and social problems. Home economics offers ample opportunity for the recognition, discussion and inclusion of cultural differences in diet, food preparation, family roles, and childrearing, and much scope for building bridges between minority and majority cultures. Modern language teaching which is inextricably bound up with the study of other cultures, is coming to include some of the overseas languages widely spoken in pupils' homes, and can very often draw upon the bilingual experience of many pupils. Geography has long ceased to be about 'capes and bays', and cannot escape consideration of social life, and of world trading relationships. In both ITT and INSET, permeation is a responsibility for each subject specialist, assisted perhaps by the lecturer/adviser more knowledgeable in multicultural education.

In this way and using the resource materials now becoming available (Craft and Klein, 1986; Craft and Bardell, 1984; Lynch, 1981), it is possible for ITT and INSET to modify curricula in the interests, first, of the minority pupil whose heritage will no longer appear to be undervalued; second, of the majority culture pupil whose schooling will now be less ethnocentric and more educative; and third, of working towards less prejudiced (or 'racist') attitudes and values, a matter which is taken up in the next section. Nor, as suggested at the outset, should all this be seen as new-fangled and revolutionary. More than three decades ago a UNESCO study of history textbooks and international understanding declared that, 'this is no time for maintaining ancient hatreds which cloud the understanding and befog the judgement' (Lauwerys, 1953).

But permeation is a sizeable, long-term enterprise, and it is easy to appear glib (Bliss, 1987). To teach students to teach children in a non-ethnocentric way, requires non-ethnocentric teacher educators, which brings us back to the central question of staffing and to the staff development policies of ITT institutions and of LEAs (in respect of INSET advisers). Secondly, syllabuses and teaching methods are operationalized by the use of appropriate textbooks and other materials. Some of these teaching resources may include racist language or imagery and be quite unsuitable; but other resources which embody ethnocentric approaches may provide an excellent stimulus to classroom discussion. No one should envisage a wholesale 'burning of the books', but students will nonetheless require careful guidance on how best to select and use teaching materials, for educating *all* children in a multicultural society (Klein, 1984).

Intercultural Relations

This third aspect of pedagogic strategy for multicultural teacher education is labelled 'intercultural relations' in preference to the narrower and more restricted term 'race relations'. Given the kind of world we inhabit, some awareness of the nature and origins of intercultural prejudice and discrimination ought to find a central place in the curriculum of ITT and INSET. It should not be forgotten that a British Home Secretary not so long ago declared that,

> . . . the anxieties expressed about racial attacks are justified. Racially motivated attacks, particularly on Asians, are more common than we had supposed; and there are indications that they may be on the increase. (Whitelaw, 1981)

More recent studies have substantiated this fear (CRE, 1987). Clearly, teacher education carries a major responsibility here.

Work on prejudice and discrimination might include, for example, the examination of stereotyping on ethnic, racial, religious and regional lines, and immediately raises the question of where this can be best located in the ITT curriculum. It is often included in core studies in the sociology of education or the psychology of perception. It could also be raised in every part of the ITT curriculum when ethnocentric or racist texts and other classroom materials are discussed with students (Klein, 1985). Secondly, students need to be introduced to techniques for managing classroom discussion on issues relating to race and racism which can often be highly emotive (Stradling *et al.*, 1984), a further task for the professional studies area. But *how* an element on intercultural relations should be included in initial or in-service training is also important. In all the foregoing, there has been the assumption that *information* is decisive, conveyed either through ITT options, core courses or permeation, or through INSET workshops or named awards. This cannot be lightly dismissed. Reports of an important cohort study of student teachers' awareness of cultural diversity in the UK appear to reveal a large degree of sheer ignorance (Hodgkinson, 1984; see also Chapter 9 in this volume). On the other hand, 'intercultural relations' is much more firmly in the area of *attitudes:* is the development or change of students' attitudes best achieved through lecture courses, through the more active involvement of participants in seminars and discussions, through practical work with children in schools (or with parents in minority communities), or through workshops (Burtonwood, 1986)?

Work on intercultural relations sometimes uses workshop introspection (or 'race awareness' sessions) as a means of getting below the surface into the deeper assumptions which motivate behaviour. Opinions vary about the efficacy of such an approach (Banton, 1985), and some prefer the more oblique and less confrontational mode embodied in techniques such as the University of Nottingham 'Lifestyles' pack, developed for the Schools Council and in use by teachers' centres and police training courses in many parts of the country. As regards ITT and INSET coursework, active and prolonged *discussion* (perhaps including simulations) should be an essential supplement to reading, essay writing and lectures; and sustained *practical work* may be an even better supplement to the formal acquisition of information. The practice of attaching students from rural colleges of education to inner city study centres for teaching practice, for example, certainly appears to be beneficial. There may also be distinctive needs according to whether ITT students are training for work in primary or secondary schools (Carrington *et al.*, 1986). It may be that further systematic study of the appraisal of attitudes towards cultural diversity among practising and student teachers needs to be undertaken, as is being attempted in the United States (Giles and Sherman, 1982).

It will by now be clear that this third category, 'intercultural relations', is really an aspect of the education of all children; it is, after all, an extension of what was suggested earlier in respect of combating ethnocentrism. But intercultural relations has been separated out in order to give it a special emphasis, for prejudice and discrimination on grounds of ethnicity, race and religion are undoubtedly realities in most, if not all, contemporary societies, and teacher educators must take account of this. A tough-minded approach to prejudice and discrimination must surely be part of the professional awareness of all teachers in a plural society, requiring teacher educators to prepare their students for participation in whole-school appraisal schemes, and for self-evaluation in the classroom, as a central element of professional practice. Every student in initial or in-service training should be adequately equipped to examine the organization of his/her school, the structure of its curriculum and the nature of his/her classroom practice to ensure that minority children are not being disadvantaged, however unwittingly, by discriminatory cultural assumptions or other practices. All teachers must be sensitive to discrimination, for example, in the provision of school meals, or in the insistence upon school uniform in the case, say, of Muslim girls or Sikh boys. Minority mores in respect of diet or modesty may be involved. The 'tracking' of certain pupils into maths/science streams, into PE and sports activities, or into early leavers' classes may result from an unintended labelling of aptitudes and abilities (for example, Carrington, 1986). Racist remarks should not be tolerated, either in the staffroom or the classroom, and offensive graffiti should be removed immediately. In all schools, multiethnic or not, teachers need to call attention — across the curriculum — to derogatory interethnic and interracial perceptions and disadvantage, both historically and in the present. Staff appointments — in all schools, not just those in multiethnic localities — should aim to reflect the nation's cultural diversity, while maintaining equal standards of professional qualification and ability (Berkshire LEA, 1983; Brent LEA, 1983b; ILEA, 1983), and to this end ethnic monitoring is now being introduced nationally.

This 'anti-racist' perspective is sometimes contrasted with 'multicultural' education (for example, NAME, 1984) and this is unhelpful, for activities such as the above are clearly an essential part of any multicultural programme. But some commentators would go much further and would attribute *all* ethnic minority disadvantage in education to 'racism'. Parekh (1983), however, has argued persuasively against 'the fallacy of the single factor' in the analysis of what are obviously highly complex phenomena; and in any case, 'race' and 'racism' are vague and less than meaningful terms (Patterson, 1985). For some enthusiasts, 'anti-racism' is fundamentally concerned with structural inequality (Hannan, 1983), and can involve putting a particular gloss on all history teaching, an explicitly anti-capitalist gloss (Institute of Race Relations, 1982). For Mullard (1984), 'anti-racist' education is part of a vast process of 'liberation from social bondage (oppression, exploitation and discrimination) of Black and other similarly situated groups'. These more extreme viewpoints on the left thus seem to redefine 'education' as traditionally understood, and in over-simplifying very complex questions perhaps have more in common with comparable views on the extreme right (for example, Pearce, 1985) than they might care to recognize.

Cohesion and Diversity

Underlying many of the debates about multicultural education is the question as to how we should resolve the competing pressures for social cohesion and for social diversity. At what point does the acculturation necessary for full participation in society become a repressive assimilation? At what point does the celebration of diversity cease to enrich and become a source of social instability (Craft, 1984)?

As we know, the prevailing social and political climate has moved towards pluralism in values of all kinds in the past twenty-five years. As was indicated above, perhaps only 5–6 per cent of the British population are members of ethnic minority groups, a very small proportion, and one which might reach 10 per cent by the end of the century. But *our view* of minorities of all kinds has altered. At the time of the New Commonwealth immigration of the 1950s and '60s, the prevailing ethic was one of *assimilation*, immigrants were to be absorbed into the population as quickly as possible — linguistically and culturally. *Integration* was a term which then came into use, and this also implied assimilation but allowing for some linguistic and cultural residues. Roy Jenkins' celebrated statement in 1966 referred to 'not a flattening process of assimilation, but . . . equal opportunity accompanied by cultural diversity in an atmosphere of mutual tolerance'. In the 1970s and '80s, we have come to talk of *cultural pluralism*, a term which places greater emphasis on diversity and the intrinsic validity of different cultures. And then there is *segregation*, which is a *de facto* reality in some inner urban districts and in a handful of urban schools; but which is also an objective for some minority communities who seek their own schools on grounds of religion.

The trend is clear. It is now increasingly acceptable to recognize linguistic and cultural pluralism. In 1980, the DES Curriculum Document, it will be recalled, stated:

> What is taught in schools, and the way it is taught, must appropriately reflect fundamental values in our society.

and it continued:

> Our society has become multicultural; and there is now among pupils and parents a greater diversity of personal values.

This was a significant statement for our society has not 'become multicultural'. It has always been multicultural, in terms of ethnicity, social class, religion and region (to say nothing of age and sex); it is simply more acceptable nowadays to recognize the fact. Furthermore, not only is the trend towards the celebration of diversity very evident here, it is also found in many other societies. There is now a sizeable literature, with titles such as *The Ethnic Revival* (Smith, 1981), *The Re-Discovery of Ethnicity* (Te Selle, 1973), and *The Rise of the Unmeltable Ethnics* (Novak, 1973). But it is important to be quite clear about the line of argument. There can be little doubt that a basic acculturation for all children is the essential key to full participation in society. It greatly increases equality of life-chance, it provides access to the opportunity structure. But beyond that basic acculturation the celebration of diversity enriches us all; and for the individual, it may be a very necessary source of identity in the alienating conditions of a complex, industrial society. It is a delicate balance: acculturation up to a point, pluralism beyond that point.

For teacher educators, this balance lies at the heart of language policy, for example. All children will need a sound basic grounding in written and spoken English; and it may be that teaching some young children through the mother tongue will facilitate this — a transitional bilingualism. On the other hand, the pursuit of culture maintenance would argue that opportunities for sustaining mother tongue teaching into secondary education to public examination level should be available for those children who wish it, and teacher education should be making provision for this. Equally, all children in British schools need to acquire a detailed knowledge and appreciation of British social institutions and the British cultural heritage; to neglect this on ideological or other grounds would simply perpetuate educational and social disadvantage, as many argued some years ago in respect of proposals for a 'relevant' curriculum for working-class children (for example, Shipman, 1973). But to fail to widen the curriculum, by means of permeation, in order to reduce ethnocentrism or to highlight the contributions of all peoples to world culture —

nor to prepare teachers for this role — is surely to miss valuable opportunities. As Gay (1983) has put it, 'ethnic and national loyalties and affiliations are not necessarily contradictory or mutually exclusive'.

Course Content

Finally, a few further comments on course content. So far as work in educational theory and professional studies is concerned, the knowledge-base for multicultural teacher education is likely to be drawn largely from the social sciences, but also from linguistics and curriculum theory. For example, a short specialist *option* in ITT might include work on migration, demographic distribution and social policy in the area of race relations; work on the psychology of learning and on the sociology of the school with particular reference to underachievement, examining sub-cultural factors in both home and classroom and the implications for teachers as well as parents; studies in the psychology and sociology of prejudice, including discrimination and 'racism'; work in the several sociological perspectives, for theories of consensus, conflict or interaction suggest alternative implications for multicultural education; work in sociolinguistics; and a programme on the content and structure of a multicultural curriculum, taking account also of school ethos and organization, pastoral care and home–school relations. Naturally, none of this should be presented uncritically and as a form of crusade; all of it should be infused with the informed scepticism characteristic of higher education, with an awareness of the paradoxes and dilemmas, and with the aim of cultivating the capacity for informed, critical judgment.

A multicultural element in the ITT *core*, as suggested earlier, can most easily be incorporated into the sociology of education component where there is a foundation disciplines programme. But not in illustration of any single theoretical paradigm, nor to the neglect of relevant empirical studies and their practical, policy implications. The multicultural aspect of the analysis of home and school factors in educability might, of course, be considered in either the sociology or psychology elements of an educational theory core. At all events, as indicated above, psychologists can quite easily include reference to multicultural aspects in the discussion of measured ability, 'culture fair' testing, underachievement and what used to be called 'cultural deprivation'. Similarly, core courses in the philosophy of education and in curriculum studies offer scope for pointing up the particular dilemmas relating to the aims of education, to the definition of school knowledge, and to curriculum construction in a culturally plural society. History of education and comparative education now appear less frequently in educational theory courses, and may often be incorporated within broader programmes of professional studies. But any historical strand would surely need to include reference to the changing social composition of urban schools in recent years, to central government initiatives in educational disadvantage, and to some of the reports from central and local government and from HM Inspectorate which have been specifically concerned with minority group children, community involvement and equal opportunity. Comparative education specialists dealing with education in the United States can hardly avoid discussing desegregation — and the bussing parallels in Britain; or, in considering European educational systems, the efforts being devoted to the education of migrant workers' children — a massive programme in culture maintenance. Ten per cent of the population of Portugal now lives in France, at least 25 per cent of that of Cyprus resides here in Britain.

Work in professional studies might include 'whole school' issues such as the framing of school policy statements, which may for example consider the use of corridor, library and classroom displays reflecting the plural ethos of modern Britain. Provision for pastoral care and careers guidance has a further dimension in the multiethnic school, as has the monitoring of pupil progress, and the discussion of relations between home, school and community. But schools in all regions can benefit from reflecting in some degree the religious diversity of our present-day society, through the morning assembly; and a review of pluralist teaching resources would be equally valuable for core course discussion.

These suggestions are merely illustrative and a number of ITT institutions have gone very much further. As to whether a modified core course in education requires additional time, a great deal can be achieved, as suggested earlier, simply by altering the range of exemplification to take account of cultural diversity. This may lend a multicultural perspective without extending the total course load, and is in fact 'permeation'. Permeation of BEd main subjects, PGCE method courses or in-service workshops can be achieved in the same way, and examples were suggested earlier. But the success of across-the-board permeation depends far more upon an institution's *overall* teaching resources than does the provision of an option or a core element which might be taught by one or two lecturers, and this raises the central question of staffing. Teaching and teacher education are labour-intensive processes, the success of which depends very largely upon the quality of the teaching, lecturing or advisory staff involved. In the absence of any regional programme to 'train the trainers', and these have operated in a number of areas (Atkins and Craft, 1988), it will be for individual institutions and LEAs to organize their own staff development programmes. A first step is often the identification of someone to act as a convenor, who will call together ITT team leaders or INSET advisers to talk through some of the central issues, perhaps together with one or two colleagues from a neighbouring institution or LEA with more experience in the field; or with an HMI, a polytechnic or university specialist, a representative of a local minority community or the local Community Relations Council. American teacher educators have advocated a similar kind of 'multicultural task force' (Hicks and Monroe, 1984).

As the influence of a rapidly developing literature (including government and HMI reports), the operation of CNAA validation, and DES Circular 3/84 (DES, 1984b) with its criteria and approvals mechanism become felt, perhaps a greater number of institutions and LEAs will set up a multicultural working group to consider possible lines of curriculum development, as have many schools. Much can be achieved, in fact, if the ten BBC films on multicultural education, produced in 1981, are used as a starting point for (critical) discussion. Other readily available resources include the annexes to Chapter 9 of the Swann Report (which includes sample syllabuses), and policy statements published by the National Association of Teachers in Further and Higher Education (NATFHE), the various teachers' unions, the former Schools Council, and numerous LEAs (including the particularly useful ILEA *Aide-Memoire for the Inspectorate*, issued in 1981). The Schools Council's comprehensive resources manual is now in a revised edition (Klein, 1984) and the Open University's third level course in educational studies (E354: *Ethnic Minorities and Community Relations*) is readily available. The School Curriculum Development Council's *Agenda for Multicultural Teaching* (Craft and Klein, 1986) also deals with the permeation of main subjects.

It may well be that the schools and LEAs are farther ahead than ITT and ITT-based in-service training in recognizing the need to review their practices, but the situation is improving. Those new to the field will have discovered the new variety and depth that multicultural development can bring. It can offer considerable *enrichment* to teacher education, strengthening and enlivening courses, and adding both to their intellectual demands and to their professional relevance. This is not a problem area, but a new avenue of opportunity for teacher education, and one that it would, indeed, be irresponsible to ignore.

References

ATKINS, M.J. and CRAFT, M. (1988) 'Training the trainers in multicultural education: The evaluation of a national programme', *British Journal of In-Service Education*, 14, 2, pp. 81–91.

BANKS, J.A. and LYNCH, J. (Eds) (1986) *Multicultural Education in Western Societies*, Eastbourne, Holt, Rinehart & Winston.

BANTON, M. (1985) 'Race awareness training: Back to the drawing board', *New Community*, 12, 2, pp. 295–7.

BERKSHIRE LEA (1983) *Education for Racial Equality*, Reading, Berkshire Education Committee.

BLISS, I. (1987) *Multicultural Permeation: A Case-study in Initial Teacher Training*, Nottingham, University of Nottingham.

BRENT LEA (1983a) *Mother Tongue Teaching* (Report No. 47/83 from the Director of Education, presented to Brent Education Committee on 4 July 1983).

BRENT LEA (1983b) *Education for a Multicultural Democracy*, Brent, Brent LEA.

BURTONWOOD, N. (1986) 'INSET and multicultural/anti-racist education', *British Journal of In-Service Education*, 13, 1, pp. 30–5.

CARRINGTON, B. (1986) 'Social mobility, ethnicity and sport', *British Journal of Sociology of Education*, 7, 1, pp. 1–18.

CARRINGTON, B. *et al.* (1986) 'Schools in a multiracial society: Contrasting perspectives of primary and secondary teachers in training,' *Educational Studies*, 12, 1, pp. 17–35.

CASTLES, S. *et al.* (1984) *Here for Good: Western Europe's New Ethnic Minorities*, London, Pluto Press.

COLEMAN, D.A. (Ed.) (1982) *Demography of Immigrants and Minority Groups in the United Kingdom*, London, Academic Press.

COMMISSION FOR RACIAL EQUALITY (1987) *Living in Terror: A Report on Racial Violence and Harassment in Housing*, London, CRE.

CRAFT, A.Z. and BARDELL, G. (1984) *Curriculum Opportunities in a Multicultural Society*, London, Harper & Row.

CRAFT, A. Z. and KLEIN, G. (1986) *Agenda for Multicultural Teaching*, London, School Curriculum Development Committee.

CRAFT, M. (1981) 'Recognition of need' in CRAFT, M. (Ed.) *Teaching in a Multicultural Society: The Task for Teacher Education*, Lewes, Falmer Press.

CRAFT, M. (1984) 'Education for diversity' in CRAFT, M. *Education and Cultural Pluralism*, Lewes, Falmer Press.

CRAFT, M. and ATKINS, M.J. (1983) *Training Teachers of Ethnic Minority Community Languages*, Nottingham, University of Nottingham.

CRAFT, M. and CRAFT, A.Z. (1983) 'The participation of ethnic minority pupils in further and higher education', *Educational Research*, 25, 1, pp. 10–19.

DEPARTMENT OF EDUCATION AND SCIENCE (1981) *West Indian Children in Our Schools: Report of the Committee of Enquiry into the Education of Children from Ethnic Minority Groups* (The Rampton Report), Cmnd. 8273, London, HMSO.

DEPARTMENT OF EDUCATION AND SCIENCE (1984a) text of Sir Keith Joseph's speech to the EEC Mother Tongue Colloquium in London, 26 March.

DEPARTMENT OF EDUCATION AND SCIENCE (1984b) *Initial Teacher Training: Approval of Courses* (Circular 3/84), London, HMSO.

DEPARTMENT OF EDUCATION AND SCIENCE (1985) *Education for All: Report of the Committee of Enquiry into the Education of Children from Ethnic Minority Groups* (The Swann Report), Cmnd. 9453, London, HMSO.

EGGLESTON, S. J. *et al.* (1981) *In-Service Teacher Education in a Multicultural Society*, Keele, University of Keele.

FIGUEROA, P. (1984) 'Minority pupil progress' in CRAFT, M. (Ed) *Education and Cultural Pluralism*, Lewes, Falmer Press.

FISHER, S. and HICKS, D. (1985) *World Studies 8–13: A Teacher's Handbook*, Oliver & Boyd.

GAY, G. (1983) 'Why multicultural education in teacher education programs?', *Contemporary Education*, 54, 2, pp. 79–85.

GILES, M.B. and SHERMAN, T.M. (1982) 'Measurement of multicultural attitudes of teacher trainers', *Journal of Educational Research*, 75, 4, pp. 204–9.

HANNAN, A.W. (1983) 'Multicultural education and teacher education', *European Journal of Teacher Education*, 6, 1, pp. 79–86.

HICKS, R.D. and MONROE, E.E. (1984) 'The infusion of multicultural education in teacher education programmes', *Journal of Multilingual and Multicultural Development*, 5, 2, pp. 147–58.

HODGKINSON, K. (1984) reported in *The Times Educational Supplement*, 27 July, page 1.

HOME OFFICE (1981) *The Brixton Disorders* (The Scarman Report), London, HMSO.

HOULTON, D. (1986) *Teacher Education in a Multilingual Context*, Nottingham, University of Nottingham.

HOUSE OF COMMONS (1981) *Racial Disadvantage, 5th Report from the Home Affairs Committee*, Vol. 1, London, HMSO.

ILEA (1981) *Education in a Multi-ethnic Society: An Aide Memoire for the Inspectorate*, London, ILEA.

ILEA (1983) *Multi-ethnic Education in Schools*, London, ILEA.

ILEA (1987a) *1987 Language Census*, London, ILEA.

ILEA (1987b) *Ethnic Background and Examination Results, 1985 and 1986*, London, LEA.

INSTITUTE OF RACE RELATIONS (1982) *Roots of Racism*, London, Institute of Race Relations.

JENKINS, R. (1966) address to the National Committee for Commonwealth Immigrants, on 23 May 1966.

KELLY, A. (1987) 'Ethnic differences in science choice, attitudes and achievement in Britain', paper presented to the annual meeting of the British Educational Research Association, Manchester, September.

KLEIN, G. (1984) *Resources for Multicultural Education* (2nd edn), London, Schools Council.

KLEIN, G. (1985) *Reading into Racism: Bias in Children's Literature and Learning Materials*, London, Routledge & Kegan Paul.

LATHAM, J. (1982) 'Exceptional children and exceptional teachers? An alternative policy for teacher education in a multiracial society', *Journal of Further and Higher Education*, 6, 2, pp. 40-7.

LAUWERYS, J.A.(1953) *History Textbooks and International Understanding*, Paris, UNESCO.

LINTON, R. (1936) *The Study of Man*, New York, Appleton, pp. 326-7.

LMP (1983) *Linguistic Minorities in England*, London, University of London Institute of Education.

LYNCH, J. (1981) (Ed) *Teaching in the Multicultural School*, London, Ward Lock Educational.

LYNCH, J. (1985) 'An initial typology of perspectives on staff development for multicultural teacher education' in MODGIL, S. *et al.* (Eds), *Multicultural Education: The Interminable Debate*, Lewes, Falmer Press.

MULLARD, C. (1984) *Anti-Racist Education: The Three O's*, London, NAME.

NAME (1984) *Teacher Education*, London, NAME.

NCATE (1977), *Standards for Accreditation of Teacher Education*, Washington, DC, NCATE.

NOVAK, N. (1973) *The Rise of the Unmeltable Ethnics*, New York, Macmillan.

PAREKH, B. (1983) 'Educational opportunity in multi-ethnic Britain' in GLAZER, N. and YOUNG, K. (Eds) *Ethnic Pluralism and Public Policy*, London, Lexington Books/Heinemann.

PATTERSON, S. (1985) 'Random samplings from Swann', *New Community*, 12, 2, pp. 239-48.

PEARCE, S. (1985) *Education and the Multiracial Society*, Monday Club Policy Paper.

RUNNYMEDE TRUST (1980) *Britain's Black Population*, London, Heinemann.

SCHOOLS COUNCIL (1981) *Multi-ethnic Education: The Way Forward*, London, Schools Council.

SELECT COMMITTEE ON RACE RELATIONS AND IMMIGRATION (1969) *The Problems of Coloured School Leavers*, London, HMSO.

SHIPMAN, M.D. (1973) 'Curriculum for inequality?' in HOOPER, R. (Ed) *The Curriculum: Context, Design and Development*, London, Oliver and Boyd, pp. 101-6. (See also the proposals by Bantock and Midwinter, in the same volume.)

SMITH, A.D. (1981) *The Ethnic Revival*, Cambridge, Cambridge University Press.

STRADLING, R. *et al.* (1984) (Eds) *Teaching Controversial Issues*, Arnold.

SUZUKI, B.H. (1984) 'Curriculum transformation for multicultural education', *Education and Urban Society*, 16, 3, pp. 294-322.

TANSLEY, P. and CRAFT, A.Z. (1984) 'Mother Tongue teaching and support: A Schools Council enquiry', *Journal of Multilingual and Multicultural Development*, 5, 5, pp. 367-84.

Te Selle, S. (1973) *The Re-Discovery of Ethnicity*, New York, Harper Colophon.

Tomlinson, S. (1986) *Ethnic Minority Achievement and Equality of Opportunity*, Nottingham, University of Nottingham.

Washburn, D.E. (1982) 'Curriculum pluralism: Are teachers prepared?', *Phi Delta Kappan*, 63, 7, pp. 493–5.

Watson, K. (1984) 'Training teachers in the UK for a multicultural society', *Journal of Multilingual and Multicultural Development*, 5, 5, pp. 385–400.

Whitelaw, W. (1981) Foreword to *Racial Attacks*, London, Home Office.

Wilce, H. (1984) 'Walking the tight-rope between two cultures', *Times Educational Supplement*, 10 February.

Chapter 9

Ignorance, not Hostility: Student Teachers' Perceptions of Ethnic Minorities in Britain

Louis Cohen

Introduction

The Swann Report (DES, 1985) *Education for All* identified three forms of response to multicultural education: 'permeation', 'core studies' and 'optional studies'. The Report regarded these three approaches as having equally important and complementary roles, but it noted with regret that far too often the only response from teacher training institutions has been to provide optional multicultural courses. This, it considered as 'entirely inadequate'.

This chapter reports a study of student teachers' perceptions of ethnic minorities in Britain. As a prelude to its presentation it is essential to site teacher education in its multicultural context. Developments in multicultural education in Britain are well-documented by Lynch (1982), Cohen and Manion (1983), Jeffcoate (1984), Craft (1981), Craft and Bardell (1984) and Tomlinson (1984). Inter alia, they deal with diverse issues such as government policy, curriculum design and development, bilingualism, linguistic diversity, racism and community initiatives. Several of the above texts address problems in teacher education but none reports substantive studies of practising teachers or students in training.

The year 1981 represented something of a watershed of concern and comment on multicultural education provision in teacher education in Britain. In that year the report of the Schools Council enquiry into multicultural education analyzed data from 525 schools in ninety-four local education authorities. The report laid great emphasis on the need for in-service courses for teachers in areas of varying concentration of ethnic minority groups and urged that there should be a 'consideration within other in-service courses of the implications of a multi-ethnic society' (Schools Council, 1981). Specifically, teacher education institutions were encouraged to review the implications of a multiethnic society for the training of all student teachers and to make provision within their programmes for specialist options and a range of in-service courses. They were further urged to develop, as a priority, appropriate award-bearing courses for teachers. Criticisms of the lack of provision of multicultural education courses in teacher training appeared in the Rampton Report (DES, 1981). The Report talked of an 'overwhelming picture of the failure of teacher training institutions to prepare teachers for their role in a multi-racial society'. It went on to observe that, 'in very few institutions is a grounding given to all students in how to appreciate and understand the experiences and cultures of ethnic minority pupils or of how to help ethnic minority parents who may not have much personal experience of this education system'. Shortly after the publication of the Rampton Report an equally scathing comment on the paucity of multicultural provision appeared in a House of Commons Home Affairs Committee Document (House of Commons, 1981). Progress in teacher education had been slow, the Committee observed; moreover, it was no longer acceptable to wait for the administrative structure of teacher training to come to terms in its own good time with the challenge presented by the multiracial classroom. The immediate need, the Committee felt, was for a recognition that Britain is a multiracial society and it was this reality that ought to permeate the whole of initial teacher training.

A survey of courses in multicultural education in teacher training programmes was conducted by Giles and Cherrington (1981). It showed that almost half of the universities, polytechnics and colleges of higher education sampled in the study made some provision in multicultural studies for their intending teachers and that among those not presently providing courses, there were many where offerings in multicultural education were in preparation. One particular conclusion of the Giles and Cherrington survey is germane to the present study. It was reported that multicultural education courses were seen by many student teachers and tutors as an exploration of problems faced by black people in white British society. Rather, the authors asserted, a more desirable way to approach education for a culturally plural society would be to 'widen the cultural content of the teacher training syllabuses to reflect elements representative of all the various cultural groups that comprise the United Kingdom'. A central premise of the present study is that initial and in-service programmes of multicultural education need to draw upon accurate and up-to-date information about the knowledge that intending and practising teachers have of the many ethnic minority groups in present day Britain (not just visible ethnic minority people). Equally important, there is a need to know something about the attitudes and the beliefs of initial and in-service teacher-trainees towards ethnic minority groups in contemporary society. Eggleston (1981) makes a similar plea:

> At a time when there is a widespread acceptance of the need for further development of in-service courses in multiracial education, there is a disturbing lack of firm evidence on which policies may be based. . .In the area of knowledge content our conclusions are therefore unambiguous: to ensure that the information presented is sensitive

to the needs of the teachers, their classrooms and above all their pupils,
it must be illuminated. . . by up-to-date theoretical understandings. . .

Whilst the Giles and Cherrington survey data are now out-of-date, it is probably
true to say that until very recently the *ad hoc* and piecemeal approaches to
multicultural education provision in teacher training to which they drew
attention continued to be the modal response of teacher education institutions
in general.

A second watershed for teacher education has been identified in the
contents of two important documents published in 1984 (Lynch, 1986). The
first was a discussion document produced by a working party of the Council
for National Academic Awards, suggested 'principles in respect of multicultural
and anti-racist education' with appended a checklist of items for possible
inclusion in courses of teacher education (CNAA, 1984). The document
identified five necessary areas of professional education which would equip
teachers (i) to prepare all young people for life in a multicultural and racially
harmonious society; (ii) to have awareness and understanding of racism; (iii)
to have awareness of intercultural relations; (iv) to be able to teach, recognizing
any particular needs of ethnic minority pupils and students; and (v) to interact
effectively with colleagues in relation to these issues.

The second document was that published by the National Association
for Multiracial Education (NAME). It called for the conferment of qualified
teacher status to be dependent on students' demonstration of 'skills, knowledge
and personal qualities appropriate to teaching in a multiracial society', and
their adoption of 'an anti-racist approach in classroom practice'. The NAME
statement also demanded essential changes in teacher education; in particular,
it suggested that all courses of professional training should be monitored so
as to ensure that due weight is given throughout to anti-racist perspectives
and to the development of strategies for anti-racist teaching (NAME, 1984).

Lynch's (1986) speculation as to whether these two documents on
multicultural provision in teacher education will have any more effect than
'two decades of previous exhortation' has been overtaken by events. The
government's systematic aggrandizement of power over the education system
so carefully documented by Troyna and Williams (1986), culminated in the
teacher education sector in the setting up of the Council for the Accreditation
of Teacher Education (CATE).

The inspection of all teacher education courses by HMI and the
requirement that all teacher education institutions present detailed course
outlines for approval by the CATE in the light of certain criteria has significant
implications for the implementation of programmes of multicultural education
in initial teacher education. The criteria of approval were set out in Teacher
Training *Circular Letter 7/84*, having been originally laid down in DES Circular
3/84. Under Section 5.8:

Students should be prepared for the diversity of ability, behaviour,
social background and ethnic and cultural origins encountered in

ordinary schools; and in how to respond to that diversity and guard against preconceptions based on race or sex.

Scrutiny of courses of initial teacher education is followed first, by *administrative course approval*, second by *academic approval* and third, approval by the Secretary of State for Education and Science as a course suitable for the professional training of teachers. In future, this final approval (Schedule 5 approval) will be conditional (inter alia) upon the inclusion of a multicultural programme of work that reflects the spirit and the implicit content of Section 5.8 above.

It is axiomatic that to be relevant and effective, courses in multicultural education must begin at the levels of knowledge and understanding of those for whom they are intended.

The Sample

A total of 392 first-year student teachers in the first month of their teacher education courses in a university, a polytechnic, and two colleges of higher education in the United Kingdom completed an anonymous questionnaire which included:

(i) a measure of ethnocentricity;
(ii) a 'knowledge of ethnic minorities' test;
(iii) a projective technique designed to elicit student perceptions of, and feelings towards coloured[1] ethnic minority groups;
(iv) an invitation to comment on the concepts of:
    (a) *assimilation/integration* and
    (b) *cultural pluralism*.

The questionnaire also asked for information about a student's sex, age, home region and subject specialism. Three hundred and seventy-eight usable questionnaires were returned.

Instruments

1 *A Measure of Student Teacher Prejudice*
The 48-item measure of ethnocentrism selected for use in the research was developed by Green (1984) in his study of the behaviour of prejudiced teachers towards black pupils.

Twenty-four of the forty-eight items are scored for prejudice on a 7-point scale (very strongly agree, strongly agree, agree, neither agree nor disagree, disagree, strongly disagree, very strongly disagree). The other twenty-four items are *distractors*, designed to disguise the true purpose of the questionnaire.

Typical prejudice items include:

Item 19 - One big trouble with Indians is that they are never contented, but always try for the best jobs and the most money.

Item 30 - It is probably true to say that one fault of the Jews is their conceited idea that they are a chosen race.

Typical distractor items include:

Item 25 - The teaching profession should determine the content of the curriculum.

Item 39 - Large schools multiply large problems.

2 Knowledge of Ethnic Minority Groups in Britain
The test consists of a list of thirty words referring to cultural and/or religious artifacts of (a) the indigenous 'British' culture (for example, MATINS = the morning service in the Church of England and the Roman Catholic Church; (b) the cultures of various ethnic minority groups distinguished in terms of their *longer history of settlement* in Britain, for example, Jews (for example, BARMITZVAH = the 'coming out' ceremony for an adolescent Jewish boy), or their *more recent history of settlement* in Britain, for example, Sikhs (for example, GURDWARA = a Sikh temple).

Students were required to write a short sentence to explain each of the thirty words and were given the following example:

SITAR = a stringed instrument used in India.

The researchers were lenient rather than strict in scoring students' answers, a mark being awarded for a reasonably accurate response to an item.

3 Students' Perceptions of and Feelings towards Visible Ethnic Minority Groups and Their Experiences of Visible Ethnic Minority People
A sentence completion technique was chosen as an appropriate way of eliciting students' perceptions of visible ethnic minority groups and their experiences of visible ethnic minority people.

Respondents were asked to complete the following sentences:

When I think of coloured people...
My experience of coloured people is...

In order to establish coding frames for the open-ended comments generated by the two sentences, an initial 10 per cent of the responses of the total sample was randomly-selected and scrutinized by three researchers working independently. When satisfactory coding frames were finally agreed, one researcher then completed the classification of the responses of all respondents with the added safeguard that another member of the research team took random spot checks to verify the accuracy and consistency of the classification process.

Sentence completion No. 1 (*when I think of coloured people...*) employed the following classificatory system:

Louis Cohen

> *positive, 'mixed', neutral, negative, no response.*

Sentence completion No. 2 (*my experience of coloured people is*...employed the following classificatory system:

> positive, negative, wide-ranging experience, little or no experience, no response.

4 *Students' Orientation towards the Concept of Multiculturalism*

The elicitation of students' views was introduced as follows:

Over the past twenty years or so, immigration to Great Britain has brought about fundamental changes in our society. We are now an ethnically-mixed and a culturally-varied nation. One consequence is that our institutions have had to adapt in order to reflect and to cater for the many mixed communities that now exist throughout Great Britain. Schools particularly have had to change to accommodate too the needs of immigrant pupils in many areas.

Like other members of society, teachers differ in their opinions about the policies which best ensure that the education system reflects and caters for the needs and aspirations of all in multiracial Britain.

One commonly-held viewpoint can be described as an *assimilation/integration* stance. It argues that whilst newly-arrived immigrants should be supported and helped to acquire a working knowledge of English so that they can be quickly absorbed by the host society, more detailed, planned programmes of educational and social support may also be needed to enable immigrants to integrate with the majority society.

An alternative point of view has to do with the idea of *cultural pluralism*. It argues that while immigrants share many of the same interests and aspirations of host society members, they may wish to retain their involvement in the richness and diversity of their own minority cultures. Cultural pluralism implies a system that accepts that people's lifestyles and values are different and operates so as to allow opportunity for all to play a full part in society.

AS AN INTENDING TEACHER, please say:

> (i) which, if either of these two perspectives *assimilation/integration*, OR *cultural pluralism* best reflects your present viewpoint; and

write a brief argument in support of your stance.

The classification of students' responses proceeded as follows:

Ten per cent (10 per cent) of the replies were randomly-selected and initial coding frames were devised by each of the three researchers working independently. An agreed coding frame was then used by one researcher to classify all responses with the safeguard of random spot checks being made by another member of the team to ensure consistency and accuracy in classification.

The final classificatory system consisted of:

assimilation/integration only; cultural pluralism only; largely assimilation/integration with some cultural pluralism; largely cultural pluralism with some integration/assimilation;

156

cultural pluralism and assimilation/integration equally weighted; inexplicable response; no response.

RESULTS : PART 1

The first part of the analysis presents a picture of the student teachers as a whole.

1 *Student teacher prejudice* (range 24–168).
The mean score and standard deviation for the whole group was:

$$\bar{x}. = 76.70 \quad s.d. = 13.90 \quad n = 377$$

2 *Knowledge of ethnic minority groups* (range 0–30)
The mean score and standard deviation for the whole group was:

$$\bar{x} = 6.96 \quad s.d. = 4.58 \quad n = 378.$$

The percentages of correct responses to each of the items were calculated and put in rank order. The following table extrapolated from the results shows the percentages for the items at the top and bottom end of the rankings.

Table 9.1.

Ranking	Item	Description	Correct responses %
1	Rosary	Beads used by Roman Catholics as a guide to devotions.	82
2	Barmitzvah	'Coming out' ceremony for adolescent Jewish boy.	67
3	Wesleyan	Followers of John Wesley; Free Church; Methodism.	55
4	Wake	A vigil; sitting with corpse before burial; Irish R.C.	53
5	Matins	Morning service in Roman Catholic and Church of England.	51
6	Vespers	Evening service in Roman Catholic and Church of England.	51
7	Punjabi	Indian language.	45
21	Gujarati	Indian language.	6
22	Imam	Religious leader in Muslim world.	6
23	Diwali	Festival of lights in Hinduism and Sikhism.	4
24	Upanishads	Hindu religious books; Indian literature c.800 B.C.	3
25	Pushto	Language of North West Pakistan.	2
26	Halal	'Clean' according to Muslim ordinances for preparation of meat.	2
27	Granth	Sikh holy book.	2
28	Gurdwara	Sikh temple.	2
29	Salavars	Trousers worn by women in India and Pakistan.	0
30	Anansi	Mythical figure in West Indian folklore and children's stories.	0

3 *Perceptions of and feelings towards visible ethnic minority groups and experience of visible ethnic minority people.*

The frequencies of students' responses to the two open-ended sentences are classified below.

(a) *When I think of coloured people* . . .

Response	n	%
Positive	255	67
'Mixed'	16	4
Neutral	48	13
Negative	18	5
No response	41	11
(n = 378)		

(b) *My experience of coloured people is* . . .

Response	n	%
Positive	124	32
Negative	10	2
Wide ranging experience	22	5
Little or no experience	175	46
Inexplicable response	22	5
No response	39	10
(n = 378)		

4 *Concepts of multiculturalism*

The frequencies of students' responses to the item on multiculturalism are classified below.

Response	n	%
Assimilation/integration only	89	24
Cultural pluralism only	194	51
Largely assimilation/integration with some cultural pluralism	11	3
Largely cultural pluralism with some assimilation/integration	10	3
Cultural pluralism and assimilation/ integration equally weighted	38	10
Inexplicable response	4	1
No response	32	8
(n = 378)		

RESULTS: PART 2

The second part of the analysis focuses upon sub-groups of the total student sample. In particular, it explores associations between *levels of prejudice* and

respondents' orientation towards multiculturalism, their knowledge of ethnic
minority groups, their perceptions of ethnic minority groups, their experience
of ethnic minority groups, their sex, and their home region in Britain.

5 *Prejudice and orientation towards multiculturalism*
   In testing the association between levels of prejudice and orientation towards
   multiculturalism, the categories *assimilation/integration only* and *largely
   assimilation/integration* were combined. So too were the categories
   cultural/pluralism only and *largely cultural pluralism*. Tables 9.2 and 9.3 show
   the associations between multicultural orientation and levels of prejudice
   when the prejudice score is dichotomized at the mean (Table 9.2) and then
   at ±1 s.d. around the mean (Table 9.3).

Table 9.2

Multicultural orientation	Prejudice	
	LESS	MORE
Assimilation/ integration	11%	22%
Cultural pluralism	37%	30%
(n = 304)		

$x^2 = 10.40$ df = 1   p = < 0.001

Table 9.3

Multicultural orientation	Prejudice VERY LOW	VERY HIGH
Assimilation/ integration	4%	26%
Cultural pluralism	48%	22%
(n = 99)		

$x^2 = 22.98$ df = 1   p = < 0.001

It is clear that higher levels of prejudice tend to be associated with an
assimilation/integration perspective and lower levels of prejudice tend to
be associated with a cultural pluralist perspective.

6 *Prejudice and knowledge of ethnic minority groups*
   Tables 9.4 and 9.5 show the associations between knowledge of ethnic
   minority groups and levels of prejudice when the prejudice score is
   dichotomized at the mean (Table 9.4) and then at ± s.d. around the mean
   (Table 9.5).

Table 9.4

Knowledge score	Prejudice	
	LESS	MORE
Below the mean	24%	32%
Above the mean	23%	21%
(n = 350)		

$x^2 = 2.49$ df = 1   p = ns

Table 9.5

Knowledge score	Prejudice VERY LOW	VERY HIGH
Below the mean	22%	38%
Above the mean	27%	13%
(n = 114)		

$x^2 = 9.11$ df = 1   p = < 0.01

The results show that prejudice tends to be associated with lower scores
on the test of ethnic minority group cultures but only among students
classified as VERY HIGH on prejudice.

Louis Cohen

7 *Prejudice and perception of visible ethnic minority groups (when I think of coloured people. . .)*

Tables 9.6 and 9.7 show the associations between perceptions of visible ethnic minority groups and levels of prejudice when the prejudice score is dichotomized at the mean (Table 9.6) and then at ±1 s.d. around the mean (Table 9.7).

Table 9.6		
	Prejudice	
Comment	LESS	MORE
Positive	44%	34%
'Mixed'	1%	4%
Negative	<1%	2%
Neutral	5%	10%
(n = 327)		

$x^2 = 19.85$ df = 3   p = <0.001

Table 9.7		
	Prejudice	
Comment	VERY LOW	VERY HIGH
Positive	48%	28%
'Mixed'	1%	3%
Negative	0%	7%
Neutral	3%	10%
(n = 112)		

$x^2 = 18.88$ df = 3   p = <0.001

Analysis shows that higher levels of prejudice tend to be associated with comments about visible ethnic minority groups that are 'mixed', negative and neutral, and lower levels of prejudice tend to be associated with comments that are positive.

8 *Prejudice and experience of visible ethnic minority groups (my experience of coloured people is. . .)*

Tables 9.8 and 9.9 show the association between experience of visible ethnic minority groups and levels of prejudice when the prejudice score is dichotomized at the mean (Table 9.8) and at ±1 s.d. around the mean (Table 9.9). These two analyses deal with *positive* and *negative* responses by the student teachers.

Table 9.8		
	Prejudice	
Comment	LESS	MORE
Positive	60%	33%
Negative	0%	7%
(n = 134)		

$x^2 = 13.44$ df = 1   p = <0.001

Table 9.9		
	Prejudice	
Comment	VERY LOW	VERY HIGH
Positive	60%	28%
Negative	0%	12%
(n = 49)		

$x^2 = 7.32$ df = 1   p = <0.01

Tables 9.10 and 9.11 show the associations between experience of visible ethnic minority groups and levels of prejudice when the prejudice score is dichotomized at the mean (Table 9.10) and then at ±1 s.d. around the mean (Table 9.11). These two analyses deal with the *degree of experience* reported by the student teachers.

Table 9.10				Table 9.11		
	Prejudice				*Prejudice*	
					VERY	VERY
Comment	*LESS*	*MORE*		Comment	LOW	HIGH
Wide-ranging experience	7%	4%		Wide-ranging experience	12%	7%
Little or no experience	31%	58%		Little or no experience	31%	50%
(*n* = 197)				(*n* = 58)		
$x^2 = 5.43$ df = 1 p = <0.05				$x^2 = 1.42$ df = 1 p = *ns*		

The above table indicates that higher levels of prejudice tend to be associated with more negative and less positive comments about visible minority groups and with less experience of them.

9 *Prejudice and sex of the student*
Tables 9.12 and 9.13 show the associations between the sex of the student and levels of prejudice when the prejudice score is dichotomized at the mean (Table 9.12) and at ± 1 s.d. around the mean (Table 9.13).

Table 9.12				Table 9.13		
	Prejudice				*Prejudice*	
					VERY	VERY
Sex	*LESS*	*MORE*		*Sex*	*LOW*	*HIGH*
Male	7%	8%		Male	6%	11%
Female	40%	45%		Female	45%	38%
(*n* = 371)				(*n* = 124)		
$x^2 = 0.003$ df = 1 p = *ns*				$x^2 = 1.69$ df = 1 p = *ns*		

Sex was not found to be associated with level of prejudice in this sample of student teachers.

10 *Prejudice and home region in Britain*
Tables 9.14 and 9.15 show the associations between the students' home region in Britain and levels of prejudice when the prejudice score is dichotomized at the mean (Table 9.14) and at ± 1 s.d. around the mean (Table 9.15).

Home regions are grouped as follows:

FEW, IF ANY Visible immigrants and/or British citizens of visible immigrant origin = Northern Ireland, Scotland, Wales, South West England, North East England.

SOME, MANY Visible immigrants and/or British citizens or visible immigrant origin = London and the South East of England, Midlands, North West England.

Louis Cohen

Table 9.14		
	Prejudice	
Home region of Britain	LESS	MORE
Few, if any visible minorities	26%	41%
Some, many visible minorities	21%	12%
(n = 233)		

$x^2 = 12.77$ df = 1   p = < 0.001

Table 9.15		
	Prejudice	
Home region of Britain	VERY LOW	VERY HIGH
Few, if any visible minorities	17%	31%
Some, many visible minorities	41%	11%
(n = 99)		

$x^2 = 16.81$ df = 1   p = < 0.001

It can be concluded that higher levels of prejudice tend to be associated with students' home regions where few if any visible immigrants and/or British citizens of visible immigrant origin are domiciled.

Summary

Several tentative conclusions arise from the analysis of the data.

1 Most of the student teachers' responses to questions to do with their perceptions and feelings about visible ethnic minority people are classified as *positive* or *neutral*. By and large, their comments are *liberal*, *respectful*, and frequently expressed in such terms as '*live and let live*'. Only a small proportion of the student group is antagonistic or hostile to visible ethnic minority groups.

2 A substantial minority of the sample of student teachers has little or no experience of visible ethnic groups in contemporary Britain. Only a small proportion of the student group has had wide-ranging contacts with visible ethnic minority people.

3 Most student teachers subscribe to a cultural-pluralist viewpoint (Education for All). That is to say, they support the position that while ethnic minorities might share many interests and aspirations of ethnic majority members, they may wish to retain their involvement in the richness and diversity of their own cultures. Such a viewpoint implies an acceptance that people's lifestyles and values are different and that society, in general, is the better for such diversity. A not insignificant minority of intending teachers supports an assimilation/integration position. These students subscribe to the view that planned programmes of educational and social support are necessary to enable ethnic minorities to integrate with the majority society.

4 Student teachers generally exhibit considerable ignorance of ethnic minority groups. Not only are many respondents unable to identify religious and/or cultural artifacts of the indigenous 'white' culture but their knowledge of the religions, customs and languages of ethnic minority groups with a history

of recent settlement in Britain is extremely sparse and in the case of certain groups (for example, Sikhs, Muslims, Hindus), virtually non-existent.

5 Intending teachers who exhibit higher levels of prejudice are more likely to:

(i) hold an assimilation/integration viewpoint;
(ii) lack knowledge of visible ethnic minority groups in Britain;
(iii) express negative, 'mixed' or neutral comments about visible ethnic minority people;
(iv) have little or no experience of visible ethnic minority people;
(v) come from regions in Britain where few if any visible ethnic minority groups live.

Discussion

The sample of student teachers whose knowledge and beliefs are examined here were contacted during the first month of their first year of teacher education. In effect, they had come fresh from their secondary schooling, save for the small percentage of 'mature' entrants drawn in the sample. To no small extent, therefore, the degree of ignorance of ethnic minority groups that they exhibit points directly to lack of opportunities during their later school years to familiarize themselves with the multiracial and composition of contemporary Britain. That notwithstanding, the inability of many intending teachers to identify salient aspects of indigenous 'white' culture let alone religious, linguistic and cultural artifacts of 'visible' ethnic minority groups bears directly on the types of initial training responses that teacher education institutions make to the requirements for multicultural provision as set out by the Council For the Accreditation of Teacher Education (see Chapter 8 by Craft in this volume).

The Swann Report (DES, 1985) *Education For All* identified three forms of response to multicultural education: 'permeation', 'core studies' and 'optional courses'. The Committee regarded these three approaches as having equally important and complementary roles but it noted with regret that far too often the only response of teacher-training institutions has been to provide optional multicultural courses. This, it considered as entirely inadequate.

If the lack of knowledge and understanding of multicultural Britain identified in this opportunity sample of intending teachers is in any way representative of the degree of ignorance in initial teacher trainees generally, then there is an urgent need for the whole of their professional studies in education to be permeated by knowledge and experiences that prepare them for life in a pluralistic society. Moreover, given the brief set out in the CATE document (1984) Section 8 quoted earlier, one would want to underscore the comment contained in the CRE response to Swann (CRE, 1985) that:

> It would be insufficient for teacher training to confine its course development to the issue of cultural diversity; attaining the objectives of *Education For All* will require also an examination of teacher

attitudes and behaviour and the development of an anti-racist ethos and practice.

The comments of student participants on the general findings of the present study (see below) bear out the Commission For Racial Equality statement above.

The Swann Report was also concerned with selection procedures for entry to teacher training and with the granting of qualified teacher status. The Committee took the view that any teacher exhibiting negative attitudes towards ethnic minority groups will be 'an inadequate teacher of any child in any school'. Moreover, any person holding racist opinions should be considered as unlikely to be able to fulfil the professional responsibilities required of a teacher.

Given the limitations of the questionnaire as a research instrument, the present study identified only a small proportion of intending teachers who fitted the description of *inadequacy* outlined above. Nonetheless, it is imperative that such individuals be identified as soon as possible and be directed away from teaching. This viewpoint was clearly endorsed by the student participants themselves. It is to a report of student participants' observations on the results of the study that attention is now turned.

Respondents' Comments

Small opportunity samples of the original respondents were gathered together in each of the cooperating institutions some eighteen months or so after the analysis of the questionnaire data.

Because they were volunteers there is no way of ascertaining whether the comments of these self-selected groups are representative of the original sample of 392 students. In the university, the polytechnic and the colleges of higher education, the author alone met the student groups and offered to share with them the results of the questionnaire and to explain to them, in simple non-statistical terms, the interpretations that he placed on the questionnaire data.

What follows is an *account of accounts*: that is to say, the researcher's construction of the major comments that the students made concerning his analyses, together with the feelings and worries which they communicated during the course of the free-flowing discussions.

Student Teacher Prejudice

It was generally acknowledged (and regretted) that there are student teachers who are racially prejudiced. Many of the group members expressed genuine concern lest they themselves exhibit prejudice *of which they are unaware*. There was little faith in effectiveness of psychological/personality testing as a way of screening intending teachers for prejudices. Yet there was a common concern that teachers need to be selected in respect of certain characteristics, not least, that they should be free from prejudice! All groups spent some time in discussing the problem of teacher selection in a multicultural society.

Student Teachers' Knowledge of Ethnic Minority Groups

If anything, there was even greater dismay at the researcher's account of widespread ignorance about ethnic minority groups in Britain among those intending to be teachers. In all four groups there were students who were extremely embarrassed by the findings. Others, however, did not react in this way. One intending teacher of secondary school English was of the opinion that her lack of knowledge would not directly affect her teaching in Northern Ireland, 'since there are so few blacks there anyway'. The relevance of teacher knowledge about ethnic minority groups and the need for multicultural education courses in teacher education was raised by a small number of the Northern Ireland group, generally in the context of the small representation of non-white minorities in the six counties.

In all four groups there was a fairly consensual view that to no small extent the lack of knowledge about ethnic minority groups arose out of *lack of instruction in secondary schools*. The priorities given to 'A' level teaching, it was felt, excluded discussion and reading about important social issues such as racial prejudice in many sixth forms. There was no support for the view that teacher education institutions were the principal culprits.

Students' Orientations — Assimilation/Integration: Culture Pluralism

The opinions of the discussion groups reflected general support for a *cultural pluralist* rather than an *assimilation/integrationist perspective*. However, several members of the groups, principally male students, questioned whether cultural pluralism had 'paid off' in light of events in Toxteth, Handsworth and Tottenham. Discussions in two groups (N.W. England and N.E. England) moved from questions to do with cultural pluralism to an *anti-racist education stance*. Opinions were quite firm about the desirability of race-awareness courses for teachers although there was very little knowledge of ILEA documents on race awareness and policy. When these were explained, there was a broad rejection of *compulsory* teacher attendance at race awareness courses.

Multicultural Education Courses in Teacher Training

Whilst all four groups acknowledged the need for courses of multicultural education in their professional training as teachers there was a general feeling that what was currently on offer fell short of what was needed. In one group a mature student commented that she 'had never had the change to air her own fears and ignorance about race and ethnic minority people'. Another mature student in the same group said, 'We have to sit and listen to experts telling us about this, that and the other. Most of the time we don't even understand the words they are using!' Discussion in the N.W. England group led to the researcher sending on to the participants photocopies of polemic material from an extreme right wing journal. Members of the group expressed disappointment that, to date, they had not had opportunities in their college studies to explore the role of propaganda in the creation and dissemination of racial prejudice.

The broad feeling in the discussion groups was that not enough time was devoted to work in multicultural education; that what was done was rather conventionally didactic; that there was a need to allow students to come to grips with their own feelings and fears before embarking on lecture-discussion type courses that were largely knowledge-based.

Typical Examples of Student Teachers' Responses[2]

Cue statement: 'When I think of coloured people, I think . . .

1   When I think of coloured people I think, often, of them in ways different to my own race. This is not something that brings out personal bias or prejudice but merely illustrative of the fact that when necessary I have to make a special consideration, a specific focus. This is something that I would not normally do. I, for instance, believe that it is not necessary to make an extreme fuss of handicapped people, wishing to make them feel as ordinary as the rest of us. In the same way in thinking of coloured people I am loath to make them objects of special/different consideration.

In my intended career the problem of individual differences will be continually to the fore. Hopefully, in any consideration of the needs, etc. of coloured people/pupils I will be able to approach a solution in the same way I approach any other solution. It is largely cultural reasons that make me in many ways think of coloured people in anyway differently to any others — feeling these differences force some specific consideration. Often the pressure for this comes from coloured people, who may well avoid integration. At college or in any other working environment that has shown me a wide cultural mix I like to think that I have thought of coloured people in the same way as my own race. Most certainly avoiding giving them secondary consideration just because they are coloured.

2   I think of coloured people as a minority group in this country. I don't tend to think of them in terms of a separate population living in their native countries!

I see them generally as a group experiencing a lot more problems than white people. I appreciate this is not always the case, with many blacks finding success, at least financially, in this country. Even those who do seem to me to be disadvantaged by their colour. There always seems to be some people attacking coloureds as a group, irrespective of their social status, income, behaviour, etc.

I see them as either being placed in, or choosing to go in, their own areas of the community. My main image of where black communities are to be found is in the centres of large cities, generally in run down areas.

I feel coloureds should be treated as total equals to whites in every respect. However, I do not think that the number immigrating to this country should be unlimited. With the economic problems faced by this country at the moment I think it is essential we look after the people already here, regardless of race, before we can consider taking in more people which may only perpetuate the problem. Once people are residents in this country I feel we have a moral responsibility to treat all as equals.

3 When I think of coloured people I think that fundamentally they are the same as white people. I am interested in their background/culture equally as I am with a white person there is no difference. My experience of coloured people has been through dance and living in Liverpool. Consequently I have no more or less respect for a coloured person than white. I judge them on personality, and if they are from Liverpool I identify with them immediately same as other Liverpudlians.

4 When I think of coloured people I think the situation we find ourselves in is one of our own making. My own feelings of how I relate and react to coloured people tends to depend on what group of coloured people is being referred to.

The 'send them home brigade' I don't believe are right in their outlook. I believe we've no right to dictate where people ought to go. Again how I feel about coloured people depends on who they are, and this in turn modifies my attitude to different groups. I also think some of the problems we have in society are because we have coloured people in our midst. Not that removing them from our society will cure these problems like any group of people there are good and bad, conformists and non-conformists, so I only have strong feelings against people who perpetuate violence and create and foster suffering and if that includes some coloureds then I dislike them, but principally for their attitude and not their colour.

Cue statement: 'My experience of coloured people...

1 My experience of coloured people is quite limited. Having lived in an area that has a very low coloured population, I am unaware of multiracial problems in society at a first hand level. There is just one ethnic family along our road and no where in my home town can really be isolated as having a high coloured population.

2 My own experience of coloured people is fairly limited. There were no coloured people in my school or childhood neighbourhood. During my working life I've come across very few coloured people, and those I have varied from likeable characters to downright nasties, but no more so than mature white people I've been in contact with. There have been some interesting encounters where race has caused friction in a work situation but the one's that stick in my mind are those between people of Indian origin and Pakistan origin.

3 My experience of black people is mixed. I know quite a lot as I live in a very racially mixed town and play the sport favoured by Asians. (I don't know many non-Asian coloured people, but have only positive things to say about those I do know.)

When I came to university I would defend black people all of the time as I rated 'coloured' with my many friends at home. However, my views have changed somewhat. Being able to see the situation at home, without being involved, is a help. Friends and family have been badly let down, to some extent used and abused by those who were my friends. I used to feel — 'some coloured people may not be very nice, but the ones I know are'. Now I feel that I would not trust an Asian again. This is only Asians. I feel that West Indians tend to be more straight forward — they say what they think. At the moment I am very bitter — but it only takes one good friend to change attitudes a little.

4 I regard myself as an understanding and openminded individual with a basic view to all means of 'Live and Let Live' (please excuse the corny cliche tone). Therefore as regards ethnic minorities in the UK I see them initially as visitors who should they wish to stay and naturalize as citizens of the UK may do so very much the same as if I emigrated to Australia, America or Africa.

I therefore see coloured people as individuals in the first instance, i.e. I form views about them as I would another Englishman or woman.

I have had coloured friends and still have some coloured friends. The friendships have been based upon common pursuits in life, for example, one-year students from the same area or snooker partners. It is not colour that determines the relationship but common interest or purely having to cooperate in a particular situation, for example, a nextdoor neighbour in hall may be black.

Whilst I would say that I do not therefore openly love or hate people for their colour I do dislike people who persecute ethnic minorities.

What also comes into mind in this case is that these minorities ought to have similar opportunities to us in all aspects of life I would strongly guess this is not, of course, so.

Obviously if the people come from another culture I would not expect them to abandon their beliefs or traditions, I would not expect them to 'force' their culture upon us. I would not like to see our culture 'forced' upon them.

I feel that they should still feel that they are visitors if they wish to retain their own cultural views and would not expect us to change our education system to cope with this. If Africans or Chinese, etc. wish to be taught in their own languages or of their own cultures then I feel that they should make provisions for this. Otherwise, I feel that they should adopt the culture of the country they visit to some extent. To what degree, is their choice. If they do not like what is here then they must of course return to their homeland. It may help by saying that should I visit Africa permanently or with this view of settling in mind, I would not demand to be dealt with especially, I would expect to have to adapt my way of life to mix in with theirs. A sort of mutual respect between cultures from which would naturally I hope develop a desire to learn about the others' culture without making great changes to the host's social systems or the visitors beliefs.

I feel it is wrong for people to visit this country or ethnic minorities that have been here for several generations to segregate themselves and see the country as a hotel just as I feel it is wrong for us to treat them in a hostile manner.

5 My own experience of coloured people is extremely limited. I knew one black boy before coming to university. He was treated equally by all the people I knew and to my knowledge never suffered from any discrimination. At university I have got to know a few coloured people fairly well and have found no difficulty in communicating with them.

I do know a few people who live in areas with high percentages of coloureds and the impression I get is that they do hold a lot more prejudice than I do. In fact one very good friend of mine would go so far as to say that he positively dislikes Asians. When I've asked him about this and told him I think it's a stupid view to hold he quite rightly says that I wouldn't know what they are really like. He sees them as unclean and invading the opportunities of white people in terms of employment.

I don't agree with his views but have to admit that I've never actually had experience to prove that he is wrong.

I must admit, however, that I wouldn't feel totally at ease if I had to move into the middle of a coloured community, where I was in the minority. I'm sure I would find it harder to go out and try to meet people and build up relationships.

Cue statement: 'My views about what future education should be are . . .

1 The main way I feel future education should be structured with respect to the coloured population is in terms of integration. I feel that coloured people should be helped to adopt the English culture as that is the culture in which they are going to live and which many of them want to adopt.

However, there is the reverse of this whereby many want to hang on to their own cultures. In this respect I feel that the idea of pluralism is taking the matter too far. I do feel coloureds should be able to hold onto their own beliefs and that whites should probably understand them more.

However, I feel that coloureds need to be able to fit their beliefs into the basic structure of the English culture. After all they are moving into 'our' country and by making such a choice should be prepared to accept our way of life. By all means they should keep their religious beliefs but they must also recognize it may well be different from the religious beliefs of the majority.

2 I see reason for lack of integration but no reason to change our present education system or social system. Perhaps we should be more aware of ethnic minorities or more accepting.

I feel they must adapt to our system just as I would adapt to theirs if I had to. Otherwise we both have the choice to return home. Integration yes — changing curriculum no!

Respect for each other is important. If a black man hit me I would hit him back because he hit me, not because he is black, or turn the other cheek irrespective of colour.

3 My views about what future education should be in this country with regard to coloured population are:

Integration would be best. Avoiding the question of religion initially (I believe in freedom of choice). Wanting primary schools separate (as has been suggested recently) only means that coloured children will have more language problems when they do eventually need to learn English.

England is a free country in its culture whereas some coloured people do not seem to be free. Arranged marriages and the roles of women in an Asian society (they are slaves) cannot be encouraged. Bigamy is still illegal — which prevents Mormons from living in their way, yet arranged marriages still go ahead. This is not a legal but a cultural problem — a black Asian may go out with a white girl (if his parents don't find out) but if he chose to marry her not only would he be thrown out of the family, his friends would abandon him. No law can change this.

I believe that children should be taught English values, principles and culture if they want to live in England. If I wanted to live in Spain I would expect a Spanish education for my children. They would have to 'be' Spanish.

I don't think colour is a problem — many coloured people live within the English culture very happily. Many, however, are determined not to.

Religion: if any is to be taught in primary schools — it should be Christianity — it is too complicated for children to understand the ins and outs at a very young age — it is also very confusing. If ethnic minority groups want their children to learn another religion they should teach it themselves, and if they want to keep their kids out of school assemblies.

4 I believe in the ideal of pluralism, that incoming immigrants have much to offer and could enrich our culture (not only through Indian restaurants!). However I feel there are practical problems with this method, in that the ideologies on which our societies are based (freedom, democracy {Christianity?} egalitarianism, etc) would not change overnight, and I would therefore move somewhat towards integration, i.e. a pluralistic curriculum,

with an emphasis on the host country's culture. As the majority of people outside school in society at large are not multicultural, immigrant children have to be 'integrated' by the school curriculum for practical reasons. But I feel it should not be forgotten that they have something to offer. I do not choose the host culture to teach immigrants out of any inbuilt superiority of that culture, but simply because it is the culture of the majority of the population, and is therefore *practically* the most suitable.

Cue statement: Assimilation/integration or cultural pluralism?

1 Until I have investigated further I cannot give a good argument for or against either theory, but can only put forward my personal ideas, which come closer to cultural plurisum that assimilation/integration. It would seem that aspects of both ideas could be useful, as any immigrant to any country should accept the laws of the society they are entering, but there is no reason for them to abandon their own culture.
2 Immigrants must want to be integrated into English society, if they do not they shouldn't come to England, but stay in their native country in order to carry out their cultural activities.
3 The idea of cultural pluralism, best coincides with my own beliefs. I feel that immigrants should be made at home in England, but should be allowed, within our laws, to express their beliefs in the way that they have been brought up to. Through this they may be able to bring changes for the better in our society and vice versa.
4 I support this view because if newly-arrived immigrants wish to be accepted in our society they should live by our social standards. However, more support should be given to the natives of our country to improve their education.
5 Although immigrants are entering a new country which has a different background and culture to their origin it is still essential in their cultures while still becoming involved in those of their new home.
6 Integration is a necessity in that colour and religious barriers can be broken by means of an understanding of each other. However, cultural-pluralism is valuable in that individuals can maintain an identity they have been 'brought-up' in and probably strongly believe in. Therefore, neither one nor the other should dominate because as human beings each and everyone of us is an individual in his/her own right and we should respect our fellow men's beliefs.

An Atypical Example of a Student Teacher Response

There were very few examples of student teacher responses such as the one cited below. It is worth quoting in full, however, to illustrate the intensity of attitudes and beliefs held by this particular respondent.

Louis Cohen

Cue statement: 'When I think of coloured people, I think . . .

When I think of coloured people I think of people who live in their own countries but are ruled by white people because they would not be able to rule their own countries in, what is considered, a modern civilized manner. Also of black people who live in countries other than their own where they fight to 'be treated equally' with white people in such a way that any differences become more exaggerated and prejudices, towards either colour, are increased. I consider pure coloured people, that is not including half castes, to be fairly simple people who, if left to themselves in their own environment, are concerned with the business of living from day to day. I think of coloured people as a very physcially able race, many top athletes and sportsmen/women are coloured and even those who do not pursue such activities appear strong and fit. They are often tall people. Coloured people often have complexes which are partly of their own making and partly due to the views of some white people. They smell differently.

Cue statement: 'My experience of coloured people . . .

In spite of the view that all African countries should be ruled by a majority government I don't think this is so and the evidence in both Kenya and Zimbabwe shows that the coloured people are unable to run their countries as efficiently as the Europeans who did so before independence. There is very little bad feeling towards whites from coloured people and on the whole they are very happy people and happy-go-lucky too. They are often very lazy and will not bother to find employment if they can be supported by the state. They have a very practical nature and this type of employment suits them far better than anything requiring particular intellectual powers, although there are always some exceptions. They do not forget things easily and although they may take a long time to learn how to do a task, once it is learnt they will always remember how to do it, and do it in exactly the same fashion as they have been taught. They have very little respect for machinery and this does not usually last very long in their case. They love bright colours.

Cue statement: 'My views about what future education should be are . . .

My views about what future education should be in this country with respect to coloured population are that everyone should stay in the same system. All should be educated together. It is important that the coloured populace in this country learn to live as everyone else does because there will only be greater emphasis on and differences if they continue to live in a different fashion. Children are very quick to notice differences and this could lead to unhappiness for whichever group is in the minority. Therefore I would agree with integration in education since if they wish to live here they should adopt the local lifestyle; if they are against doing this they should not really be living in this country and would be better to find another place where their own life-style will fit into the society already present. I would be against pluralism since I do not agree with religion being taught in schools — it is a personal, or at the widest a family, matter.

Notes

1 '*Non-white*' or '*visible*' ethnic minorities would have been the preferred terminology. Pilot testing the questionnaire indicated that '*coloured*' was the word used by the majority of student respondents in speaking about non-white groups in contemporary Britain.
2 The transcripts are reproduced exactly as written by the student teachers.

References

COHEN, L. and MANION,L. (1983) *Multicultural Classrooms*, London, Croom Helm.
CNAA COMMITTEE FOR EDUCATION, MULTICULTURAL WORKING GROUP (1984) *Multicultural Education: Discussion Paper*, London, CNAA.
CRAFT, A.Z. and BARDELL, G. (1984) *Curriculum Opportunities in a Multicultural Society*, London, Harper & Row.
CRAFT, M. (Ed) (1981) *Teaching in a Multicultural Society: The Task for Teacher Education*, Lewes, Falmer Press.
CRE (1985) *Swann: A Response from the Commission for Racial Equality*, London, CRE.
DEPARTMENT OF EDUCATION AND SCIENCE (1981) *West Indian Children in Our Schools: Report of the Committee of Enquiry into the Education of Children from Ethnic Minority Groups* (The Rampton Report), Cmnd. 8273, London, HMSO.
DEPARTMENT OF EDUCATION AND SCIENCE (1985) *Education for All: Report of the Committee of Enquiry into the Education of Children from Ethnic Minority Groups* (The Swann Report) Cmnd. 9453, London, HMSO.
EGGLESTON, J. (1981) 'Present provision in in-service training' in CRAFT, M. (Ed) *Teaching in a Multicultural Society: The Task for Teacher Education*, Lewes, Falmer Press.
GILES, R. and CHERRINGTON, D. (1981) *Multicultural Education in the United Kingdom: A Survey of Courses and Other Provision in British Institutions of Higher Education*, London, CRE.
GREEN, P.A. (1984) 'Teachers' influence on the self-concept of ethnic minority pupils', unpublished PhD thesis, University of Durham.
HOUSE OF COMMONS (1981) *Racial Disadvantage, 5th Report of the Home Affairs Committee*, Vol. 1, London, HMSO.
JEFFCOATE, R. (1984) *Ethnic Minorities and Education*, London, Harper & Row.
LYNCH, J. (1982) *The Multicultural Curriculum*, London, Batsford Academic and Educational Ltd.
LYNCH, J. (1986) 'An initial typology of perspectives on staff development for multicultural teacher education' in MODGIL, S. *et al.* (Eds) *Multicultural Education: The Interminable Debate*, Lewes, Falmer Press.
NAME (1984) *Statement on Teacher Educators*, London, NAME.

Louis Cohen

SCHOOLS COUNCIL (1981) *Multi-Ethnic Education: The Way Forward*, London, Schools Council.
TOMLINSON, S. (1984) *Home and School in Multicultural Britain*, London, Batsford Academic and Educational Ltd.
TROYNA, B. and WILLIAMS, J. (1986) *Racism, Education and the State*, London, Croom Helm.

Chapter 10

'A New Planet'? Tackling Racial Inequality in All-white Schools and Colleges

Barry Troyna

Lecturer:	I don't know what problems there are in, say, Bradford or Birmingham — there are certain schools where there are more overseas nationals than there are English people. I don't know what problems these people have.
Researcher:	Well, they wouldn't be overseas nationals would they; they'd be British citizens.
Lecturer:	Oh, they'd be British citizens of foreign origin.
Researcher:	But probably they'd be British citizens born here.
Lecturer:	Oh yes, but although they would be born here they would have the culture of their original country (cited in Troyna and Selman, 1988, p. 29).

...the work of all schools should be informed by a policy that recognizes the pernicious and all-pervasive nature of racism in the lives of students, teachers, and parents, black and white, and the need to confront it. We further emphasize that this is not only a task facing schools in the inner cities or in what some people still insist on calling 'immigrant areas'. It is incumbent upon schools and colleges everywhere to tackle the issue of racism...(MacDonald, Bhavnani, John and Khan, 1988, p. 2)

All-white Areas: A 'New Planet'?

Whether *Education for All* is a landmark in pluralism is not the most pressing concern of this chapter. This is partly because I am not convinced that the

Committee's conception of pluralism should constitute an informing principle of the UK's educational system (Troyna, 1986). I'll have more to say on this later in the chapter. More importantly, however, I do not think that it is a question which should be uppermost in our minds in the post-Swann period. Instead I would contend that the limited impact of the report and related initiatives on the way schools are organized and administered should be our focus of concern. In particular, the failure of the report to stimulate changes along multicultural and anti-racist lines in schools and colleges where there are few black students is profoundly disturbing. And it is this broad issue which I will address in the chapter.

For Shanin and Keith Popple (1987), active campaigners for anti-racist education, the move from the metropolitan centres of the North and Midlands to the rural south-west of England was, it seems, traumatic. They compare the experience to 'stepping onto a new planet where even the language around race relations is dissimilar from that in vogue nationally' (p. 28). Their impressions, of course, have been confirmed by various studies of the way in which policy-makers and teachers in predominantly/all-white areas of the UK view multicultural (MCE) and anti-racist education (ARE) (for example, Townsend and Brittan, 1972; Little and Willey, 1981; Troyna and Ball, 1987). The studies show conclusively that neither MCE or ARE has made an impact on the educational landscape beyond the inner cities. Indeed, it is salutary to be reminded of the fact that a number of schools in predominantly/all-white areas have yet to 'adapt to the cultural pluralism that is now a fundamental aspect of British society' (Taylor, 1987, p. 45). Fewer still have taken on board the more radical conception of ARE as a procedural value or coherent set of practices.

In a (forlorn) attempt to mobilize change along MCE/ARE lines in ethnically homogeneous settings[1], academics, practitioners and others have developed an impressive array of tactics and approaches (for example, Brown, 1988; Gaine, 1987; Taylor, 1987). This development has been facilitated by the availability of Education Support Grants (ESG) and Grant Related In-Service Training (GRIST) funding from the DES since the mid-1980s. But whilst these initiatives have been important, and, in general, welcome, we should not lose sight of the fact that they are piecemeal tactics, not comprehensive strategies. In the event, then, their influence on (and attraction to) educationists outside the urban centres of the UK is unpredictable and erratic; plausible and acceptable in some contexts, less so in others. In 1985 I argued that with one or two conspicuous exceptions 'multiculturalists have not attempted to ground their arguments (for reform) in a convincing educational framework' (Troyna, 1985, p. 222). By and large I think this is still the case, especially with regard to ethnically homogeneous areas. Although some theoretical advances have been secured in the last few years these have not engaged directly with the particular circumstances under which educationists operate in predominantly/all-white institutions. I would go further. Wittingly or otherwise, some theorists have circumvented this issue entirely (for example, Brandt, 1986; Troyna and Williams, 1986). What is more, the Swann Committee and educational policy-makers have followed this same track, as I will show later.

It seems to me that it is now time for those committed to the espousal and legitimation of ARE to treat seriously the question of how effective and persuasive strategies might be formulated for predominantly/all-white schools and colleges. From an instrumental point of view, at least, this is important. As Peter Newsam, former Chairperson of the Commission for Racial Equality informs us,

> . . . to dodge the issue of racial injustice in all-white schools may be racist because it disproportionately disadvantages black youths when some of those untaught white youngsters later become employers, football fans, union officials or join the police. (Newsam, 1986, p. 80)

But 'means-end' arguments are not sufficient, in themselves, to dislodge entrenched views about the supposed causal link between black residents and a 'race relations' problem. In Gus John's words, professionals in all-white areas are unlikely to give a 'monkey's toss about the fact that with increased mobility students in Chichester might well end up managing a black or multiracial workforce in Birmingham' and should therefore be prepared for that possibility (John, 1987, p. 20). Rather, our commitment to developing a broadly conceived ARE policy in which the particular circumstances of ethnically homogeneous schools and colleges are acknowledged should derive from the conviction that all students must be incorporated in the development of more emancipatory forms of education. The realization of this goal cannot, and should not, be dependent on spatial, residential or demographic factors. As the enquiry into the murder of Ahmed Iqbal Ullah at Burnage High School, Manchester revealed, an anti-racist movement which does not (or refuses to) recruit the support of white citizens is bound to fail; it is likely to exacerbate differences and polarize students according to perceived racial differences (MacDonald *et al.*, 1988). The imperative then must be to move beyond the identification of tactics and reliance on opportunism. We must aim to formulate an interventionist strategy which has a clearly specified *raison d'etre*. Put simply, we must try and ensure that our various initiatives cohere into an organized model which has a distinctive theoretical base and is invested with intellectual rigour and rationality. Ambitious goals, certainly; nonetheless, these must be our target if the failure of the Swann Committee is not to be repeated.

I want to concentrate on the following things in this chapter. To start with, I want briefly to trace the emergence of inclusive conceptions of MCE and ARE in the UK in recent years. I will then consider some of the reasons why these programmatic sets of reform have failed to secure a firm toe-hold in schools and colleges outside the main urban centres. From there I will offer a framework for intervention along ARE lines based on the concepts of 'selection' and 'learning'. This is intended to have relevance to all educationists, irrespective of their location or the demographic and ethnic profile of their students. The model will be fleshed out with some comments about curriculum content, materials and pedagogy. Finally some formative comments on the model will be made in the light of its implementation in a college of further education (FE) in an all-white borough[2]. Let's begin, however, with what can now be construed by antiracists as the relative optimism of the late '70s and early '80s.

From 'Special Needs' to 'Education for All'

In sharp contrast to the late 1980s the first two Thatcher administrations saw the proliferation and expansion of race equality policies at the local state level. Within this progressive approach to race-related matters it was possible to discern a shift in the specific debate about 'MCE'. Without wishing to oversimplify the complex nature of this debate it could be said to have focused primarily on the orientation and emphasis of this educational philosophy. Originally conceived as an educational response to what white policy-makers and educationalists defined as the 'special needs' of students from Afro-Caribbean and South Asian backgrounds, MCE is now increasingly interpreted as a philosophy and set of practices which has implications for all schools and colleges, irrespective of their location or the ethnic backgrounds of their students. This concept of MCE constituted the essential motif of the Swann Committee's final report and underpinned the principle of 'Education for All' which it commended to the Secretary of State for Education in March 1985 (DES, 1985). This inclusive definition has also figured increasingly in the policy statements on MCE issued by local education authorities (LEA), schools and colleges (Troyna and Williams, 1986).

If there is now general agreement about the orientation of multicultural education the same cannot be said about its proposed emphasis in policy or practice. On the one hand are those committed to cultural pluralism. On this view, teaching from a multicultural perspective prioritizes the inclusion and promotion of ethnic minority lifestyles and cultures in the curriculum and teaching aids. The rationale for this approach derives from the assumption that it encourages white students' empathy with (and tolerance of) ethnic minority groups and mitigates their prejudice and discrimination against those groups. This conception of MCE figured prominently in *Education for All* and is pre-eminent in the UK and elsewhere (Banks and Lynch, 1986; Bullivant, 1981) despite the questionable, some might say spurious status of its underlying principles and assumptions (Troyna, 1987). On the other hand, there has been the more recent emergence and gradual diffusion of anti-racist conceptions of educational change. Here, the concern is with white institutions rather than black groups. That is to say, 'us' rather than 'them'. In this model we find less emphasis on the lifestyles and cultures of ethnic minority groups and greater attention to the structures which produce, sustain and legitimate values and practices which help maintain racial inequality. Furthermore, this conception eschews the conservative model of schooling which gives vent to rationalist models of reform and demands a radical and comprehensive reappraisal of the nature and function of formal education. To a greater or lesser extent, ARE principles informed the policies of LEAs such as Berkshire, Brent, Haringey, Manchester and the Inner London Education Authority (ILEA), although in some of these LEAs the commitment is becoming increasingly hesitant and ambiguous. However, because of their ostensibly radical approach to change within and beyond their individual educational institutions these LEAs have been demonized in the media and denunciated by Margaret Thatcher, Kenneth Baker and other 'anti-antiracists' as anathema to 'good' education. The veracity of these criticisms need not detain us here. But it is important to acknowledge their role in inhibiting the diffusion of ARE and strengthening professional (and political) resistance to its adoption. We must also recognize that policy pronouncements on MCE and ARE since 1981 have been more in evidence than the enactment of the practices they are intended to prompt. Put another way, there is often a great divide between the principles espoused in LEA, school and college policies and what takes place on 'the chalk face' (Troyna and Ball, 1987). And I've already hinted that this divide is often not attenuated by policy-makers, writers and spokespersons on MCE and ARE who, when presented with the opportunity to exemplify their philosophy in practice, fail to do so. This criticism is especially pertinent in the two contexts which compel attention in this chapter: predominantly/all-white areas and the post-16 further education sector. Now, on the face of it there has been a growing demand for the infusion of MCE (and, to a lesser extent, ARE) principles in colleges of FE where there are few, if any, ethnic minority students. For instance, the former Chief Officer of the Further Education Unit (FEU) of the Department of Education and Science insisted in his endorsement of the Unit's policy statement on MCE that changes are 'important not only in inner-city colleges with substantial numbers of black students, but in all establishments and types of courses, whatever the composition of the student body' (FEU, 1985, p. i). This commitment also has been espoused in publications issued by the Commission for Racial Equality and the National Association of Teachers in Further and Higher Education. However, a critical perusal of these documents shows that the examples of 'good practice' to which they allude and the curricular changes they prescribe are, by and large, derived from and relevant to inner-city, multi-ethnic colleges. Three recent examples should be sufficient to illustrate this point. Let's begin with Lord Swann's report, *Education for All*.

Despite the commitment to an inclusive definition of MCE Lord Swann and his colleagues abdicated responsibility for demonstrating how this might be operationalized beyond multiethnic contexts. Instead, as Steve Harrison (1986) has pointed out, the approach and format of the report was at variance with its central proposition of 'Education for All'. For instance, all the parental forums organized by the Committee were held in ethnically-mixed areas. Furthermore, language and religious education, the curriculum areas put under the microscope by the Committee, were appraised only 'from the perspectives of second language learners and those who follow religions other than Christianity' (*ibid.*, p. 184). Clearly, the relevance of these deliberations to the institutions in predominantly/all-white areas is at best limited, at worst non-existent. The Swann Committee offered little concrete guidance as to how the philosophy, 'Education for All', might be taken to obviate teachers' resistance (or just plain indifference) to its proposed reforms.

Further evidence of this discrepancy between espoused philosophy and specific guidance on its implementation could be found in the borough where Libby Selman and I carried out our action research project. Along with its neighbouring LEAs the borough had formulated a policy on MCE which we were told had been circulated on publication to all local schools and colleges. The policy is firmly based on what I have already characterized as a multicultural paradigm. Its main thrust, after a synoptic account of its responsibilities under Section 71 of the 1976 Race Relations Act[3], is an analysis of the perceived linguistic, religious and dietary needs of the various local ethnic minority communities and advice on how these might be satisfied within the borough's provision of services. The policy shares with the Swann Report support for cultural pluralism as an informing principle of how educational provision should be formulated and delivered. It encourages a firm rejection of an educational service premised on traditional ethnocentric, even racist assumptions. We are told that the benefits for all pupils of an education service delivered from, and underpinned by, a cultural pluralist perspective are *independent* of the local presence or otherwise of ethnic minority communities. This inclusive conception of MCE, justified primarily on instrumental grounds, is stressed in the introduction to the policy:

> To believe that there is no need to consider the cultures of others since they are not within our own parish is utterly to ignore the changes in our society in mobility and in what constitutes being British in the 1980s. (n.d., p. 1)

Having provided a rationale for a philosophy of MCE which implicates all local colleges and schools the policy then provides examples of 'good practice' and *modus operandi* which are limited exclusively to relations between staff and ethnic minority pupils. In short, the policy defines and confines MCE to a conception of reform which has relevance only to ethnically-mixed settings. It therefore provides an emphatic denial of its own apparent philosophy! But more than this. The reproduction of this restrictive definition of MCE at borough level has the potential to sanction its restricted implementation to ethnically-mixed contexts. By failing to offer specific advice on how predominantly/all-white educational institutions might contribute towards the promotion of cultural pluralist ideas (and, more especially, the enhancement of racial equality in education) the policy can be viewed as the borough's benediction of the 'no problem here' posture already adopted by most practitioners in the area.

Nor are so-called radical contributors to the debate immune from criticism.

In his book, *The Realization of Anti-racist Teaching* (1986) Godfrey Brandt provides a careful and detailed exposition of ARE principles and pedagogy. He then turns to exemplars of ARE teaching by what we are told are ' "ordinary" teachers in "ordinary" schools' (p. 148). Unfortunately, however, these vignettes are all based in ethnically-mixed settings and are therefore discrepant with the fact that 'the majority of Britain's population does not live in inner cities, nor is it in regular contact with non-white people' (Taylor, 1984–5, p. 1).

Framework for Intervention: 'Selection' and 'Learning'

It was impatience with these sleights of hand in policy and theory on MCE coupled with the more general malaise affecting the organization of MCE and ARE beyond inner-city contexts which prompted an attempt to develop a clear rationale for intervention in ethnically homogeneous schools and colleges. Elsewhere I have suggested that the distinction between the 'selection' and 'learning' aspects of education provides an expedient context for crystallizing appropriate strategies. The analytical distinction derives from the work of Lyn Yates in Victoria, Australia. She found it useful in highlighting the different ways in which sexism impacts on the experiences of students in schools (Yates, 1988). For us it helps clarify the complex nature and dimensions of racial inequality in a range of educational settings and suggests the sort of strategies needed to combat their expression, reproduction and legitimation (Troyna, 1988a). I want to argue that 'learning' provides a rationale for interventions along ARE lines in institutions where there are few, if any, black students. But let me begin by unpacking these two concepts.

In multiethnic schools and colleges concern about the educational experiences and progress of students centres largely on matters of 'selection' or 'who gets what' in the allocation and distribution of educational rewards. Efforts are geared towards exploring the opportunities available, courses followed and qualifications obtained by students; to tease out any discrepancies which might exist along ethnic (class or gender) lines and to introduce strategies which might counteract these disparities. It was due to concern about 'who gets what' that the Swann Committee was set up in 1979[4].

In the late 1970s the apparent discrepancy between the educational outcomes of black and white pupils had compelled the attention of the Select Committee on Race Relations and Immigration (SCRRI) and in its final report to the Labour government the Committee had recommended the setting up of 'a high level and independent enquiry into the causes of underachievement of children of West Indian origin' (1978, p. xx). Indeed since the early '60s the issue of 'who gets what' has dominated the debate about the education of black pupils in the same way as it had earlier characterized policy initiatives on the experiences of working-class pupils in British schools (Williams, 1986) The result has been the introduction of various 'do-able' initiatives to stem the tide of differentially worse outcomes and opportunities for black students.

'Selection', then, has provided a justificatory framework for MCE and ARE reforms.

Quite obviously, however, 'selection' — the issue of how scarce educational rewards are distributed amongst students of different ethnic origins — is not a pressing matter in predominantly/all-white establishments. Therefore neither this criterion of racial inequality nor the strategies which stem from it are suitable for these schools and colleges. But, this is not to say that racial inequality is not a feature of the experiences of students here. Following Lyn Yates, then, I would suggest that in these settings the theme of 'learning' must become the fulcrum around which MCE and ARE initiatives should operate. Thus there is less emphasis on the overt and quantifiable aspects of racial inequality, more on the ethos, curriculum and pedagogical features of educational institutions which contribute to what young people learn about themselves, others and their social world. The central imperative then becomes: to what extent are the educational experiences and *learning* contexts of young people in these establishments structured in ways which will challenge those less obvious, more diffuse but no less insidious means by which racism and the practices it gives rise to are maintained and reproduced?

This, then, constitutes the rationale for intervention in predominantly/all-white areas of the country, and it is to the elaboration of this that the chapter is geared. To start with we need to be clear about the precise form this intervention should assume. Well, I noted earlier that prevailing models of MCE which emphasize the celebration of ethnic lifestyles in the hope that this will improve the life chances of black youth are premised on shaky ground. This is not the place to develop an elaborate critique of MCE. A number of attacks on this philosophy have already been mounted (for example, Mullard, 1984; Brandt, 1986; Hatcher, 1987; Troyna, 1987). A more pressing concern is to specify principles which will inform an effective, intellectually rigorous and politically defensible campaign against racial inequality in *all* schools and colleges.

In my view, it is important to organize interventions around ARE principles. From this vantage point, the main goal is to empower students to challenge the practices and ideological supports of racial injustice. Now, this does not discard entirely the value of white students learning about the religions and experiences of Britain's black communities. But neither does it distort its significance by privileging this dimension above all others. It may be a necessary but certainly not a sufficient consideration in the framing of the intervention. As the Institute of Race Relations (1982) has put it: 'Just to learn about other people's cultures is not to learn about the racism of one's own. To learn about the racism of one's own culture, on the other hand, is to approach other cultures objectively' (p. iv). Building on Stuart Hall's seminal contribution to the debate about 'race' and education (1980) I would contend that ARE must be geared towards probing the manner in which racism rationalizes and helps maintain injustice and the differential power accorded to groups in society. This eschews approaches which focus narrowly on individualized forms of racism within institutions and concentrates instead on broader social relations. That is to say, what is studied from this perspective is the social and racial formation of the state and how it might be possible to transform it. Quite clearly such complex and sophisticated considerations cannot logically be broached if the issues of 'race' and racism are dislocated from the broader social, political and historical processes of society which have institutionalized unequal power. However, the tendency in 'race relations' teaching has been to do just that and convey to students a distorted and misleading view of how 'race' constitutes an organizing and discriminating variable in UK society. The result: what Paul Gilroy (1987) calls 'the coat-of-paint theory' prevails (p. 5). This state of affairs is naive and politically maladroit. It obfuscates the role of racism, sets up in effect (if not intent) a hierarchy of oppression and has the potential to induce feelings of guilt amongst white pupils. In short, it is divisive. What is more, its effacy as a teaching strategy is erratic, to say the least (Stenhouse *et al.*, 1982). What I am suggesting then is that ARE, whilst not obscuring the salience and specificity of racial inequality, needs to lay 'bare the *various* forms of oppression' (John, 1987, p. 21, my emphasis). In this way it avoids the trap of reductionism and essentialism (Wolpe, 1988), characteristics which continue to dominate interventionist strategies in so-called Racism Awareness Training programmes and, as the Burnage High School episode showed, in certain school-based anti-racist strategies.

In more precise terms, this conception of ARE takes as its starting point the view that racism constitutes an ideological lens through which people perceive and interpret their reality. This interpretation has parallels with Cashmore's insistence that there is a 'logic of racism'. As he argues, the particular circumstances in which people live their lives heighten the potential of racism as an appealing and plausible mode of reasoning; an explanatory framework which is seen to be logical and which 'informs many day-to-day judgments and, in turn, actions' (Cashmore, 1987, p. 3). There is a range of empirical studies of 'commonsense racism' which support Cashmore's argument. These include Husbands' exploration of the reasons for National Front (NF) support in various urban settings (1983); the study of racism on the football terraces completed by John Williams and his colleagues (Williams, Dunning and Murphy, 1984) and the analysis of adolescents and politics by Raymond Cochrane and Michael Billig (1984). In the last study, for instance, we are provided with vivid snapshots of the way in which the logic of racism operates with young white people and encourages some of them to support NF policies. As the researchers inform us, the NF constituted a clearly articulated symbol for many youngsters who saw their life chances threatened by the local presence of black people: 'Feeling that something must be done in the face of economic decline, they were drawn to the conclusion that the repatriation of non-white immigrants was the only possible policy' (Billig and Cochrane, 1987, p. 50). If this 'logic', or conception of reality is to be challenged seriously then superior and more plausible explanations need to be provided.

And, as I said earlier, this cannot be achieved through a narrow, exclusive focus on 'race relations'. The aim must be to achieve horizontal rather than vertical connections in the exploration and understanding of inequality and oppression. To highlight the interconnecting role of gender, class as well as racial divisions as constitutive elements in the maintenance of hegemonic domination. Needless to say, this broadly conceived intervention eschews the rationalist approach favoured by exponents of MCE (for example, Lynch, 1987) who continue to ignore both its pedagogical and political frailties and the objections to the conservative model of school reform which it implies (Amir, 1969; Connor, 1972; Brewer and Miller, 1986). Amongst a range of dubious features of the liberal premises on which rationalist pedagogy is based it is important to recognize its potential to induce guilt, and to stigmatize and exclude white youngsters from the struggle to combat oppression; to put into motion, in other words, the tragic spiral of events which followed the death of Ahmed Iqbal Ullah at Burnage in September 1986. Rather than imposing the burden of racial inequality on white youngsters (*qua* white youngsters) the aim of ARE must be to encourage them to recognize not only the specific nature of racial discourse and practice but the forms of inequality they, themselves, experience and share with black people: as women, students, young people, residents in an economically depressed area of the UK or as members of the working class. To distil commodities within a framework where differences are recognized[5].

So, how do we operationalize this strategic model? Well, it seems to me that it calls for the identification of core concepts around which teaching sessions revolve, materials emerge and analysis develops. As Bernard Crick (1978) reminds us: 'We perceive and think in concepts'; they are the 'building blocks with which we construct a picture of the external world' (p. 47). Margaret Robson (1988) has shown how the concepts 'struggle' and 'shortage' might be used as the basis for anti-racist interventions whilst my research with Libby Selman indicated that 'rights' and 'bias' were particularly appropriate concepts around which sessions could be organized. But the identification of core concepts through which students can interrogate beliefs, values and ideologies does not, and should not, comprise the whole story of ARE. Although I agree with Ian Lister (1987) that 'progressive' forms of education have tended to be 'process rich/content poor', nonetheless, we must be sensitive to the influential role played by school/college organization, patterns of classroom control and pedagogy in relation to the transmission of values and assumptions. It is important, then, that organizational, administrative and pedagogical arrangements are congruent with (and supportive of) ARE principles as they are promulgated through the 'formal' curriculum (see Carrington and Troyna, 1988).

In all, then, the framework for intervention comprises the following discrete but complementary strands: learning about rights, learning about collaboration and learning new perspectives. The substantive representation of these strands is presented in Figure 10.1.

Figure 10.1: A Framework for Multicultural and Anti-Racist Education

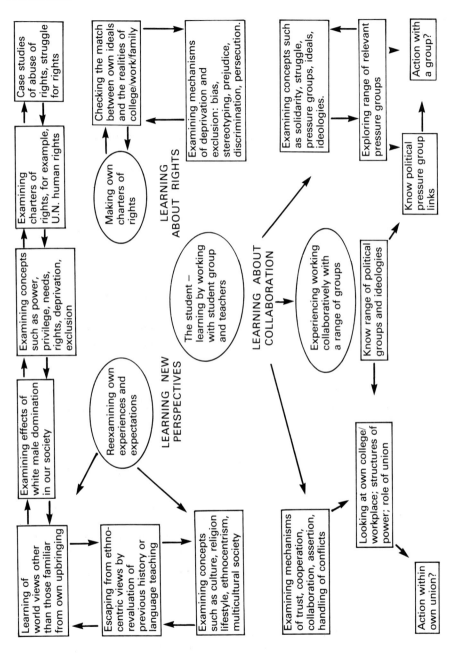

It should be clear from the framework that whilst it departs from Swann's exhortation for moves towards cultural pluralist approaches it shares many of the properties of political education as it is defined by the Swann Committee and Billig and Cochrane (1987), as a means of subverting the attraction of racist politics to young people. As the Swann Committee put it:

> Effective political education should...lead youngsters to consider fundamental issues such as social justice and equality and this should in turn cause them to reflect on the origins and mechanism of racism and prejudice. (DES, 1985, p. 336)

I want to turn now briefly to a discussion of the implementation of the model in a college of further education in the North of England (fuller details of the action research project can be found in Troyna and Selman, 1989).

The Project: 'Monoculturalism Thrives...'

I have already noted that the borough in which the college is located has made only gestural noises about racial equality. It is an area of the UK where 'monoculturalism thrives' in the formulation of social and educational policy (Keel and Briggs, 1986). However, the region has also witnessed increased attacks on black council housing residents, the widespread distribution of racist propaganda and vigorous recruitment campaigns organized by the National Front and British National Party. Against this background a recent survey in the region revealed that 40 per cent of a sample of teachers insisted that multicultural education was not relevant to their school (Biott, *et al.*, 1983).

Neither the college nor the Liberal Studies Department (where the project formally was based) had a policy on race-related matters, handling racist incidents or the teaching of controversial issues. These matters were dealt with in an *ad hoc* and inconsistent manner. Racism, on the whole, was conceived by staff in psychologistic terms; a personal and aberrant disposition which should be dealt with in an individualistic and incremental manner, if and when necessary. It was not interpreted as an ideology which, along with sexism, channelled political oppression and demanded coherent and systematic opposition. As a member of the college's senior management said: '...a direct attack on racist attitudes leads to entrenched positions...a direct frontal approach, assault, sometimes worsens the situation'. The institutional ethos and routinized practices of the college exemplified the 'no problem here' ideology. However, this is not surprising given the salience of 'who gets what' in the popular rationale for MCE.

Our research project suffered from the usual problems associated with externally-funded research. At best, then, it constituted a brief, episodic intervention into the learning experiences of three groups of students following vocational and academic courses[6]. Any lasting impact was likely to be vitiated by a range of extraneous factors: the utilitarian ethds of the college and student cultures; the marginal role of liberal studies in the students' personal curricula and the limited time available for the research. What is more, we were intervening at a late stage of their educational careers. This had two major implications for the initiative. First, by late adolescence political (and racial) assumptions and convictions are entrenched and difficult to dislodge (White, 1983, pp. 110–4). Second, whilst it may be relatively easy to eschew the 'benign authoritarianism' which prevails in classrooms and encourage more participatory methods of learning, it is more difficult at this stage to initiate and sustain genuine cooperation. For students who have already experienced 15,000 hours of formal education competitive individualism is considered *de rigueur*. Reflecting on her own experiences Judy Gallaghan (1988) has noted that by this stage of their educational lives students have

> . . . always studied on (their) own. You couldn't let anyone see your work in case they copied it and managed to squeeze through the gate ahead of you. You knew the fewer the people pushing at the gate, the better your chances of getting through. (p. 5)

Michael Marland (1987) has lamented the absence of research into the causal link, if any, between 'specific teaching about racism' and 'children's theories and their attitudes' (p. 127). I suspect he will be frustrated by this research. We made no attempt to collect quantifiable data about the efficacy of the project in relation to individual attitudes. Our concern was less with changes along psychologistic lines, more with encouraging a general realization amongst students (and staff) of the pernicious and pervasive nature of racism and its dialectic relationship with gender and class-based forms of oppression. Above all, we were interested in generating sufficient concern amongst students that they might assume responsibility in collaboration with staff for the development of an anti-racist ethos in the college. By this I mean a determination to ensure that the norms, beliefs, attitudes which are reflected in institutional patterns and routinized practices should be compatible with, rather than discrepant from, the principles of anti-racism which I proposed earlier. Given the enormous constraints imposed on the project a formal evaluation of the interventionist model I have recommended must be held in abeyance, at least until it can be implemented across a broader range of courses and for a more prolonged period. My tentative assessment of the project is based on various and diffuse qualitative sources: discussions with students; comments submitted on the evaluation sheets; remarks made to college lecturers; discussions during the teaching sessions and so on. As might be expected these discursive data are diverse, fragmented and contradictory; they are impossible to cohere into a distinctive and organized pattern. Perhaps a better indication of the impact of the project has been the range of initiatives along MCE and ARE lines which has taken place since we entered the college in April 1987. For instance: the Students' Union has formulated an equal opportunities policy and appointed an officer with responsibilities for its implementation. The senior management of the college has accepted the need for a more coherent and effective approach to anti-racist, anti-sexist education and is in the process of adopting a formal policy affirming its commitment to these principles. It has also endorsed proposals for a programme of staff development. Changes have also taken place in the college library. The presence of the project helped sensitize both students and the librarian to the anachronistic and offensive titles on the library shelves. These have been removed. Now it would be disingenuous for the project to assume entire responsibility for this progress. Nonetheless, its presence clearly had a catalytic effect. For these educationists working in multiethnic areas where the LEA has a clearly articulated policy on ARE and the necessary services and resources to facilitate its diffusion amongst local schools; or, for those activists whose campaigns for racial equality crystalize around the observable and quantifiable matter of selection (or 'who gets what') these initiatives may appear piecemeal — tentative steps along the road to racial equality in education. They are. But in an educational setting where, in the words of one lecturer, 'you hardly see a black face'; where Swann's calls for action have fallen on deaf ears and where, historically, racist views have been expressed almost with impunity and racist recruitment drives outside school gates have intensified in recent years, these developments could be seen as an important challenge to the status quo. In the context of the 'new realism' where more and more LEAs are cutting their programmes on race equality we shall be increasingly dependent on exploiting 'loopholes' in legislation (Ouseley, 1988) and 'goodwill' to secure gains in the campaign for ARE. The imperative must be to build on these initiatives.

Acknowledgment

I would like to thank Fazal Rizvi for his constructive comments on an earlier draft of this chapter.

Notes

1 The designation of areas as 'ethnically homogeneous' does, of course, reproduce racist understandings of diversity. Such areas commonly include considerable diversity but this is often overlooked because it is not structured along perceived racial lines. I have discussed the problematic notion of 'ethnicity' in educational research elsewhere (Troyna, 1988c).
2 The research project referred to in this article was funded by the Further Education Unit of the Department of Education and Science. I am grateful to Alan Murray (formerly of the FEU) and Libby Selman, the Research Associate on the project for their guidance and support during the research period: April 1987–September 1988. Full details of the research project (RP 412) can be found in Troyna and Selman (1989).
3 Section 71 of the 1976 Race Relations Act places a general statutory duty on local authorities 'to eliminate unlawful racial discrimination, and to promote equality of opportunity and good race relations'.

4 Of course the narrow concern with the educational issue of 'who gets what' was inextricably linked to the view that the persistent 'underachievement' of black pupils would threaten the credibility of the meritocratic ideal and have profound social and political implications. I have addressed this question elsewhere (Troyna, 1986 and 1988b).
5 This approach has also been recommended for community workers in multiethnic settings (Thomas, 1986, for example).
6 The three groups comprised full-time students following GCSE integrated humanities; first year catering students and second year nursery nursing students. In combination, the selected groups offered variations of vocational choice, and a major contrast between the context of a GCSE course and the non-examined liberal studies hours. In terms of gender, the contrast was only between all-female and mixed groups. There was little variation in age since all groups included students aged between 17 and 23, with the majority at the younger end of the range.

References

AMIR, Y. (1969) 'Contact hypothesis in ethnic relations', *Psychological Bulletin*, 71, 5, pp. 319–42.
BANKS, J. and LYNCH, J. (Eds) (1986) *Multicultural Education in Western Societies*, Eastbourne, Holt, Rinehart and Winston.
BILLIG, M. and COCHRANE, R. (1987) 'Adolescents and politics' in MCGURK, H. (Ed.) *What Next? An Introduction to Research on Young People*, London, Economic and Social Research Council.
BIOTT, C. *et al.* (1983) 'Beyond the policy threshold', unpublished working paper, Sunderland Polytechnic.
BRANDT, G. (1986) *The Realization of Anti-racist Teaching*, Lewes, Falmer Press.
BREWER, M. and MILLER, N. (1986) 'Contact and co-operation: when do they work?' in KATZ, P. and TAYLOR, D. (Eds) *Eliminating Racism: Profiles in Controversy*, London, Plenum Press, pp. 315–26.
BROWN, C. (1988) 'The "White Highlands..." Anti-racism?', *Multicultural Teaching*, 6, 2, pp. 38–9.
BULLIVANT, B. (1981) *The Pluralist Dilemma in Education*, London, Allen and Unwin.
CARRINGTON, B. and TROYNA, B. (Eds) (1988) *Children and Controversial Issues: Strategies for the Early and Middle Years of Schooling*, Lewes, Falmer Press.
CASHMORE, E. (1987) *The Logic of Racism*, London, Unwin.
COCHRANE, R. and BILLIG, M. (1984) 'I'm not National Front myself, but...' *New Society*, 17 May, pp. 255–8.
CONNOR, W. (1972) 'Nation-building or nation-destroying', *World Politics: A Quarterly Journal of International Relations*, 24, pp. 319–55.
CRICK, B. (1978) 'Basic concepts for political education' in CRICK, B. and PORTER, A. (Eds) *Political Education and Political Literacy*, London, Longman, pp. 47–62.
DEPARTMENT OF EDUCATION AND SCIENCE (1985) *Education for All: Report of the Committee of Enquiry into the Education of Children from Ethnic Minority Groups* (The Swann Report) Cmnd 9543, London, HMSO.
FURTHER EDUCATION UNIT (1985) *Curriculum Development for a Multicultural Society: Policy and Curriculum*, London, FEU.
GAHAGHAN, J. (1988) 'Wisdom and wealth, *the* Great education hoax', *New Internationalist*, February, pp. 4–6.
GAINE, C. (1987) *No Problem Here*, London, Hutchinson.
GILROY, P. (1987) *Problems in Anti-racist Strategy*, London, Runnymede Trust.

HALL, S. (1980) 'Teaching race', *Multicultural Education*, 9, pp. 3–12.

HARRISON, S. (1986) 'Swann: The implications for schools', *Journal of Education Policy*, 1, 2, pp. 183–95.

HATCHER, R. (1987) ' "Race" and education: Two perspectives for change' in TROYNA, B. (Ed.) *Racial Inequality in Education*, London, Tavistock, pp. 184–200.

HUSBANDS, C. (1983) *Racial Exclusionism and the City*, London, Allen and Unwin.

INSTITUTE OF RACE RELATIONS (1982) *Roots of Racism*, London, Institute of Race Relations.

JOHN, G. (1987) 'Antiracist education in white areas: A movement in search of a focus', *Sage Race Relations Abstracts*, 13, 3, pp. 17–24.

KEEL, P. and BRIGGS, M. (1986) 'Introduction', *Multicultural Teaching*, 4, 3, p. 3.

LISTER, I. (1987) 'Global and international approaches in political education' in HARBER, C. (Ed.) *Political Education in Britain*, Lewes, Falmer Press, pp. 47–62.

LITTLE, A. and WILLEY, R. (1981) *Multi-Ethnic Education: The Way Forward* (Schools Council Pamphlet 18), London, Schools Council.

LYNCH, J. (1987) *Prejudice Reduction and the Schools*, London, Cassell.

MACDONALD, I., BHAVNANI, R., JOHN, G. and KHAN, L. (1988) *Racism and Racial Violence in Manchester Schools,* Press Release.

MARLAND, M. (1987) 'The education of and for a multi-racial and multi-lingual society: Research needs post-Swann', *Educational Research*, 29, 2, pp. 116–29.

MULLARD, C. (1984) *The Three O's*, London, NAME.

NEWSAM, P. (1986) 'Beating bias', *Times Educational Supplement*, 27 June.

OUSLEY, H. (1988) 'Resisting Institutional Change', Unpublished paper presented to the conference, Local Authorities and Racial Equality: Policies and Practice, University of Warwick, 24–25 September.

POPPLE, S. and POPPLE, K. (1987) 'Antiracist work in the South West', in TAYLOR, B. (Ed.) *Ethnicity and Prejudice in 'White Highlands' Schools*, Exeter, School of Education, University of Exeter (Perspectives 35), pp. 27–30.

ROBSON, M. (1987) *Language, Learning and Race*, London, Longman for FEU Publications.

SELECT COMMITTEE ON RACE RELATIONS AND IMMIGRATION (1978) *The West Indian Community (Vol. 1)*, London, HMSO.

STENHOUSE, L. *et al.* (1982) *Teaching About Race Relations: Problems and Effects*, London, Routledge and Kegan Paul.

TAYLOR, B. (1984/5) 'Multicultural education in a "monocultural" region', *New Community*, 12, 1, pp. 1–8.

TAYLOR, B. (1987) 'Anti-racist education in predominantly white areas', *Journal of Further and Higher Education*, 11, 3, pp. 45–50.

THOMAS, D. (1986) *White Bolts, Black Locks: Participation in the Inner City*, London, Allen and Unwin.

TOWNSEND, H.E.R. and BRITTAN, E. (1972) *Multi-racial Education: Need and Innovation* (Schools Council Working paper 50) London, Schools Council.

TROYNA, B. (1985) 'The great divide: Policies and practices in multicultural education', *British Journal of Sociology of Education*, 6, 2, pp. 210–24.

TROYNA, B. (1986) ' "Swann's song": The origins, ideology and implications of Education for All', *Journal of Education Policy*, 1, 2, pp. 171–81.

TROYNA, B. (1987) 'Beyond multiculturalism: Towards the enactment of anti-racist education in policy, provision and pedagogy', *Oxford Review of Education*, 13, 3, pp. 307–20.

TROYNA, B. (1988a) ' "Selection" and "learning": Frameworks for anti-racist initiatives in education' *Multicultural Teaching*, 6, 3, pp. 5–7.

TROYNA, B. (1988b) 'British schooling and the reproduction of racial inequality' in CROSS, M. and ENTZINGER, H. (Eds) *Lost Illusions: Caribbean Minorities in Britain and the Netherlands*, London, Routledge, pp. 166–84.

TROYNA, B. (1988c) 'Paradigm regained: A critique of "cultural deficit" perspectives in educational research', *Comparative Education*, 24, 3, pp. 273–83.

TROYNA, B. and BALL, W. (1987) *Views From the Chalk Face: School Responses to an LEA's Policy on Multicultural Education*, (2nd edn), Coventry, University of Warwick, Centre for Research in Ethnic Relations.

TROYNA, B. and SELMAN, L. (1989) 'Implementing multicultural and antiracist education in all-white colleges' (RP 412), London, Longman for FEU publications.

TROYNA, B. and WILLIAMS, J. (1986) *Racism, Education and the State*, London, Croom Helm.

WHITE, P. (1983) *Beyond Domination: An Essay in the Political Philosophy of Education*, London, Routledge.

WILLIAMS, J. (1986) 'Education and race: The racialisation of class inequalities', *British Journal of Sociology of Education*, 7, 2, pp. 135–54.

WILLIAMS, J., DUNNING, E. and MURPHY, P. (1984) *Hooligans Abroad*, London, Routledge and Kegan Paul.

WOLPE, A.M. (1988) ' "Experience" as analytical framework: Does it account for girls' education?' in COLE, M. (Ed.) *Bowles and Gintis Revisited*, Lewes, Falmer Press, pp. 131–57.

YATES, L. (1988) 'Does "all students" include girls?: Some reflections on recent educational policy practice and theory', *Australian Educational Researcher*, 15, 1, pp. 41–57.

Chapter 11

Warnock and Swann: Similarities and Differences

Peter Mittler

Towards Education For All

The aim of this chapter is to invite comparisons between developments in the fields of special educational needs and multicultural education. It is suggested that the goal of *Education for All* is now at the heart of both movements and that a joint approach to its realization might be productive.

The Warnock and Swann reports (DES, 1978 and 1985) represent a convenient point of departure for such a journey. Both reports are in the great British tradition of committees of enquiry. Both stimulated much public and professional debate and are likely to continue to be influential for some time to come. Both are concerned with the response of society in general and of the education system in particular to children and young people who have been denied equality of opportunity within the education system or in society as a whole and who have suffered varying degrees of deprivation, discrimination and marginalization. Both reports seem to have been motivated by the wish to work for equality of opportunity within the educational system, in the hope that this would at least lay foundations for fuller participation in community life on leaving school. Above all, both reports call for a radical reappraisal of the whole curriculum in the interests of all children, not just those with whom the reports happen to be concerned.

The point has now been reached where 'education for all' can be regarded as equally the goal of the special needs as of the multicultural movement. Although origins can be detected in Warnock and in some of the evidence submitted to it, the demand for a radical reform of the whole curriculum with the aim of ensuring full access for all children in schools is being increasingly clearly articulated from within both the special needs and multicultural constituencies. Unfortunately, but understandably perhaps, the movements are working in parallel rather than in concert.

The Warnock Report and its Aftermath

The Warnock Committee was established in 1974, after years of campaigning by professional and voluntary organizations and pressure groups. It was argued that a committee of enquiry into handicapped children would be the last of the great series of major enquiries since the Second World War into primary, secondary, tertiary, adult and higher education. Successive governments showed little enthusiasm but eventually the Secretary of State for Education and Science of the day (Margaret Thatcher) agreed to the establishment of the committee, and appointed as its chairperson Mary Warnock (now Baroness Warnock, Mistress of Girton College, Cambridge), an Oxford philosophy don and ex-headteacher of a prestigious independent girls' school.

The Committee was established to:

review educational provision...for children and young people handicapped by disabilities of body or mind, taking account of medical aspects of their needs, together with arrangements to prepare them for entry into employment.

One of the first achievements of the Warnock Committee was to broaden its terms of reference to encompass a much larger group — all those children who experience difficulties in learning or in adapting to the demands of school and who therefore required special provision to meet their needs. This difference is referred to in the categorical jargon of the field as that between the 2 per cent and the 18 per cent, the former being mostly children in special schools, the latter consisting of the much larger number of children in ordinary schools who were experiencing problems of learning or adjustment. Accordingly, the Committee recommended that

the planning of services for children and young people should be based on the assumption that about one in six children at any time and one in five children at some time during their school career will require some form of special educational provision.... Our concept of special education...embraces the notion of any form of additional help, wherever it is provided and whenever it is provided, from birth to maturity, to overcome educational difficulty.

Ironically enough, it was a later Secretary of State (Sir Keith Joseph) who, without referring to children with special needs or to children from ethnic minorities, insisted that up to *40 per cent* of children were failing to benefit from schooling and that major educational reforms to the curriculum and management of schools were needed to bring about change.

Can Schools Cause Special Needs?

The shift of emphasis from children with identified handicaps and disabilities to the much larger number who are not deriving full benefit from schooling contributed to the growing conviction that the origins of difficulties lay not merely within the children themselves but were to be sought, in part at least, in the schools, particularly in the design and delivery of the curriculum and in their organization and management. These concerns, echoed by many professionals of very different political and ideological persuasions, led to a number of major developments designed to modify both the school curriculum and the examination system. Although the reforms are intended to benefit all children, those from ethnic minorities and those with special educational needs would stand to gain most if these changes were implemented.

For many years, special education operated on a 'defect' or 'deficit' model, sometimes confused with a medical model. Traditionally, the causes of learning difficulty have been seen as lying largely within the child. First, doctors, then psychologists and teachers, developed increasingly refined diagnostic tests in an effort to pinpoint the nature of the difficulty, in the hope that this knowledge would lead to individually designed remedial programmes. Even though these hopes have remained largely unfulfilled, the within child model is still strongly held by many teachers. Of course, children do have specific impairments, including physical, sensory, intellectual and communication difficulties. But these can never provide the sole explanation for a child's difficulties. The roots of underachievement cannot be simplistically attributed to factors within the child, whether these arise from low intelligence, specific physical, sensory or cognitive deficits or impaired motivation or self-esteem.

The education of children from ethnic minorities has also, in the past at least, operated on a deficit model: it was believed that special measures were needed to compensate either for innately lower intelligence or for inferior linguistic skills.

But if schools are in part contributing to, or causing, underachievement or somehow actually creating special needs, which particular aspects of school practice might be involved? What could be done to identify such influences in the hope that greater awareness might suggest ways in which adverse influences might be addressed?

The conceptual framework now under discussion calls for an attempt to understand the interaction between the child's impairments (if any) and the various environments in which the child is living and learning. Clearly, the micro and macro environments of home, community and school are central to such an understanding (Galloway and Goodwin, 1987; Mittler, 1987).

Whole School Policies

The response of the educational system to this challenge has taken the form of an attempt to modify the curriculum and organization of the school as a whole. An uneasy but productive alliance was formed between the left and right of the educational establishment, resulting in a number of developments designed to reform the organization and delivery of the curriculum in such a way as to make it more accessible to *all* pupils. The most recent and so far untested product of this alliance is the General Certificate of Secondary Education (GCSE). Both the course work and the assessment process of the GCSE represent a major departure from traditional public examinations, designed in part to enlarge the number of pupils who will have access to the Certificate. The extent to which GCSE courses and examinations are truly open to all remains to be seen. So far, the indications are that practice varies greatly from subject to subject and area to area.

A steady stream of HMI and DES documents on curriculum and good practice were issued from the centre during the 1970s. With the publication of the Warnock Report, these documents made increasing reference to ways in which schools could not only more effectively meet special educational needs but actually prevent such needs arising in the first place.

At a general level, concern was focused on the inaccessibility of the full curriculum to many of the children in the school. Some subjects and courses were not thought suitable for certain children. Other children were withdrawn from particular subjects for additional work in English or in order to provide extra help with literacy. National surveys suggested that children with special needs tended to lose out on science and languages (Clunies-Ross and Wimhurst, 1983). At a specific level, concern was expressed about the language of instruction, children not understanding what was required of them and worksheets and textbooks with readability and comprehension levels pitched too high for a significant number of children.

Seen from a special needs perspective, a 'whole school' approach calls for a re-examination of all aspects of the curriculum for all children. Instead of removing children into special schools or special classes or units, it seeks to do everything possible to support both the teacher and the child in the classroom. The avoidance of isolation and segregation is the prime aim, coupled with curriculum modification, curriculum access and in-class support (see Dessent, 1987; Sayer, 1987; and Wolfendale, 1987, for more detailed statements both of the principles and practice of a whole school approach).

A whole school policy is also concerned with ways in which the school is organized and managed and with the value systems which underlie the way the school is run. *Fifteen Thousand Hours* (Rutter, Maughan, Mortimore and Ouston, 1979) emphasized ways in which schools do influence outcomes and life chances for pupils. The study highlighted major differences in 'ethos' between twelve London inner city schools. Above all, the study showed how opportunities for children were related to the characteristics of schools as social institutions. These included a range of factors, such as the extent to which children were able to exercise choice and responsibility, the availability of incentives, an emphasis on activity and engagement, as well as staff teaching styles and behaviour in the classroom.

Another seminal influence from mainstream education has been the series of curriculum reports from the ILEA. Hargreaves' book, *Challenge for the Comprehensive School* (1982), called for a radical reappraisal of the secondary curriculum, a major shift of emphasis from the 'cognitive-academic' curriculum to one which would provide a much wider range of experiences and pupil choice and which would enhance rather than undermine the dignity of the pupil. Some of these ideas were incorporated into the ILEA report *Improving Secondary Education* (ILEA, 1984) which envisages a major reorientation of the curriculum. Parallel reforms of the primary curriculum were proposed in the Thomas Report (ILEA, 1985a). Finally, the Fish Report on special needs, significantly entitled *Equal Opportunities for All?* (note the question mark) is probably the most important policy document on special needs since the Warnock Report some ten years ago (ILEA, 1985b). The report is a landmark because it relates special needs firmly to the equal opportunities movement. A similar demand is articulated by people with disabilities themselves, particularly since the 1981 International Year of Disabled Persons and the foundation of organizations of, rather than for, disabled people.

A number of other developments and suggestions for better practice have been proposed for ordinary schools. If implemented, these would almost certainly benefit all children in schools but particularly those with special needs and from ethnic minorities, though the demand for these changes did not necessarily originate from either of these groups but from a perceived need for change within mainstream education itself. These include records of achievement and profiling, an increasing emphasis on the contribution of pupils themselves in choosing modules of study and in formulating their own profiles. Such pupils would also benefit from different approaches to school-based assessment, with less emphasis on norm-referenced tests which compare pupils with one another or against local or national norms, in favour of criterion-referenced assessment which is concerned with the attainment of skills and competencies in specific tasks.

Common Elements

Clearly, the special needs and multicultural lobbies have much in common. Both are aiming to achieve a higher quality education not only for the children in their 'constituency' but for all children. Both are concerned with the prevention of underfunctioning and low achievement and with the costs to be paid in a sense of failure and in low self-esteem. Both are concerned with the effects of teacher under-expectation and under-demand. Both therefore depend for progress on the willingness of teachers to re-examine not only what and how they teach but how schools are organized and managed (Sayer, 1987).

The Swann Report (DES, 1985) discusses ways in which underachievement and low attainment are related to racist and stereotyping attitudes in society in general and in schools in particular. One expression of stereotyping is the expectation that certain groups are 'unlikely to benefit' from certain experiences and resources—whether they be children from ethnic minorities, girls or children with special needs. The equal opportunities movement aims to confront these dangers by a policy of awareness followed by active monitoring and, where necessary, by positive discrimination or affirmative action.

Policy and practice issues relating to children with special needs and children from ethnic minorities thus have much in common, even though their advocates may prefer for a variety of reasons to fight for the same goals from different vantage points. A brief consideration of some of the common ground will highlight the sensitive nature of the overlap.

Over-representation of Ethnic Minorities in Special Schools

In the first place, it has long been a matter of criticism and controversy that children from Afro-Caribbean families are greatly overrepresented in special schools, particularly those for children with moderate learning difficulties and those for children with emotional and behavioural problems (the former 'ESN(M)' and 'maladjusted' categories). This has understandably been deeply resented by the West Indian community (Coard, 1971). Tomlinson (1981) has documented the process by which children are assessed as failing and the step-by-step decisions that lead to their removal from ordinary into special schools. Her research confirmed that a disproportionate number of children sent to special schools for children with moderate learning difficulties are from Afro-Caribbean families.

The defence offered by LEAs and by the professions has always been that this was in the interests of children who were failing badly in the ordinary school and who needed the small classes and specialized methods which only special schools could offer. Educational achievement, as measured by attainment tests, was stated to be a more important criterion than intelligence, as measured by IQ tests which may be culturally inappropriate.

The 1981 Education Act has sought to avoid confusion and the risk of discriminatory procedures by laying down that children whose language of origin was not English should not be regarded as having special educational needs within the meaning of the Act. But this makes it difficult to help children from homes where English is not the first language; clearly, such children may experience difficulties in school for a variety of reasons, not necessarily connected with language.

Social Disadvantage

A second area of overlap arises from low income, severe poverty and unemployment and their consequences in overcrowding and sub-standard housing and poor health. The Swann Report summarizes evidence on ways in which low income, unemployment (particularly youth unemployment) and poor housing are even more likely to be experienced by certain ethnic minority groups than by the indigenous working-class community.

The association between low achievement and social class has been fully documented for many years and is regarded as an endemic feature of British society and social structures. Fifteen years ago, the National Child Development Study showed that children from socially disadvantaged homes were seven-and-a-half times as likely to be sent to the then ESN schools as other children (Wedge and Prosser, 1973). Despite this, it cannot be sufficiently emphasized that most children from socially disadvantaged families are not sent to special schools and produce average or above average school work and examination results. Even so, such children are almost certainly 'at risk' of having their abilities underestimated in school. Douglas's (1964) early work showed that decisions on streaming in the primary school tended to be influenced by home background, even when children were in the same IQ band.

The links between social background and educational attainment are highly complex and not at all well understood. Much the same can be said of the causes of underachievement in children from ethnic minorities, as the Swann Report has again demonstrated. The technical appendix by Mackintosh and Mascie-Taylor, after an exhaustive discussion of the research evidence, concludes that the small residual differences in educational attainment between British West Indian and indigenous children can largely be attributed to differences in their social circumstances. These are particularly powerful factors in all sections of British society, with a strong advantage for children from middle class backgrounds and professional families at all stages of development and schooling, from the nursery to the university and beyond.

Families of children with special needs tend to come from the poorest and most disadvantaged sections of society. The majority of children in schools for children with moderate learning difficulties, many of those in schools for children with emotional and behavioural difficulties and a substantial number of children in ordinary schools with mild or moderate learning difficulties live in families with low or below average incomes and housing and above average rates of unemployment and ill health. Children with physical and sensory disabilities are more evenly distributed across all social classes. It used to be thought that this also applied to children with severe learning difficulties but more recent evidence suggests that children from working-class backgrounds are somewhat overrepresented (Fryers, 1984).

Professional Ignorance

A third common element is ignorance and lack of information. Understandably, teachers have little experience of children with disabilities who have traditionally been placed in special schools. The current emphasis on returning such children to ordinary schools means that teachers will need to be helped to avoid stereotyped judgments about such children and learn to assess and meet their needs as individuals, rather than as members of a category known as 'handicapped child'. Hence the insistence on the use of non-discriminatory language: we talk less about 'the deaf child' than about 'children with impaired hearing'. The emphasis on the needs of the individual child is another example of the attempt to think first about the child rather than about the disability.

On the other hand, teachers are well aware of the existence of the broader group of children with special needs, not only the one in five in ordinary schools but also those that have been sent to special schools for children with moderate learning or emotional and behavioural difficulties after being judged to be unsuitable for ordinary schools. The success of current policies to reintegrate these children and to retain a new generation in ordinary schools is largely dependent on teacher attitudes which, in turn, depend on accurate information.

Generalizations about children with particular disabilities are as suspect as generalizations based on race or gender. The danger of stereotyped judgments based on lack of information applies as much to children from ethnic minorities as to those with special needs. Just as teachers may lack experience of some groups of children with special needs, so they may lack information about children from ethnic minorities. This is reflected in generalizations about 'Asian' children which ignore major differences within, as well as between, various communities.

At a time when attempts are being made to introduce notions of multicultural education to all schools, including those without any children from ethnic minorities, teachers' lack of experience of such children is a considerable handicap. However, the Swann Report emphasizes that teachers may not always be well informed about the cultures and belief systems of minority groups whose children do attend their schools. This is the background for the Report's insistence that all our schools have to come to terms with the realities of an unequal but rapidly changing pluralist society.

Separate Provision

A fourth set of common and controversial concerns relates to the whole question of separate provision. The Swann Report rehearses the arguments for and against separate schools, particularly in the context of the strong advocacy presented by the Muslim community for single sex schools, as well as the demand for Black schools articulated by sections of the West Indian community. The language of the Swann Report will be familiar to special educators:

> While we fully appreciate the concerns which have led some sections of the Asian community to press for the establishment of their own schools, we do not believe that creating an artificially separate situation in which groups of children are taught exclusively by teachers from the same ethnic group is desirable from the point of view of the children, the minority community or society as a whole and we are not therefore convinced that 'separate' schools can be supported on these grounds. (DES, 1985, para. 2.12)

In the field of special education, the issue of integrated provision has become the central question of special education. Although the principle that handicapped children should be educated in ordinary schools has long been accepted in general terms and has been frequently reiterated as a central plank of national and local policy, the process of implementation has been slow and uneven.

Unlike separate schools for children from ethnic minorities, there has long been a strong tradition of separate special schools. In 1985 there were some 1500 special schools in England and Wales, catering for about 114,000 pupils, an average size of some seventy-five children. The largest number are for children with moderate learning difficulties (55,000), severe learning difficulties (24,000), emotional and behavioural difficulties (13,000) and physical disabilities (11,000) (DES, 1986).

The debate about the integration of children now in special schools into ordinary schools is taking place at several levels. At a moral or ideological level, it is argued that children have a right to be educated alongside their peers and that it is wrong to deprive them of the opportunity of doing so. On this argument, educational integration is part of the equal opportunities movement. Furthermore, pupils should get to know children with disabilities as part of their own personal development and also because this will eventually result in more tolerant and better informed citizens. At the same time, it is argued that ordinary schools should provide for all children in their community even if this entails major changes in their curriculum and organization. Such changes are in any case regarded as inherently desirable because they will benefit all children in the school.

Special schools are criticized because their isolation from other schools and ordinary children provides a poor preparation for life in an integrated adult community. Their teachers are accused of having low expectations and sometimes of over-protecting their children. Also, many special schools can only provide a restricted curriculum — for example, for physically handicapped children of normal intelligence.

On the other hand, the quality of teaching in special schools is often very high. Other strengths include small classes, high adult–child ratios, the availability of welfare assistants and non-teaching assistants in the classroom, flexible timetables, an absence of examination demands, the possibility of mobilizing support from relevant professionals such as psychologists, doctors, therapists and social workers. The challenge to the education system is to ensure that the benefits and strengths of special schools are transferred to the non-segregated setting of the ordinary school.

The demand for integration has been strongly articulated by many professionals and parents of children with disabilities. On the other hand, the views of parents of children with moderate learning difficulties, with emotional and behavioural difficulties and above all of parents of the 18 per cent of children already in ordinary schools are not known. There are no parent organizations to speak for these groups comparable to those representing children with disabilities, such as the Royal Society for Mentally Handicapped Children and Adults, the Spastics Society, the National Deaf Children's Society, the Royal National Institute for the Blind or the Association for All Speech Impaired Children.

Despite a general consensus in favour of integrated education, there is little evidence so far of a major reduction in the proportion of children attending special schools, with the possible exception of children with sensory impairments and physical disabilities. The proportion of children in special schools remains constant, once allowance has been made for falling rolls; indeed, the number of children in schools for children with emotional and social difficulties seems to be increasing (Swann, 1985).

Most LEAs are now establishing special needs departments in secondary schools and designating specialists in primary schools. In addition, strong special needs advisory services are becoming available to support children and teachers in the ordinary school. Special needs teams are also relying less on withdrawal of children from mainstream lessons, as this is simply another form of segregation. Instead, they are seeking to develop a 'whole school' approach which seeks to make the curriculum more accessible and to remove barriers to full participation in the life of the school. This involves in-class support in the ordinary class (Moses, Hegarty and Jowett, 1987).

Recent critics of developments since the 1981 Education Act have highlighted the inherent weaknesses of current provision. Dessent (1987) and Galloway and Goodwin (1987) suggest that some of the new developments are inherently divisive and segregationist. For example, the creation of special needs departments or faculties in secondary schools can lead to other teachers regarding special needs as someone else's responsibility. Similarly, the management and staffing of special needs posts both within schools, in the support services and in the management structures of LEAs themselves can strengthen the very divisions which they are designed to remove. Indeed, the increasing contact between special and ordinary schools can actually lead to an increase in referral of children to special provision.

The success of current efforts clearly depends on the willingness of ordinary schools not only to retain children but to meet their needs. Schools' tolerance thresholds, especially for behaviour that they regard as difficult or disruptive, varies greatly from school to school), as the *Fifteen Thousand Hours* study showed (Rutter *et al.*, 1979). Such children are still sent in large numbers not only to 'schools for the maladjusted' but also to other special schools, including those for children with moderate learning difficulties, and even schools for the delicate. In addition, increasing use is made of what is euphemistically termed 'off-site provision'—better known as 'sin-bins' (Lloyd-Smith, 1984).

The barriers to fuller integration of children now in special schools are therefore partly attitudinal, partly financial and partly a matter of tradition. But despite the slow pace of progress in practice, there is strong agreement with the principle of integration among the majority of professionals, policy makers and parents. This commitment is frequently expressed in the language of *Education for All*.

Home–school Relationships

Parents and teachers have traditionally kept each other at arms' length, despite the demonstrated benefits of collaboration. In the field of special needs, however, bridges between home and school have begun to be built even though most examples of successful partnership have come from the field of severe learning difficulties (Mittler and McConachie, 1983). Families of children with moderate learning difficulties and emotional and behavioural difficulties, far less families of the broader group of children with mild learning difficulties already in ordinary schools have not on the whole benefited from the 'parents as partners' platform so strongly established in the Warnock Report and developed in later practice.

Families of children with special needs are all too easily stereotyped by teachers. A comment such as 'What do you expect from a child from that kind of family?' can be considered as damaging as any racist or sexist stereotype. Parents who do not attend parent meetings held at school are dismissed as 'not interested in their children's education' or as 'hostile to the school and all it stands for'.

On the other hand, an increasing number of schools are finding new ways of working with parents. The 'paired reading' movement has highlighted the advantages of teachers and parents working together in listening to children read (Topping and Wolfendale, 1985). A number of community education projects have brought parents and teachers into productive working and social relationships (Widlake, 1985). The parents have come not from traditional affluent, middle-class areas but from inner city areas characterized by deprivation and disadvantage.

Families from ethnic minorities have also been the victims of stereotyped attitudes and judgments not only on account of their ethnic origins but also because it was assumed that communication problems would make contact and collaboration difficult or impossible. Teachers have also been anxious not to intrude on the privacy of such families and feared they would not be welcome.

Projects reported by Widlake (*ibid.*) have richly demonstrated the possibilities of developing effective and supportive relationships between parents and teachers, once traditional assumptions and practices are put aside. For example, teachers should not be discouraged when parents fail to attend school meetings but should explore the possibility of their visiting families at home. The day may come when visits to the home are accepted as part of the work of all teachers, not only those working with special children.

Once again, successful practice in one field raises questions for the whole of education. Why should home–school links only work for children with special needs or those from ethnic minorities? Does not the success of such work suggest that we need to rethink our whole approach to all parents?

Teacher Education

Changes as fundamental as those demanded in the Warnock and Swann reports call for matching initiatives in the field of teacher education. The reorientation of the whole curriculum demanded in these reports requires a reappraisal of the whole of teacher education, at pre-service and in-service levels. Every area of the curriculum will need re-examination in order to ensure that special needs and multicultural elements have been included. The Warnock Committee went as far as to say that every serving teacher should be given the equivalent of a five-day awareness course. Ten years later, it is ironic to recall their calculation that 200 additional lecturers would be needed to implement this recommendation alone.

Exhortation and rhetoric, even when matched by institutional commitment, will not change teacher education. So how much can be achieved with the staffing and funds currently available?

Special needs and multicultural education are now the twin imperatives of teacher education. The central government and its agencies have begun to insist that institutions involved in initial teacher training demonstrate not merely that special needs and multicultural elements are available as options but that both are regarded as compulsory features of the course for all teacher training students. Failure to do so could result first in an adverse HMI report, then an injunction to change by the Council for the Accreditation of Teacher Education (CATE). The final sanction is withdrawal of accreditation for teacher training from the institution as a whole.

The teacher education recommendations of the two reports are broadly similar, though Swann is considerably more detailed than Warnock. For this reason, a brief summary of the main Swann recommendations will be given, since virtually all of them are equally relevant in a special needs context. For example, references to a pluralist society should be seen as including children with disabilities and difficulties, however these may be caused.

Initial Training (BEd and PGCE)

1 All courses to be permeated with a 'genuinely pluralist approach to education' (2.12).
2 Optional courses should also be available (2.16).
3 All students should have the opportunity to gain experience in multiracial schools (2.22).
4 HMI, CATE and training and validating institutions should monitor progress (2.24).

5 Induction training needs to pay more attention to pluralist issues (3.3 and 3.5).

In-service Courses

1 All INSET courses (including management and all award-bearing courses) should reflect 'the multiplicity of cultures, faiths and languages in present day society' (3.12–3.14).
2 Some teacher training institutions to be centres of specialism (3.15).
3 The DES should fund evaluation of Racism Awareness Training courses (3.17).
4 The DES should fund pilot projects in all-white areas to help teachers to adopt a pluralistic perspective (3.18).
5 New in-service funding arrangements such as Grant Related In-Service Training (GRIST) should enable teachers to be seconded for Swann-related training (3.20).
6 School-based INSET should be encouraged. Each school should develop its own in-service programme (3.23 and 3.24).
7 Distance education should be developed, particularly in all-white areas (3.23).
8 The DES should support and fund teacher exchanges between all-white and multiracial schools (3.23).
9 Closer links to be developed between training institutions and multiracial schools — for example, through secondment of teachers to training institutions (3.24).
10 HMI should issue guidance on 'training of trainers', in the light of a project at Nottingham University (3.25).

These recommendations seem to have been welcomed — at least in principle. Problems of implementation have arisen because of the absence of staff with the appropriate background and qualifications and because these recommendations have not been matched by funds to appoint staff to spearhead these new initiatives. The teacher education recommendations in the fields of multicultural and special needs education have coincided with a financial crisis of unprecedented severity when new appointments are out of the question.

Since the publication of the Swann Report, the government has introduced radical changes in the funding of INSET. In future, schools and LEAs will be given more freedom to plan and deliver their own INSET. Interim indications are that schools will run their own courses and make less use of courses provided in institutions of higher education. As a result of these changes, education departments in higher education may lose students to the point that their very existence is threatened. Although the government has designated both 'special needs in schools and colleges of further education' and 'teaching and curriculum in a multiethnic society' as national priorities attracting 70 per cent DES funding, the way in which schools and LEAs choose to interpret these priorities remains to be seen. Until now, courses in both these areas have recruited well, mainly because of the interest of teachers and the support of LEAs.

Despite these problems, significant improvements have been made in the field of special needs teacher education since the publication of Warnock, as suggested by HMI and conference reports since 1981 (for example, Thomas and Smith, 1985; Moses and Hegarty, 1987; Robson, Sebba, Mittler and Davies, 1987). Many teacher training institutions have tried to adopt the 'permeation' model by seeking to ensure that special needs considerations were included in all relevant courses, both in foundation subjects such as psychology, human development, sociology, history, philosophy, as well as in all curriculum subject areas, such as primary education, secondary English, maths, sciences, humanities and languages. But permeation policies depend on the interest and commitment of all members of the teaching staff and on the ability of those who represent special needs and multicultural education to convince their colleagues of the importance of enlarging their courses to incorporate these elements.

The challenge in higher education is the exact parallel of that facing the schools: to avoid the isolation and marginalization which comes from merely grafting on additional components on the curriculum. At the same time, all members of staff need to be convinced that special educational needs and education for a pluralist society are the responsibility of every member of staff and not the preserve of a few specialists.

Conclusions

The significance of Warnock and Swann far transcends the interests of particular minorities. The reports raise fundamental questions concerning the work of the education system as a whole and of each school and educational establishment in the country. The reports do not confine themselves to a demand for equal opportunities for 'their children' but call for a reappraisal of what our educational system should be offering to all children. Does the curriculum cater for all children in the school? Are there children who are denied full access to the curriculum? If so, how can schools examine their assumptions and their practice, become aware of varying degrees of stereotyping and labelling concerning particular groups of children, their families and the communities and neighbourhoods from which they come? What values and assumptions does a school convey in the ways it treats its children, their families and the communities in which they live?

What about the future? Although the Warnock and Swann reports have stimulated a great deal of discussion and debate and initiated a reappraisal of current assumptions and practices, how much real progress has been made and what can reasonably be expected in the future?

Unfortunately, neither report can be said to have received enthusiastic government backing. The Warnock Report was sent out for lengthy consultation without any official indication of government reaction. The 1981 Education Act is but a pale shadow of the report and is now under heavy attack for having spawned a divisive bureaucratic process which separates 'statemented' from 'non-statemented' children within ordinary schools and which has not resulted in a significant increase in integrated provision within ordinary schools. Similarly, the government's reception of the Swann Report can hardly be described as one of enthusiasm and has been marked by semantic and ideological battles over the anti-racism issue.

Lack of government commitment does not normally stifle local innovation; indeed, practice in some LEAs is substantially ahead of government leadership both in the field of special needs and multicultural and anti-racist education. In the field of special needs, national surveys have shown that initiatives do not generally spring from LEA policies but from leadership by schools and individual teachers (Hegarty, 1987; Jowett, Hegarty and Moses, 1987).

Unfortunately, recent government initiatives suggest that LEAs and schools will experience a significant reduction in their freedom to innovate. Over and above the problem of dwindling financial resources, the imposition of a national curriculum and the introduction of regular testing of children threatens many of the whole-school, cross-curricular approaches which lie at the heart of the Warnock and Swann reports. If the emphasis is to be on assessment of competencies in the core curriculum, what are the implications for children with special needs? What priority can in future be given to the reform of each area of the curriculum to ensure that it is fully accessible to all children in the school? Once headteachers and schools are given more financial autonomy, what priority will they give to 'minority interests', and to under-functioning children, particularly if it is precisely these interests that are raising questions about the work and priorities of the school as a whole? And how will such children fare in the new grant-maintained schools once they are removed from LEA control?

These are serious questions which face both the special needs and ethnic minority constituencies. Until now, they have been working in parallel rather than together. The time has surely come for them to join forces and make a common cause to work for 'education for all'.

References

CLUNIES-ROSS, L. and WIMHURST, S. (1983) *The Right Balance: Provision for Slow Learners in Secondary Schools*, Windsor, NFER/Nelson.

COARD, B. (1971) *How the West Indian Child is Made Educationally Subnormal in the British Educational System*, London, New Beacon Books.

DEPARTMENT OF EDUCATION AND SCIENCE (1978) *Special Educational Needs: Report of the Committee of Enquiry into the Education of Handicapped Children and Young People* (The Warnock Report), Cmnd. 7212, London, HMSO.

DEPARTMENT OF EDUCATION AND SCIENCE (1985) *Education for All: Report of the Committee of Enquiry into the Education of Children from Ethnic Minority Groups* (The Swann Report), Cmnd. 9453, London, HMSO.

DEPARTMENT OF EDUCATION AND SCIENCE (1986) *Statistics of Education. Vol. 1: Schools*, London, HMSO.

DESSENT, T. (1987) *Making the Ordinary School Special*, Lewes, Falmer Press.

DOUGLAS, J.W.B. (1964) *The Home and the School*, London, McGibbon and Kee.

FRYERS, T. (1984) *The Epidemiology of Severe Mental Handicap: The Dynamics of Prevalence*, New York and London, Academic Press.

GALLOWAY, D. (1985) *Schools, Pupils and Special Educational Needs*, Beckenham, Croom Helm.

GALLOWAY, D. and GOODWIN, C. (1987) *The Education of Disturbing Children: Pupils with Learning and Adjustment Difficulties*, London, Longman.

HARGREAVES, D. (1982) *Challenge for the Comprehensive School: Culture, Curriculum and Community*, London, Routledge and Kegan Paul.

HEGARTY, S. (1987) *Meeting Special Needs in Ordinary Schools: An Overview*, London, Cassell.

ILEA (1984) *Improving Secondary Education* (The Hargreaves Report), London, ILEA.

ILEA (1985a) *Improving Primary Education* (The Thomas Report), London, ILEA.

ILEA (1985b) *Equal Opportunities for All?* (The Fish Report), London, ILEA.

JOWETT, S., HEGARTY, S. and MOSES, D. (1987) *Joining Forces: A Study of Links between Special and Ordinary Schools*, Windsor, NFER/Nelson.

LLOYD-SMITH, M. (Ed.) (1984) *Disrupted Schooling*, London, Murray.

MITTLER, P. (1987) 'Towards education for all: Editorial introduction', *Special Needs in Ordinary Schools*, London, Cassell.

MITTLER, P. and MCCONACHIE, H. (Eds) (1983) *Parents, Professionals and Mentally Handicapped People: Approaches to Partnership*, Beckenham, Croom Helm.

MOSES, D. and HEGARTY, S. (1987) *Developing Expertise: INSET for Special Needs*, Windsor, NFER/Nelson.

MOSES, D., HEGARTY, S. and JOWETT, S. (1987) *Supporting Ordinary Schools*, Windsor, NFER/Nelson.

ROBSON, C., SEBBA, J., MITTLER, P. and DAVIES, G. (1987) *In-service Training and Special Educational Needs: Running Short, School-Focused Courses*, Manchester, Manchester University Press.

RUTTER, M., MAUGHAN, B., MORTIMORE, P. and OUSTON, J. (1979) *Fifteen Thousand Hours: Secondary Schools and Their Effects on Children*, London, Open Books.

SAYER, J. (1987) *Secondary Schools for All: Strategies for Special Needs*, London, Cassell.

SWANN, W. (1985) 'Is the integration of children with special needs happening?', *Oxford Review of Education*, 11, pp. 3–18.

THOMAS, D. and SMITH, C. (1985) 'Special educational needs and initial training' in SAYER, J. and JONES, N. (Eds) *Teacher Training and Special Educational Needs*, Beckenham, Croom Helm.

TOMLINSON, S. (1981) *Educational Subnormality: A Study in Decision Making*, London, Routledge and Kegan Paul.

TOPPING, K. and WOLFENDALE, S. (Eds) (1985) *Parental Involvement in Children's Reading*, Beckenham, Croom Helm.

WEDGE, P. and PROSSER, H. (1973) *Born to Fail?*, London, National Children's Bureau.

Peter Mittler

WIDLAKE, P. (1985) *Reducing Educational Disadvantage*, Milton Keynes, Open University Press.
WOLFENDALE, S. (1987) *Primary Schools and Special Needs: Policy, Planning and Provision*, London, Cassell.

Chapter 12

Research in a Plural Society:
Pitfalls and Possibilities*

James Cornford

Introduction

The experience of the Swann Committee (or Rampton/Swann Committee, DES, 1981 and 1985) underlined two important though often neglected truths: that research if it is to be useful must be done well before it is needed; and that research is seldom neutral. Educational research requires long lead times if it is to be convincing: any research on ethnic relations is sensitive and will probably be contested. It is not surprising, therefore, that the Committee faced a number of difficulties in finding satisfactory research to supplement and support the evidence it received from teachers, parents, local education authorities, and many other individuals and groups. The first difficulty was that the Committee was not able to consider at length a comprehensive research strategy, given the requirement to produce quickly an interim report (DES, 1981).

The second difficulty, reflected clearly in the interim report, was the inadequacy of official statistics to provide anything but the crudest indications of the extent of differences between ethnic groups in academic achievement. This is regrettable but not surprising. The School Leavers Survey, on to which additional ethnic questions were piggy-backed with the collaboration of a number of LEAs, is an administrative exercise. It was not designed for the Committee's purposes and not capable of adaptation to include the large number of additional questions about pupils, their backgrounds and the schools themselves, which would have been necessary to get behind crude ethnic categories and to give some idea of the causes as well as the extent of differences of achievement. This is not the fault of the Statistics Branch of the Department of Education and Science for whose help the Committee was grateful. The Branch was indeed quick to point out the limitations of the survey. But it is a comment on the failure of the Department to keep itself adequately informed on what has for many years been acknowledged to be an urgent problem. The Committee recommended in its interim report that the Department should

*This is a revised version of annex G *A Note on Research* published as part of the Swann Report and appearing here by kind permission of the Department of Education and Science.

institute a programme for monitoring the educational progress of children from ethnic minorities. The subsequent experience of the Committee only reinforced the need for this to be done. If this should prove too complex and too sensitive to handle as a routine administrative exercise, as may well prove to be the case, then the Department should establish a research programme to examine these problems in a regular and systematic way. Research undertaken by individual intitiative in universities, colleges and research institutes has for the most part been on a small scale, not replicated or cumulative and often indifferent in quality.

That was the third difficulty. The most important step taken by the Committee was to commission from the National Foundation for Educational Research (NFER) three reviews of research into the education of pupils of West Indian, Asian and other origins: these have been published as *Caught Between* (Taylor, 1981) and *Best of Both Worlds* (Hegarty and Taylor, 1986). In the report the Committee draws wherever possible on the findings of the research reviewed. And it must be said that whatever its shortcomings the cumulative effect of the research is to confirm and underline the seriousness and complexity of the educational problems facing ethnic minorities. The point to make again here, however, is the inadequacy of the past *ad hoc* research effort as a basis for policy, and the need for the Department to make the fullest use of the small number of first-rate research workers in the field.

The fourth difficulty facing the Committee was the sheer sensitivity of the issues it wanted to examine. This may be illustrated by a brief account of the major research initiative attempted by the Committee in response to criticisms of its interim report. This initiative originated with a proposal from the Research and Statistics Branch of the Inner London Education Authority for a project on black students and educational success. The idea was to interview about their home background and school experience, two groups of black pupils, one of which would have achieved a certain level of success in public examinations at 16 + and the other not. Matching groups of white pupils were to be interviewed at the same time. It was hoped in this way not only to shift the focus of attention from factors associated with failure to those associated with success, but to get at the pupils' own perceptions of their schooling and in particular of the influence of racial attitudes on their performance. The major limitation of the research design, of which the proponents were well aware, was that to get groups of an adequate size the sample had to be drawn from a large number of schools. This would have precluded independent examination and assessment of the policies and practices of the schools themselves which are widely recognized to be a critical factor in pupils' achievement. Despite this limitation, the Committee saw this as a promising proposal, but wished to extend its scope to include both Asian pupils and places outside London. Negotiations to modify the research design and to conduct linked projects in Birmingham and Bradford were making progress when the project had to be abandoned.

The project was criticized at a conference of the National Association for Multiracial Education (NAME), and subsequent meetings of members of the Committee, of the research team and members of the Caribbean Teachers' Association, NAME, the Afro-Caribbean Education Research project (ACER) and other teachers and community workers revealed grave doubts about the value of the project and serious criticism of its design. The central issues were the emphasis on social and cultural factors and the weakness in relation to the schools. Whatever view one took about the force of these criticisms, there could be no mistaking the strength of the conviction behind them, and without the goodwill and cooperation of the critics the project had no chance of success. It was therefore withdrawn.

The Committee agreed with its critics over the lack of research about what goes on in schools and asked the ILEA team to design an alternative project to look at such factors as streaming, subject choice, examination entry and curriculum content as they affected children from ethnic minorities. The most illuminating studies of ethnic factors in schools have been based on direct observation, carried out in particular schools and classrooms, often highly perceptive and suggestive but necessarily limited for purposes of generalization. The question is whether, drawing on these perceptions, measures can be developed which are methodologically sound, capable of replication and acceptable to LEAs, teachers, parents and pupils. This was the question to which the ILEA team now addressed itself. Unfortunately the earlier delays and the time taken to develop the feasibility study pushed the timetable beyond the anticipated life of the Committee. It was not therefore possible to fund this study from the Committee's budget and the Committee strongly recommended that the DES should fund it. The Department, however, delayed beyond the point where the ILEA team could be kept together and thus lost the opportunity to build directly on the work already done. The Committee regretted this and believed that direct research on school policy and practice was essential if progress was to be made towards understanding the dynamics of ethnic relations in schools and towards improving performance. It is also necessary to reassure ethnic minorities that serious attention is given to their complaints and that research will be conducted which is not so designed as to throw the whole burden of responsibility for low academic achievement on pupils and their families. For these reasons the Committee particularly welcomed the joint research project of the Policy Studies Institute and the University of Lancaster, funded by the DES, on 'Factors associated with success in multi-ethnic schools'. This study concentrates on the relation between school policies and practices and the achievement of pupils. The results of this study, which are not yet available, would undoubtedly have been of great value to the Committee and would perhaps have enabled many of its internal debates to be conducted more fruitfully. This study itself encountered serious difficulties in negotiating access to the schools and it was not possible to focus directly on the influence of racial factors, as some direct observational studies have done. The problem addressed by the ILEA feasibility study remain to be tackled.

Commissioned Work

The upshot of this sorry tale was that, apart from the review of existing research, the Committee was able to commission new research on a modest scale only. Its major commissions were not indeed of new research, but were subventions to current programmes to enable research teams to complete work in progress in time to be of use to the Committee. The first of these was to the ESRC's Research Unit on Ethnic Relations, at the University of Aston (now at the University of Warwick), for a study of the definition and implementation of multicultural education policy by four local education authorities, by Professor John Rex and colleagues (RUER, 1983). The second commission was to the Postgraduate School of Studies in Research in Education of the University of Bradford to enable the Committee to draw on the findings of a longitudinal study of academic achievement under the direction of Dr Gajendra Verma for which the fieldwork had been carried out in 1977–1982 (Verma, 1984; Verma with Ashworth, 1986).

Two other studies were directly commissioned on matters of particular concern to the Committee: a survey of present provision and capacity for training teachers in ethnic minority community languages (Craft and Atkins, 1983), and a study of provision for multicultural education in 'all-white' schools (Mathews and Fallows, 1985). Each of these studies produced useful information and interesting argument which are reflected at the appropriate places in the report.

Agenda for Research

There were three steps which the Committee saw as essential to provide a sound basis for future policy:

(i) the establishment of an adequate statistical base;
(ii) the setting up of a programme of longitudinal studies to monitor in greater depth the progress of ethnic minority children; and
(iii) the support of research projects which concentrated on the educational process, particularly policies and practices within schools, the relationship between home and school, and the transition from school to work.

The Statistical Base

1 In its interim report (DES, 1981) the Committee argued for the value of ethnically based statistics as follows:

Ethnically based statistics can, we believe, be of value at all levels and to all parties within education: to central government, in determining policy; to LEAs in quantifying and locating particular needs; to schools so that they can take full account of the cultural and linguistic backgrounds of pupils and see whether any groups are underachieving or are disproportionately represented in any subject or class and to make an appropriate response; and to parents so that they can assess their child's performance in relation to his peers. We are therefore wholly in favour of the collection of educational statistics on an ethnic basis where they are to be used in establishing facts about how members of the ethnic minorities are faring in the educational system.

It also made specific recommendations about pupils and teachers including:

(i) All schools should record the ethnic origin of a child's family, along with the normal standard data, when a child first enters school, on the basis of discussion with parents.

(ii) The DES should reincorporate the collection of information on the ethnic origin of all pupils in schools into its annual statistical exercise and should introduce ethnic classifications into its school leavers survey.

2 The Committee was aware that there are strong objections to the collection of ethnically based statistics including:

(a) that the information is not and will not be used to the advantage of the groups concerned: a more probable result is the perpetuation of negative stereotypes. Monitoring in the past has not led to improvements;

(b) that ethnic classifications are unsatisfactory and have no educational relevance; and

(c) that information on ethnic origin could be used in conjunction with the British Nationality Act 1981 to determine individual citizenship.

3 Although the Committee understood the fears that lay behind these objections, it nevertheless believed that the collection of ethnically based statistics was necessary both for planning the policies recommended in the report and for making sure that they were being implemented. It agreed however that:

(a) it is necessary to arrive at a commonly agreed set of classifications that can be seen to have a definite educational relevance because they correspond to real social and cultural differences which affect the relationship between schools and pupils; and

(b) that we must distinguish between information which it is in the direct interest of individual pupils and their families to have collected (for example, language, religion) and more general information, including ethnic origins, which may be of importance for LEA or DES policy, but which does not need to be collected from each pupil or recorded individually.

4 The first thing to establish is the purpose for which statistics should be collected. The following have been suggested:

  (a) The assessment of special education need (pupil).
  (b) The allocation of staffing and other resources to meet such need (LEA/school).
  (c) Monitoring of performance (LEA/DES).

5 The second thing to determine is what information is required and from whom, for example:

  (a) Pupils

    (i) mother tongue and whether used at home;
    (ii) special dietary needs;
    (iii) religion.

  (b) Schools in addition to (a) (i)–(iii) above
    (i) English language proficiency;
    (ii) standardized test results at various ages;
    (iii) admission to selective schools, composition of bands or streams;
    (iv) suspensions, referrals to special agencies outside school;
    (v) external examinations: entries and results;
    (vi) staying on into full-time education post 16;
    (vii) success in obtaining employment;
    (viii) entry into higher education.

  (c) LEA/DES in addition to above
    (i) ethnic origin.

6 This information may be collected as follows:

  (a) Pupil information from parents on entering school.
  (b) School information: compiled by school as pupil progresses through school.
  (c) LEA/DES: the important point is that information on ethnic origin need not be collected from every individual pupil at all: the information is being collected primarily for a political purpose, namely to monitor the performance of ethnic groups, not to help with the problems of individual pupils or to allocate resources which must be done on the basis of need, i.e. the numbers of pupils actually experiencing language difficulties.

7 Information on ethnic origins could of course be collected from parents when children first enter schools as the Committee originally recommended. Given the fears that have been expressed and the fact that this information is required for general policy purposes and not for direct educational decisions about individual pupils, there is a case for collecting this information by sample survey. The major problem about information collected from individuals is confidentiality: that information may be used for purposes

other than that for which it was originally required (for example, fears about nationality). The advantages of using a social survey for monitoring as against the collection of information from each and every individual include:

(i) the guarantee of anonymity and confidentiality to those questioned: the survey is a separate exercise and the information is not recorded on the individual's record card;

(ii) greater accuracy: it is much easier to collect accurate information from a sample than from routine administrative enquiry to a whole population;

(iii) greater flexibility: information sought can be adjusted in the light of experience; an administrative system is cumbersome, and expensive to alter;

(iv) more scope for gathering additional information which may be pertinent to monitoring including information on institutional factors. A regular survey could have a core of questions on ethnic background, but study in addition specific problems like the school allocation problems of an LEA or placement in special schools.

Monitoring

(a) What is proposed in effect is to include the collection of information on ethnic origins within a programme of research rather than through the administrative procedures of the school, in the belief that the survey interview is more searching, more sensitive and more secure for the informant and will avoid raising delicate issues between schools and parents. It is also likely to yield more accurate, detailed and meaningful information than that which would emerge from the necessarily rough classifications which would have to be adopted for administrative record keeping.

In any event the monitoring of performance should not be left to *ad hoc* investigation but should be the subject of a continuing research programme. The main elements of such a programme would be as follows:

(i) To obtain data on all categories of children, but with particular care to see that ethnic minority children are adequately represented in the samples.

(ii) To collect contextual data on teachers, peers and schools to ensure adequate interpretation.

(iii) To ensure acceptable measures of minority status, that is, agreed definitions of classifications of ethnic origin.

(iv) To maintain consistency and comparability of definitions, as a large part of the purpose is to establish trends.

(v) The progress of children through the system and from one point to another will be of central interest, which implies longitudinal studies following cohorts of children in the manner of the National

Child Development Study and the Child Health and Education Study.

(vi) It will be necessary to include parents in the surveys in order to obtain adequate data on key background factors such as social class.

(vii) Consideration will need to be given to the measures used to assess the outcomes or achievements of children. The use of public examination results alone is unlikely to be adequate.

(viii) There will need to be a guarantee of long-term funding to ensure continuity, to enable research procedures to be progressively improved and to allow for an adequate judgment of the success of the programme.

(b) Any such programme will need to be the responsibility of a specially designated research unit or group, either within the DES itself or in some research institute or university. To the extent that it needs to acquire the confidence and cooperation of a number of groups, parental, professional and official, there would be something to be said for a position independent of the DES and for the involvement of the various groups in the work of the unit. Its staff would need to have experience of work in ethnic relations and particular skills in the area of educational survey research. There are likely to be difficult issues both of classification and of survey design, which will need to be tackled with a combination of technical competence, imagination and political sensitivity. This will not be a routine research assignment.

The main responsibility of the unit would be to set up and run a series of overlapping longitudinal studies, perhaps three or four, covering the age ranges of interest, from infant through to post-compulsory school age, and including further education and training. The main purpose of these studies would be to compare the progress of minorities and other groups through the crucial stages of the system. Thus a study from age 13 to age 16 would look at how comparable pupils aged 13 from different groups had made out by the time of their examination year. It would be important to report these studies every two or three years to monitor change. It would be equally important to include in the design of such studies as much data as possible on the character and composition of schools. The preliminary results of the PSI/Lancaster University study demonstrate clearly the potential value of such studies.

Specific Research

Here the Committee indicated the areas of research which should enjoy priority. It did not devise or propose particular projects. There is a limited number of first rate research workers and it is seldom possible and never wise to tell them what to do. Nevertheless the Committee thought that the DES and other funding bodies should give priority, other things being equal, to research in the following areas:

1 Policy and practice in schools.
2 Multicultural policies.
3 Language.
4 The transition from school to work.
5 Pre-school learning.

Schools

In her review of research from 1960 to 1982, Tomlinson (1983) comments:

> The literature has largely documented underachievement among minority group children, particularly children of West Indian origin, and there has been an obsessive concern with 'explaining' this rather than focusing on factors which might make for children's improved education. There is very little positive literature documenting factors in and out of school which might make for more success among minority children within the existing school system, and there is no literature at all documenting particular factors within schools which might make for more effective education for the children. (p. 4)

To this one might add that there is precious little research which throws light on factors within schools which may help to explain the difficulties which children encounter, whether matters of school policy, or organization of classroom practice. To do so requires a different approach and a different kind of research from most of what has been done to date. As a perspective critique of the Committee's own aborted project on successful black students put it:

> . . . . the sponsors appear to want a particular kind of evidence, i.e. quantified information which can be quoted with ease and treated as 'proof' yet without examining internal school dynamics.
>
> Surely it seems reasonable to put the case for research of a more qualitative, interactive nature. Though this type of evidence may be less suited to 'proving' what makes a successful black student, it can give much greater insight into the complex range of variables which affect the educational life-chances of black British children. (ACER Project, 1982, p. 57)

The report goes on to suggest that eight factors should figure prominently in any research designed to look at school dynamics, namely: discipline policy, school policy on examination procedures, non-examination procedures, teachers, school management, home/school liaison, links with the community, and post-16 curriculum and opportunities. (Further specification of these factors as set out in the report is given in Appendix 1.)

The Committee agreed that there was an urgent need to look at these factors in schools and for that reason welcomed the PSI/Lancaster study. Experience of that project however suggests that there are major difficulties in carrying out an ambitious programme covering a large number of schools and that it may be necessary to restrict future research either to a relatively small number of schools, to be studied in depth, or to concentrate on a few aspects of policy and practice across a larger sample of schools. If the second approach were to be adopted, the PSI/Lancaster researchers themselves would be inclined to concentrate on home/school liaison, the curriculum in the humanities and the pastoral system.

More sensitive yet are the questions raised by research on classroom practice, and there the Committee may have fallen foul of its own usage. 'Racism' has been used to describe a wide range of attitudes and behaviour, in a way which makes perfectly good sense to those who experience it, but it is puzzling and alienating to those who do not. Experience and research (see for example the second review of research by the NFER (Hegarty and Taylor, 1986) and the study by Peter Green in the Report) both show that teachers hold marked stereotypes of children from different ethnic groups and have different expectations of them, just as they do of boys and girls and of children from different social backgrounds. Some of these prejudices may be open and some unconscious. Their effect in a mixed classroom must be complex and can only be teased out by patient and scrupulous observations. Nothing can be done without the cooperation of the teachers themselves and it cannot be emphasized too strongly that the purpose of such research is not to find another scapegoat for the shortcomings of the schools, but to help teachers to be aware of the influence of their attitudes on the learning of their pupils and the extent to which unexamined prejudices can lead to self-fulfilling prophecies, whether of success or failure. It is important to know whether or not there are regular patterns in the way teachers deal with the children from different ethnic groups, how far these patterns reflect conscious or unconscious assumptions on the part of the teachers about the character and capabilities of the children, and how far these assumptions reflect the differences of language, culture and experience which children bring with them to school. These subtle and complex problems deserve at least as much attention as, for instance, the question of mixed ability teaching has received.

Multicultural policies

It is clear from the researches of the Economic and Social Research Council's Research Unit on Ethnic Relations that multicultural educational policies have been adopted piecemeal by LEAs in response to a variety of pressures. It is not clear exactly what these policies mean in principle and still less what their implications will be in practice. The RUER is following up the question of implementation in the school as part of its programme. It is not surprising, and perhaps not regrettable, that public policy should develop in a haphazard and muddled fashion. There are, nevertheless, some sharp and difficult choices which cannot be resolved by the application of the panacea of 'multiculturalism', which have already surfaced in the field of religious education and which are going to become increasingly pressing in the field of languages and the humanities curriculum in general.

These choices are thrown into relief by the Committee's report whose emphasis shifted from a primary concern with the academic achievement of children from ethnic minority groups to a wider and more fundamental prescription about the kind of society for which schools should be trying to prepare all children. The report refers frequently to a commitment to a 'truly pluralist society' to justify various policy recommendations. But it is not at all clear what 'pluralist' means. Hegarty and Taylor (1986), in their review of research on 'Asian' children comment sharply:

> What for example is really meant by cultural pluralism? How are the cultures and their representatives to coexist? At what level, for example, are the cultures to be integrated? Would there, for instance, be a separation of public and private cultures? What implications does cultural pluralism have for social cohesion? Does cultural pluralism imply greater individuality or segregation? What links are there between cultural pluralism and equal opportunities or racial harmony?

These questions need to be further explored both generally and in relation to education. Different interpretations of pluralism have different political and educational implications, and it is likely that not only the majority and minorities may differ over which one they prefer but that both majority and minorities may also differ among themselves. Compare for the sake of argument two crudely characterized versions of pluralism:

Individualist
This view starts from the assumption of the modern, universalist, nation state in which the rights of individual citizens to life, liberty, property, association, worship and political participation are guaranteed. It is assumed that there are core values—loyalty to the regime and support for those civil rights—to which all citizens subscribe, but that beyond this there is a limited need for conformity: many things which in the past were thought to require common agreement can now be regarded as 'things indifferent'. There may need to be common road regulations, but there is freedom of religious belief and worship. This view requires assimilation on the part both of majority and minorities. Minorities have to accept the political regime; the majority should in logic modify that regime to exclude 'things indifferent' from state regulations, for example disestablish the Church

of England and end compulsory religious education in maintained schools. 'Assimilation' is to a common core with everything else left to private choice and action.

Communitarian
This view differs in that in addition to a common core of public values to which majority and minorities adhere, it demands that public recognition and support be given to the separate values and activities of majority and minorities. Public resources should be made available for activities specific to particular groups: for example, public money for compulsory religious education of whatever kind parents demand, or possibly for special provision for teaching minority languages. Separate maintained schools for Muslims are a logical consequence of adhering to the present support for compulsory religious education.

The individualist assumes that in essentials (and the essentials are liberal) there will be conformity, but limits essentials and omits some very important aspects, like religion, from the core. The communitarian assumes that in some essentials, groups will differ and can be enabled and encouraged to do so. To take the example of language: for the individualist English only may be essential. There is no official recognition of other languages, only optional study on the same basis as foreign languages. For the communitarian other community languages would be afforded some official recognition and encouragement including provision in the curriculum as a medium of instruction.

The essential distinction in this example is between the recognition of individuals with equal rights and the recognition of groups with particular claims. Other distinctions could be made with different implications. The point of the example is that it would be useful to have spelt out the implications of various definitions of pluralism, so that policy makers in the midst of their piecemeal accommodations can have a better idea of where their decisions may lead them.

There are at least three ways in which research may help:

1 By establishing what public attitudes to multicultural issues are, not because these necessarily dictate what policies should be adopted, but because it should be helpful to know what reactions to anticipate and how much persuasion may be necessary to win general acceptance for innovation. The available evidence suggests that there is a long way to go on some issues of pressing importance to minorities (see Table 12.1.)
2 By looking abroad at the policies and experience of other countries with substantial ethnic minorities. Policies can seldom be transplanted wholesale, but detached observation of other people's problems can often throw light on our own and will certainly provide warnings against exaggerated expectations of fashionable nostrums. Such research to be useful requires detailed first-hand knowledge of the countries concerned: there is nothing useful to be gained from tourism. For this reason there is much to be said

in favour of comparative research by cross-national teams. It would, for example, be of great interest to compare the development of multicultural education in Holland and the United Kingdom, preferably by a detailed case study of what is actually happening in schools.

3 By monitoring developments in the curriculum, in the absence of a centrally ordained curriculum, changes in examination syllabuses and, still more, changes in the content and emphasis of what is taught in schools take place piecemeal. No doubt HM Inspectorate are aware of what is going on and can and will draw attention to significant changes. But it may also be useful to have a deliberate look at how 'multiculturalism' is affecting the teaching of history, which conveys what one might call the authorized version of the society children are members of and how it came to be as it is. Changes in the teaching of history and related studies are bound to be contentious and for that reason alone deserve to be widely understood and debated. We are not likely to become a truly pluralist society by stealth.

Table 12.1 *Attitudes to Multicultural Education*

.... respondents were asked whether or not they thought that schools containing many children whose parents came from other countries and cultures should adopt special policies. Such policies included:

	% agreeing
Providing special classes in English if required	77
Teaching all children about the history and culture of these countries	74
Allowing those for whom it is important to wear traditional dress	43
Teaching children (from different backgrounds) about the history and culture of their parents' countries of origins	40
Providing separate religious instruction if their parents request it	32
Allowing these children to study their mother tongue in school hours.	16

Language

There has been a great deal of research and experiment on various aspects of language on which the Report drew. Problems remain to be investigated, but there are two points which have a general application but seem to be particularly worth making in the context of language:

1 The first thing is that special attention should be given to communicating the results of research both to those who commission it and to those who

are its subjects but often also active collaborators in carrying out the projects. The Language Information Network Coordination, which grew out of the Linguistic Minorities Project (LMP), is an example of an attempt to build dissemination on to a research project and to maintain the impetus and interest which the original project generated. This example should be imitated; both researchers and funding bodies need to recognize this and allow for it in their initial planning (see LMP, 1983 and 1985).

2 It has been usual to look on ethnic minorities as presenting language problems, first because they require special teaching in English in order to participate fully in education, and secondly because they make demands for special recognition for their community languages. Both have been and remain serious problems, but they should not be allowed to obscure the fact that a large British bilingual population is an asset and a resource, which ought to be welcomed and exploited. The recent DES Consultative Paper, *Foreign Languages in the School Curriculum* (DES, 1983) gives scant recognition to the possibilities. A more radical reappraisal of language policies should in future include the mother tongue of linguistic minority pupils within the compass of languages available to all pupils, as well as making greater provision for their academic study by bilingual pupils.

Some LEAs have already embarked on experiments with Faculties of Communication which bring together the various aspects of language learning. These experiments should be monitored and the results made as widely available as possible.

The transition from school to work, further education and training

It has to be faced that changes in the curriculum, however desirable in themselves, will not necessarily translate into improved academic achievement narrowly defined; nor will academic success necessarily translate into career opportunities, given the prevalence of discrimination in the labour market. As children from ethnic minorities are likely to remain disproportionately represented in non-examination classes, it will be important to monitor:

1 new developments in the secondary school curriculum, especially those that involve a move towards more practical or less academic subjects. Will ethnic minority pupils do newer, less academic and less well regarded subjects, and if so how will it affect their chances of employment?
2 the Technical and Vocational Education Initiative (TVEI). The curriculum being developed under TVEI seems to be designed to develop the sort of skills in which many minority pupils, particularly West Indians, have expressed an interest. Are they aware of the scheme and getting a chance to participate, and if so to what effect?
3 the experience of minority pupils on youth training schemes and in further

education. A comparatively high proportion of minority pupils attend further education colleges, and this, along with youth training schemes, may be the most important substitute for the education that some of them are not getting at school. How far is this the case?

4 the number and progress of minority students in higher education. This is a matter of critical importance, particularly for the future recruitment of teachers, and there is precious little information about it. There has been some monitoring of the initial stages of access courses, but it appears that the DES does not itself propose to follow this through to ascertain whether or not the policy is working. As these courses have been widely adopted, this seems a mistake, which should not need to be made good by others.

5 Finally there is a case, given the shortage of information on the post school experience of ethnic minority pupils, to exploit the data of the National Child Development Study. The proportion of ethnic minority subjects in the sample is small but the data are rich and now extend from birth to age 23, and thus include a full educational history of training and early work experience, as well as much else. At the least this would provide a basis for comparison with subsequent generations. Similar use might be made of the Child Health and Education Study at the University of Bristol.

Pre-school learning

It is well established that by the age of 7 the level of children's academic achievement is strongly related to family background factors, particularly social class and ethnicity. Research by the Thomas Coram Unit in London and the Community Education Development Centre in Coventry suggests that there is an important link between reading attainment and direct parental teaching. The Thomas Coram Unit (1983) is at present trying to tease out the effects of parental and teacher influence on children's achievement in the infant school for a sample of white British children and black British children of Caribbean descent in 33 ILEA infant schools. If this research emphasizes the importance of pre-school learning, as well as parental involvement, it will reinforce the case for looking at pre-school provision for ethnic minority children. It is already known that working mothers from ethnic minority groups make disproportionate use of child minders and that the marked variations in the use of services by different ethnic groups are not simply reflections of different patterns of maternal employment (ILEA, 1982). We need to know how far these differences may be determined by practical difficulties, such as hours of opening of nursery schools, and how much by more sensitive factors such as differences of views over child rearing, which may affect the willingness of ethnic minority mothers either to leave their children in nursery schools or to become involved with the education they are receiving there. Perhaps the most useful and important thing would be to find examples of successful to find examples of successful provision of pre-school education for ethnic minority children and how they have been organized and funded.

Conclusion

In conclusion three points:

1 The Committee stressed the importance of systematic monitoring and the collection of an adequate statistical base for policy. But it must also be recognized that to grasp what is actually going on in the schools, small scale research, often in the form of demonstration projects or experiments, is essential and that the involvement of teachers, parents and pupils in such projects is often the most effective means to change.

2 The Committee also emphasized the importance of direct research in the schools themselves: it is equally important to relate what is happening in schools to the communities in which they operate, and especially the ethnic minority communities, which like the rest of society are continuously changing. Stereotypes of these communities are as dangerous and misleading as stereoptypes of pupils.

3 Many of the recommendations of the Report resembled acts of faith, based upon experience and common sense. If they are implemented, they will become hypotheses to be tested to see whether or not they have the good results expected of them.

Appendix 1:   ACER Suggestions for Variables to be Included in Study of School Dynamics

1 Discipline Policy
  (a) Suspension.
  (b) Expulsion.
  (c) Referral procedures, for example, assessment centres, intermediate treatment centres, discipline units.
  (d) Home tuition: what is taught.

2 School Policy on Examination Procedures
  (a) Streaming and setting.
  (b) Mixed ability teaching:
     (i) Maths and English and how these subjects are taught.
     (ii) Remedial education: withdrawal procedures and who goes where and when.
     (iii) Does the school have a policy of combining mixed ability teaching methods with streaming procedures?

(c) Option choice procedures:
  (i) Does the timetable restrict flexibility of choice?
  (ii) Guidance on option choice: careers/pastoral advice and parental involvement/consultation.

3 Non-Examination Procedures
  (a) What curriculum is available for pupils not entered for exams?
  (b) Does the school provide school leavers with a record of their studies?
    (i) Does this record indicate what subjects the pupil studied?
  (c) Pupils' incentive to attend non-examinable subjects.

4 Teachers
  (a) How does the teacher see his/her role within the school?
    (i) Managerial, subject oriented, pastoral, counselling and careers advice throughout the pupil's school life.
  (b) Does the teacher see the child as a whole person or is the child simply studying English, maths, history, etc?
  (c) Teachers' expectations of pupils and pupils' expectations of teachers.

5 School Management
  (a) Does the head delegate? In what ways is the head involved in the whole life of the school?
  (b) Role of deputy head/s and senior teachers and pastoral heads.
  (c) Role of governors in decision making.

6 Home-school Liaison
  (a) Role of parent-teachers' association:
    (i) To what extent do parents influence school policy?
    (ii) Is the PTA's function purely extra curricular?
  (b) Parents' evenings: school reports and option choice?
    (i) How much consultation is there between parents and teachers?
  (c) Open evenings and cultural evenings.

7 Links with the Community
  (a) Advice centres.
  (b) Supplementary schools.
  (c) Youth clubs.
  (d) Community centres.

8 Post-16 Curriculum and Opportunities
  (a) Work experience.
  (b) Counselling.
  (c) Sixth form curriculum: academic, vocational, non-vocational.

James Cornford

References

ACER PROJECT (1982) *Racism and the Black Child*. Report of the Follow Up Groups on the Interim Rampton Report, London, Afro Caribbean Education Research Project, May.
CRAFT, M. and ATKINS, M. (1983) *Training Teachers of Ethnic Minority Community Languages*, Nottingham, School of Education, University of Nottingham.
DEPARTMENT OF EDUCATION AND SCIENCE (1981) *West Indian Children in Our Schools: Report of the Committee of Enquiry into the Education of Children from Ethnic Minority Groups*, (The Rampton Report) Cmnd. 8273, London, HMSO.
DEPARTMENT OF EDUCATION AND SCIENCE (1983) *Foreign Languages in the School Curriculum: A Consultative Paper*, London, Department of Education and Science/Welsh Office.
DEPARTMENT OF EDUCATION AND SCIENCE (1985) *Report of the National Committee of Enquiry into the Education of Children from Ethnic Minority Groups*, (The Swann Report), Cmnd 9543, London, HMSO.
DEPARTMENT OF EDUCATION AND SCIENCE (1987) *Modern Foreign Languages to 16*, Curriculum Matters 8, An HMI Series, London, HMSO.
GREEN, P. (1984) (study published as annex in Swann Report).
HEGARTY, S. and TAYLOR, M. (1986) *Best of Both Worlds*, Windsor, NFER.
ILEA (1982) *Pre-School Survey*, London, ILEA.
JOWELL, R. and AIREY, C. (1984) *British Social Attitudes–The 1984 Report*, London, SPCR/Gower.
LMP (1983) *Linguistic Minorities in England*, London, University of London Institute of Education.
LMP (1985) *The Other Languages of England* (Linguistic Minorities Project) London, Routledge & Kegan Paul.
MATHEWS, A. and FALLOWS, L. (1985) Annex to Swann.
RUER. (1983) *Development of Multicultural Education Policy in Four Local Education Authority Areas*, Birmingham, RUER, University of Aston.
TAYLOR, M. (1981) *Caught Between*, London, NFER/Nelson.
THOMAS CORAM UNIT (1983) *Current Research*, London, University of London.
TOMLINSON, S. (1983) *Ethnic Minorities in British Schools*, London, Policy Studies Institute/Heinemann Educational.
VERMA, G. K. (1984) *Ethnicity and Achievement in British Schools*, Bradford, University of Bradford.
VERMA, G. K. with ASHWORTH, B. (1986) *Ethnicity and Educational Achievement in British Schools*, London, Macmillan.

Chapter 13

The Hermeneutics of The Swann Report

Bhikhu Parekh

In this chapter I intend to discuss a rather unusual but important and neglected problem, namely how to read reports produced by independent committees or commissions of enquiry appointed by governments. We have devoted considerable attention in recent years to the problems involved and the techniques to be employed in understanding literary and philosophical texts. The reports produced by committees and commissions (reports as they will be hereafter called) are no less intriguing. They belong to a distant genre and require sophisticated hermeneutic techniques. Since we approach them with wrong expectations and judge them by irrelevant standards, we are often excessively harsh on them. We are disappointed that they do not pronounce the last word on the subject and close a controversy, that they are not sufficiently rigorous, theoretical or radical, or that they are eclectic and consensual.

The reports are paradoxical documents. Written by committees rather than individual authors, printed by governments rather than academic publishers, lacking 'jackets', cover designs and other insignia of identity, and making no claim to originality or scholarship, they almost invite us to treat them as bland and bureaucratic documents representing little more than eclectic collections of ideas drawn from diverse and sometimes incompatible sources. At the same time they are also bulky, learned, well-argued, based on the available and sometimes specially commissioned research and collectively composed by a body of generally well-known men and women including some academics. They therefore look like and demand to be treated as learned treatises. Neither glorified pamphlets or civil service memoranda on the one hand, nor scholarly academic compositions on the other, they are a distinct modern breed going back no further than a few decades. How should we view them and what are we entitled to expect of them?

I suggest that we should see them as what they claim to be, namely reports or discussion documents, both reflecting and reflecting on and, in the process, systematizing the vague but nonetheless unmistakable consensus prevailing in society and guiding the public debate on the best way of dealing with the relevant subject. The committees of enquiry do not spring up in a vacuum. They are set up when a problem has agitated the community for some time and been a subject of public debate. During the course of the debate, several solutions are canvassed — some are dismissed as implausible or unacceptable and a broad consensus is formed about the possible and acceptable range of solutions. If the public mind is already made up, a committee of enquiry is not necessary. If it is totally confused and chaotic, a committee is not possible. Then there can be no agreement either on its terms of reference for it is not clear *what* it should investigate, nor on its composition for, in the absence of well-formed points of view, it is difficult to decide *who* are competent to represent these. It is because its report is expected to reflect a consensus distilled from a dialogue between different points of view that the Committee concerned is expected to be representative in its composition. The Committee temporarily transfers the debate from the public realm to a credible and non-partisan forum where it can be conducted in a more manageable form and in a less charged atmosphere.

As a public, action-orientated and officially accredited group of people, a committee of enquiry is subject to five sets of constraints.[1] First, it is necessarily conceived and structured within the limits of its terms of reference. They constitute its source of legitimacy, its birth certificate as it were, and it cannot go beyond them without discrediting itself. The terms of reference are a distillation of the consensus thrown up by the prior public debate on the subject and are not and cannot be ideologically neutral. They identify a specific area as a problem, define its nature and broadly indicate the direction in which its solution is to be looked for, and thus at least partially predetermine the character and content of the final report. Looking like an innocuous announcement of the birth of a committee, they are really like a genetic profile predicting the story of its life. Obviously no terms of reference are or can ever be so precise as to rule out ambiguity and interpretation. And naturally a good deal of discussion in the committee centres around their divergent interpretations and the way they can be so construed as to open up or block inconvenient areas of investigation.

Second, the members of a committee each have his/her own views on how to define and tackle their subject matter and press them as vigorously as they can. The fact that the report gives them a rare opportunity to influence public opinion and shape government policy provides an additional incentive to do so. Each asks for a specific kind of research or a certain class of witnesses and interprets the evidence in a manner most likely to further his or her point of view. Though some members wield more power than others depending on their public, professional and political status, none is wholly powerless. He/she can ask awkward questions, slow down the work (a vital consideration for every time-bound committee), and threaten to write a dissenting note, thereby damaging the credibility and impugning the intellectual and moral authority of the report.

Since all arguments are inherently inconclusive, alliances get formed and deals struck. The resulting report reflects the balance of power in the committee and is generally a compromise between the contending points of view. If some members emerge dominant, as they generally do, their views form the basic thesis of the report; opinions of others get accommodated either in the relatively safe corner reserved for appendices and footnotes or get mentioned in the text but not in the list of recommendations. If the committee is deeply divided between equally powerful groups, the basic thesis of its report reflects its precarious balance of power and gestures in different directions. The nature and intensity of the struggle for ideological domination within the Committee varies with the character of the subject it is asked to examine. However, since no subject, especially one important enough to need a committee is ever non-controversial, no committee is ever immune to the struggle for ideological domination.

Third, every committee is subject to the constraints of time, energy and money. It is expected to produce its report within a specific period; its members have other commitments and cannot give it their undivided attention; the resources at its disposal are invariably limited. All this means that it has to agree upon a plan of action and decide how to order its priorities, how best to go about its business, how to organize its deliberations and collect evidence, and when to start preparing drafts. Every decision on these matters determines the general direction in which a Committee moves and shapes its final report. Not surprisingly it becomes an arena for subtle manipulation, and the unwary get hijacked. Since members of a committee have other commitments, much of the decision-making in these areas, as well as the task of preparing the final draft of the report, are left to the Chairman and the civil servants appointed to service the committee. The Chairman's personal biases and his opinion on the kind of report likely to please, or at least be acceptable to the government, cannot but influence his decisions. He is generally chosen with care and because he is believed to be 'sound'. And if he gives the impression of coming under the influence of some of his 'wild' members, he might be gently warned that his unspoken expectations of the reward for his labours might not be met. The civil servants' role should not be underestimated either. They are a vital link between the committee and the government and in constant contact with their seniors in the civil service. They have their own preferences and they know the 'departmental' view on the subject as well as what the government and the minister would find 'acceptable'. They do not merely service the committee, but also attempt to guide and steer it in a specific direction. Their degree of success depends on the watchfulness and resistance of its members.

Fourth, every report is a public document intended as a major intervention in the ongoing debate on the subject in question. When it is published the kind of impact it makes therefore depends on how the media present it. A committee wants its report to be read one way; the media may choose to read it very differently. Since they have neither the time nor the capacity to appreciate the nuances of its arguments, they inevitably abstract and abridge it and simplify its thesis. They are also never ideologically and politically neutral, and their biases inevitably influence their interpretation of it. Often they not only simplify and vulgarize it but also alter its balance, draw dubious conclusions, distort its arguments, charter it in the service of dubious causes and destroy its integrity. The danger is particularly great when the report deals with a controversial subject or advances a thesis that steps outside the prevailing consensus. A good example of this in recent years was the way in which almost all the newspapers skilfully monitored and influenced the confidential deliberations of the Rampton Committee, inspired leaks, misrepresented the report and created a climate inhospitable to its impartial discussion.

Finally, the life span of a committee comes to an end when it submits its report to the government. The government's interpretation of it is decisive and final, both because it is its intended audience and its interpretation forms the basis of its policies. By its very nature a government is never a neutral party patiently awaiting the wise guidance of the report. It has its own views on what it would like to do and what would be acceptable to its supporters in the parliament and the country as a whole and which it would generally have taken care to communicate to the committee. If the report's recommendations fall within its range of expectations, they are welcomed. They might not be acted upon, but respectful lip service would be paid to them and they would be kept alive in the public realm as desirable goals to be translated into policies at a convenient time. If, however, the recommendations fall foul of the government's expectations or other policies, the report receives a cool and even hostile reception. The way the government reacted to the Rampton Report, manipulated the media and 'reluctantly' yielded to their demands to ignore it and to sack the Chairman in 1981, was a good example of this.

I suggest that we should read the Swann Report in the light of the above discussion if we are to make sense of its apparent inconsistencies, strange gaps, hidden messages and several unusual features.

Take its terms of reference, which read as follows:

Recognizing the contribution of the schools in preparing all pupils for life in a society which is both multiracial and culturally diverse, the Committee is required to:

review in relation to schools the educational needs and attainments of children from ethnic minority groups taking account, as necessary, of factors outside the formal education system relevant to school performance, including influences in early childhood and prospects for school leavers;

consider the potential value of instituting arrangements for keeping under review the educational performances of different ethnic minority groups, and what those arrangements might be;

consider the most effective use of resources for these purposes; and to make recommendations.

Not much analytical acumen is required to see that the terms of reference are not neutral but informed by what I might call a social-democratic view of the nature and causes of the educational underachievement of ethnic minority children. This is hardly surprising for Mrs. Shirley Williams, the then Secretary of State for Education and Science, and later one of the four co-founders of the Social Democratic Party, was responsible for setting up the Committee of Enquiry in 1979 and took keen and protective interest in its deliberations. Britain is said to be a 'multiracial and culturally diverse society', a proposition either hotly disputed or taken not to entail educationally significant conclusions by many in the Conservative party. The school is expected to prepare its pupils for life in such a society, implying that it ought to cultivate tolerance of and respect for cultural diversity and impart multicultural education suited to a multicultural society. The Conservatives reject this view on the ground that the school's task is to initiate its pupils into the 'long-established' and 'common British culture' and gradually assimilate them in the 'British way of life'. The Left, especially the radical, not the traditional political Left, rejects it on the grounds that cultural tolerance has no meaning in a racist society and that the school should concentrate on anti-racist education. Again the terms of reference assert that the educational performance of ethnic minority children is influenced by three sets of factors, namely those indigenous to the educational system, economic prospects of school leavers and influences in early childhood. By and large the Conservatives do not assign much importance to the second and stress inherited intelligence and the academic quality of the school. The Left stresses parental social and economic circumstances or class on the ground that it determines the quality of early childhood influences and the kind of school to which a child goes. The Liberals are nervous and shy about the nature and importance of inherited intelligence, ambiguous about the role and significance of class and place considerable value on early childhood influences. The terms of reference of the Swann Committee of Enquiry combine and suitably dilute all three.

The terms of reference both guided the Rampton and later Swann committees' deliberations and created a measure of conflict. Since they required it to look at factors outside the formal education system, it devoted a large part of its report to social and economic factors and racism in British society. The reference to the early childhood influences raised sensitive and contentious issues. Since a large body of professional opinion unfairly tended to place disproportionate blame on the structure of the Afro-Caribbean family for the underachievement of its children, all the Afro-Caribbean and some other members of the Committee were rightly suspicious that their Report might be used to lend credence and legitimacy to such a view and distract attention from the reality of economic inequality and racism. Naturally they took every step to ensure that this part of the Committee's terms of reference did not receive more than superficial attention. If the Committee had forced the issue, as some members tentatively attempted to do, it would have split.

Take, again, the rather puzzling fact that the Swann Report devoted a good deal of space to the question of the alleged genetic inferiority of the Afro-Caribbean children. Some have contended that by doing so it conferred intellectual legitimacy and social respectability upon an absurd view. In the light of the way the media had savaged the Rampton Report, the Swann Committee had no alternative but to grapple with it. The Rampton Report had held racism in society at large and in the educational system largely responsible for the underachievement of the Afro-Caribbean children. Most of the media, some openly, others by innuendoes and insinuations, poured scorn on this and hinted that the Report had been dishonest in ignoring the 'genetic factor'. The credibility of the Swann Committee depended upon recognizing and nailing the prejudice. It rightly concluded that however painful and humiliating the exercise, the deep-seated prejudices had to be patiently analyzed and exposed. It therefore invited two distinguished Cambridge academics to produce a rigorously researched paper appropriately entitled 'The IQ Question', which was to run to forty-seven pages.

Although the Rampton (and later Swann) Committee was set up to deal with the problems of *all* ethnic minority children, it owned its existence to the widespread anxiety over the gross underachievement of the Afro-Caribbean children about whom indeed it was required to submit an interim report. This created a psychological climate from which it was not able fully to liberate itself. From the very inception, most of its members and much of the public opinion took it to be an Afro-Caribbean Committee concerned with the problems of Afro-Caribbean children and to which the other ethnic minority children were largely marginal. This was only true so far as the interim report was concerned. Once that was published the Committee was required to cast its net wider and examine the problems of other ethnic minorities as well. The gross underachievement of the Bangladeshi children was widely known and had aroused great anxiety. Some Pakistani and Turkish Cypriot children too were known to underachieve. Although the performance of the other Asian communities was not worrying, they had more specific problems. One would have thought that the Swann Committee would therefore have devoted its resources and attention to these and other related questions. That it did not adequately do so has puzzled many.

To their great credit the Afro-Caribbean members of the Committee formed a cohesive group, did their homework, spoke with one voice and coordinated their strategy. Not surprisingly they were able to set its agenda and influence its deliberations. They had the added political advantage of a concerned and well-organized Afro-Caribbean community closely watching the Committee's work. The community's invisible presence was felt by everyone on the Committee. No one wanted to alienate or lose its support, which was as important as the government's for the credibility of the report. The Afro-Caribbean members of the Committee frequently invoked this to lend weight and urgency to their views. Their Asian colleagues could not have presented a greater contrast. They were drawn from different Asian sub-communities with conflicting interests and expectations, they had no experience of fighting for a common cause, and they lacked deep roots in their communities. As for their communities they took little interest in the work of the Committee and seemed to have no strong feelings on any issue except the religious schools and, to a lesser extent, the teaching of mother tongue. They did not hold the Asian Committee members accountable for their views, nor put pressure on them, nor invite them to specially convened public forums nor even lobby them. Not surprisingly the Asian members lacked political weight, had no common cause to fight for and drifted. They tended to speak and act as isolated individuals and lacked collective presence and power, with the result that the problems of Asian children received inadequate attention. This was by no means an unusual phenomenon. In almost all areas of British public life the links between the Asian intellectuals and their community are tenuous and fragile. Unlike their Afro-Caribbean counterparts they do not feel responsible *for* let alone *to* it, and it does not feel either that it must hold them accountable. The reasons for this are too deep to explore here.

The other aspects of the Swann Report can be similarly explained. Many of its critics have commented that it gestures in the direction of both multi-cultural and anti-racist education. When the educational community in the country at large is itself divided between the two schools and has so far remained unable to evolve a consensus, the Swann Committee could hardly be expected to do much more than reproduce the wider dispute. Indeed its members too were divided into two camps and, since neither gained intellectual and political ascendancy, the Report reflected the balance of power. Again, it has been widely remarked that the Report does not fully explain why the Afro-Caribbean children underachieve. In the light of our earlier discussion the explanation is obvious. The members of the Committee had to rely on their common sense and the prevailing consensus. The former pointed in different directions, and the latter was either non-existent or biased and unacceptable. They could have thought up imaginative hypotheses, of which there were several, and commissioned research. However, the failure of imagination and nerve and, it would seem, deep ideological conflicts and political fears came in the way. The NFER's first review of research prepared by Monica Taylor had proposed an interesting study along the following lines:

> A major in-depth investigation...to study and compare the relation between the performance of West Indian pupils, their family background and factors internal to school. The emphasis in such a study would be on home–school interaction and type, size and atmosphere of school, necessitating carefully matched samples for detailed study, focusing particularly on those children who were comparatively high achievers.

According to the NFER review considerable light would be thrown on the

Afro-Caribbean pupils' underachievement by investigating the factors in the school and at home that had enabled some of them to succeed in GCE 'O' level and CSE examinations. Dr Mortimore, the Director of Research and Statistics at the Inner London Education Authority, proposed to undertake such a study, broadening it to include the Asian and White pupils as well as giving greater attention to the influence of racism. Mortimore's study did raise difficulties, one of the most important being the danger of political misuse. Though Mortimore himself would have been sensitive to the differences in family structures and seen the different factors in their complex relationship, past experience indicated that the same could not at all be said of the media and influential politicians who might have oversimplified his findings and fastened much of the blame on the Afro-Caribbean family. However, the research also had its obvious merits and could have thrown considerable light on the factors responsible for Afro-Caribbean underachievement. The Afro-Caribbean members of the Swann Committee, as well as some others, persuaded the rest that on balance the political and educational risk was not worth taking.

Whatever one may think of the final decision, the very fact that it involved delicate political calculations shows how naive it is to think that academic research can ever be politically neutral. Sometimes the research itself is biased. To choose or stress one factor rather than another is already to indicate who is likely to be responsible and deserves to be *blamed* for the problem under examination. And even if the research is itself unbiased and fully sensitive to the complex interaction between various factors, the knowledge it yields cannot remain confined to the experts accustomed to its nuances. It enters the public domain where it is seized upon, vulgarized and chartered in the service of dubious political causes. All knowledge runs that risk. The risk often *has* to be taken, but not always. And when it is taken, it must be appreciated that it is a *risk*, requiring delicate calculations and involving a measure of moral responsibility for its consequences. Truth is a great moral value not to be lightly compromised, but so is human well-being *and the two do not always coincide*. Unlike an academic whose work may or may not be widely noticed and politically appropriated, a committee of enquiry is necessarily a public body delivering a public report carrying the moral and political authority of a collective and quasi-official agency. Its decisions are necessarily subject to greater moral constraint and political pressure. However non-controversial its subject matter and however detached its members, its report is necessarily a messy and yet skilfully judged compromise.

Note

1 To avoid invidious comparisons I have not mentioned any government report other than the two I am commenting upon. Though obviously not all the following points apply to all of them, there is hardly any to which most of them do not.

Chapter 14

Postscript —
Cultural Pluralism:
Strategies for Change

Gajendra K. Verma

As was suggested in chapter one of this volume, the Swann Report represents a landmark in pluralism and one that points the way towards better things. This chapter reflects on the contribution that the pluralist approach advocated in *Education for All* can make in response to one of the major challenges facing late twentieth-century societies, at home and abroad.

It will not be enough to preach the gospel of cultural pluralism. It would be naive to assume that the development of a programme of education for all would of itself put to rights the social, cultural, political and economic disadvantages faced by ethnic minority groups. One could hardly expect that kindling a re-assessment among individuals of their cultural standpoints in relation to those of others around them would bring about dramatic changes in the situation. But who is to deny that such programmes will not have some effect and begin to create a more conducive climate?

Certain issues seem likely to be stubbornly problematic. These would appear to centre on disadvantage in housing, employment and economic circumstance. It is difficult to envisage a society in which certain sectors of the population will not always be more vulnerable than others to disadvantage. Whatever sort of safety net that a democratic society provides to cushion the worst effects of disadvantage, or relative disadvantage, there will inevitably be those who find themselves at the bottom of the ladder. If cultural pluralism were to gain a real foothold, one might expect, as the decades unfold, the incidence of disadvantage among families with ethnic minority origins will steadily fall. But in the meantime life-chances of thousands of young people from ethnic minority groups will be adversely affected because of discrimination and social rejection by the mainstream culture.

Despite the generally depressing evidence from Britain and elsewhere as to educational underachievement by ethnic minority groups, there was some evidence as the Swann Report found and as Bullivant had found in Australia that some sub-groups were performing as well as their ethnic majority peers.

That, in turn, may give rise to new problems that society and education will have to face. Bullivant (chapter 5) reported a newer phenomenon where the attitudes of disaffected youth from the ethnic majority group were beginning to rub off on some ethnic minority youngsters causing them to adopt similar anti-education attitudes. But these are problems for the future!

In the meantime, what sort of programmes will cultural pluralism have to produce to offset the disadvantages suffered by ethnic minorities? Indeed, have concepts of cultural pluralism any lasting future? How will the demands, aspirations and expectations of tomorrow's society change? Will the next decade and those ahead of it bring about an even greater polarization of cultural stances or will there be a gradual fusion towards a new culture? Will future generations of both ethnic minority and majority groups move towards the shared cultural norms within a national framework? Or will ethnic minorities look increasingly within their communities for self-expression, self-fulfilment and livelihood as an expression of their alienation? The answer to those questions is not an easy one. Much depends on the attitudes and behaviour of the mainstream society. If it allows them the opportunity to move up the occupational ladder then one might hope to see a broadening of society's cultural norms and not retrenchment into polarized and fragmentary cultures. The framework of attitudes fostered in schools through an effective 'Education for All' may indeed be contributory to a steady change in the behaviour of individuals from different ethnic groups that will point the way toward better things.

If we look around the world we find that new patterns of socio-economic-political consciousness underpin the modern pluralism that affects us all. One of the main goals of cultural pluralism within the educational context must be to provide all pupils and students with the skills, knowledge and attitudes they need if they are to function effectively in contemporary society. There has always been diversity of opinion about what constitutes education. However, since society is pluralist, education must reflect and utilize cultural diversity.

Cultural diversity is a fact of life in almost all countries of the world. Populations in the Australian continent, in North and South America, in the Indian sub-continent and in Africa have been culturally heterogenous since time immemorial. Yet, in Britain, like many Western countries, the 'pluralist' composition of society has become a matter of controversy and debate over the past twenty years. Anxiety has grown about the increase in inter-ethnic conflict in recent years. There is also ample evidence that prejudice and discrimination against ethnic minorities in matters of education, employment and housing have become part of everyday life.

In a complex situation such as this the Swann Report is a complex document providing wide-ranging evidence and analysis about the issues in the schooling of ethnic minority groups in Britain. The Report makes clear that the issues and needs of ethnic minorities are tied up with the education of white children, and hence the title 'Education for All'. It comments in the opening chapter:

We feel it important to begin by setting out clearly our view of the kind of multiracial society for which we believe the education system should be preparing all youngsters, and the extent to which the reality in Britain today is at variance with the ideal. (DES, 1985, p. 8)

Later in the same chapter it goes on to say:

We are not seeking to fit ethnic minorities into a mould which was originally cast for a society, relatively homogeneous in language, religion and culture nor to break this mould completely...We are instead looking into a form which retains the fundamental principles of the original but within a broader pluralist conspectus — diversity within unity. (p. 8)

In this statement the broad message is that both ethnic minority and majority groups have equal rights to a good education. This must be seen as a bold challenge to the traditional fabric of the educational system which no other report had ever made. This is a radical view of the nature and function of the school/institution which has given the educational debate in Britain a new direction. Yet, it attempts to preserve the core values of society.

The Report makes it clear that the ideal society is a pluralist one where diversity is acknowledged and respected within a '...commonly accepted framework of values, practices and procedures'. It maps out the kinds of response required by the educational system to meet the social, psychological and educational needs of *all* children. Furthermore, it advocates the sharing of cultures within a national identity framework and not solely the maintenance of existing cultures. Given the central philosophy of the Report's recommendations it is obvious that British society is far removed from this ideal. It is also clear that prejudice amongst white people against black people exists in all walks of life. Only radical changes in attitude reflecting equality and justice can bring about the necessary transformation in society.

Before considering some fundamental strategies for change it is worthwhile looking at various constitutents of pluralism.

Pluralism involves different cultural, ethnic and religious groups in the same society not merely existing side by side, but understanding sympathetically each other's folkways, life-styles, literature, customs and aspirations (Triandis, 1976). The alternative to pluralism in an ethnically mixed society is racialism or the absorption of minority groups by the majority.

The Report asserts that the goal of cultural pluralism can be attained by achieving equality of opportunity for *all* regardless of sex, race, creed, class, ethnic background etc. A critical element, however, in developing cultural pluralism is that the individual/the group's culture should be maintained and preserved so that they can function in society with respect and without penalty. At present it is not happening in British society either at the institutional or societal level. Indeed, ethnic minorities have been, and continue to be denied equal opportunity, and equal access to education, training and employment.

Gajendra K. Verma

In this context the thrust of the Report's philosophy is 'to identify and to remove those practices and procedures which work, directly or indirectly, and intentionally or unintentionally, against pupils from any ethnic group, and to promote through the curriculum, an appreciation and commitment to the principles of equality and justice on the part of all pupils'.

It strongly advocates that the existing monocultural education should be replaced by multicultural and anti-racist education. This implies that the system must allow for considerable variations within any context, since it is likely that some individuals are more culturally retentionist than others. Social, cultural, linguistic, religious, socio-economic, class and personal characteristics all contribute to the particular educational aspirations of ethnic groups.

The impact of the monocultural orientation of the educational system on the self-respect and identity of ethnic minority children and adolescents is shattering. The British educational system has so far failed. It fails to concern itself with the preparation of *all* individuals to function in a society composed of varied races, cultures, social norms, values and life-styles, each different but interdependent. It fails also to help pupils and students of the majority community to understand the origins and nature of racism, and the gross inequalities of power in society.

Pluralism within the political state implies that certain ethnic groups (defined by combination of religion, ethnicity or cultural values) are both relatively endogamous, and strive to retain their distinctive cultural identity through some degree of institutional separation. Berry (1979) stresses that the majority of individuals in all ethnic groups in the political state must *value* such a state of affairs before a society can be truly pluralist.

The recent overuse in Western societies of the plural society concept — originally developed in order to describe colonial societies in Burma and Indonesia and later used in a description of Dutch society (Bagley, 1972; Lijphart, 1977) — reflects a rhetorical and indeed a crude political attempt to rationalize cultural domination. The South African case is the most flagrant example of this, where the preservation of cultural differences is used as an excuse for the preservation of economic and political domination of black people by whites. Few writers would deny that the essence of pluralism is that the different ethnic, religious and social groups making up society have equal power in terms of access to economic and political resources. The question arises as to whether society at large is willing to commit itself to cultural pluralism to the extent of including ethnic minorities in the power structure.

Pluralism has considerable application in the field of race and education. This assumes that educational processes should respond to, and respect and foster the cultural identity of various minority groups in society, as well as making members of the majority group culture aware of the needs and aspirations of minority groups. The ultimate aim of education in a plural society is to produce young people who have a cognitively complex view of a world within which they are in harmony. Ethnic minorities, both in Britain and elsewhere, have their own independent historical and cultural continuity.

Although they interact with other cultures in a plural society, this does not mean that they should become a mere shadow of the majority group's tradition. Such cultural reductionism has not taken place in some plural societies such as in India, Malaysia and Singapore. Ethnic minorities in these countries have managed to preserve their cultural, religious and linguistic distinctiveness over many generations.

A number of key issues come to the fore when one considers how institutional strategies might be developed to promote understanding of cultural pluralism. Members of the white majority group require more information about different cultures, and some soul-searching about their attitudes and behaviour towards ethnic minority groups. But just providing more information about other cultures does not always result in 'increased tolerance'. This is because stereotypes of other peoples have already been learned through family, television, text books, peers etc., and through the observed social status of particular groups in society and globally.

Unless these deeply embedded notions are identified, and critically evaluated, new information tends only to reinforce existing understandings about out-groups. Teachers need to explore these issues with their pupils. Pupils should be equipped to look critically at the historical and current reasons for the continued unequal social status and disadvantaged position of different ethnic and cultural groups in society.

Any analysis of culture should take into account the social class, gender, physical mobility, experience of discrimination, political affiliations etc. Thus, the aspects of culture should not be viewed in terms of external characteristics of the individual. This strategy implies that teachers ought to use the experiences of ethnic minority children and their parents as the starting point for an understanding of 'culture' — their experience in school, at home, at work, in their communities and in society at large.

It must be recognised that ethnic minorities suffer from multiple disadvantages in all aspects of life because of discrimination which leads to injustice. Teachers can strengthen and encourage self-respect in ethnic minority pupils, provide a clear understanding to both minority and majority pupils of the way in which society works, a sense of what is fair, and a commitment to change things which are unjust.

Attainment of cultural pluralism is lodged squarely in the policy, structures, practices and beliefs not only in the educational system but in society at large. It is not an individual problem; it requires both a political commitment and institutional efforts. The school cannot and should not remain neutral in these matters. It should not passively reflect society, it must actively seek to change the attitudes and behaviour of its future citizens. Cultural pluralism challenges schools' traditional role as the transmitters of the dominant culture. In this process it should engage both those who experience injustice and discrimination and those who are members of the dominant culture in the challenge to racism.

One of the most significant contributions of the Swann Report must be that of unpacking the current situation in society in general and the educational system in particular in a way that enables and invites action to right the wrongs suffered by ethnic minorities. Men, women and children are suffering from economic, educational and social disadvantages because of race. As well as pointing up a number of fallacies in our thinking about these issues, the Report points the way to the development of a truly pluralist society. It demonstrates the vital role that schools and other educational institutions have to play in establishing it.

Time is slipping away. Government policies have yet to be clearly defined and the machinery has yet to be put in place which will result in a reduction in racial prejudice and discrimination not only in educational institutions but in society at large. If government is really sincere about its commitment to justice and the well-being of all citizens it must adopt the philosophy and strategies for change proposed by Swann for the realisation of a truly ethnically plural society as we move towards the twenty-first century.

References

BAGLEY, C. (1972) 'Racialism and Pluralism: A Dimensional Analysis of 48 Countries', *RACE* Vol. 13, pp. 347–54.

BERRY, J. (1979) 'Research in Multicultural Societies: Implications of Cross-cultural Methods', *Journal of Cross-cultural Psychology* Vol. 10, pp. 415–34.

DEPARTMENT OF EDUCATION AND SCIENCE (1985) *Education for All: Report of the Committee of Enquiry into the Education of Children from Ethnic Minority Groups* (The Swann Report) Cmnd. 9453 London, HMSO.

LIJPHART, A. (1977) *Democracy in Plural Societies: A Comparative Exploration,* New Haven: Yale University Press.

TRIANDIS, H. (1976) 'The future of pluralism', *Journal of Social Issues,* 32, pp. 179–208.

Notes On Contributors

Gajendra K. Verma is Reader in Education and Director of Centre for Ethnic Studies in Education, University of Manchester, School of Education, UK. He has researched and published widely in the field of race in education and employment, and was a member of the Swann Committee. He has also served on a number of National Committees concerned with the education of ethnic minority pupils. He is author/co-author of over a dozen books.

John Rex is Research Professor and Associate Director at the Centre for Research in Ethnic Relations, University of Warwick, UK. His pioneering work based on Sparkbrook nearly two decades ago placed issues of race and prejudice on the Social and Political agenda.

Sally Tomlinson is Professor in the Department of Educational Research at the University of Lancaster, UK. She teaches and researches in the area of race, ethnicity and education, and has published widely on educational issues relating to minority and majority society children.

Millicent E. Poole is Professor of Education at Monash University, Australia. Her main areas of concern are culture and life possibilities, and the relationship between education and social policy, especially in relation to adolescent and youth life choices associated with gender, ethnicity and social class.

Judyth M. Sachs is foundation senior lecturer in Education at the Gold Coast College of Advanced Education, Australia. Her research is sociologically based and is concerned with multicultural education policy, critiques of inservice education and teacher work.

Brian M. Bullivant is Reader in Education at Monash University, Australia. He specializes in cultural analyses of racial and ethnic relations and the dynamics of pluralism in Western societies.

Christopher Bagley is Professor of Child Welfare in the Faculty of Social Welfare at the University of Calgary, Canada. He has published widely in the field of race, education and Social Welfare. He has also conducted Cross-Cultural Research in Britain, the Netherlands, India and Japan.

James Lynch is Professor in the Faculty of Education at Sunderland Polytechnic, UK. He is also Consultant to such international organizations as UNESCO and the World Bank. He has extensive experience of working in developing countries and specializes in least developed countries (LDCs).

Maurice Craft is Professor and Chairman of the School of Education at Nottingham University, UK where he was formerly Pro-Vice-Chancellor. He was a member of the Swann Committee's Teacher Education Sub-Committee, and has written and consulted widely in multicultural education.

Louis Cohen is Professor of Education at Loughborough University of Technology, UK. He teachers multicultural education courses to undergraduate and postgraduate students.

Barry Troyna is lecturer in the social aspects of education at the University of Warwick, UK. His latest books include *Racism, Education and the State* (with Jenny Williams), *Racial Inequality in Education* (edited for Tavistock Publications) and, with Bruce Carrington, *Children and Controversial Issues* (Falmer Press).

Peter Mittler is Professor of Special Education and Director of the Centre for Educational Guidance and Special Needs, School of Education, University of Manchester, UK and is currently a member of the Schools Examination and Assessment Council. He is adviser to several United Nations agencies on aspects of disability and has been President of the International League of Societies for Persons with Mental Handicap.

James Cornford was a member of the Swann Committee and since March 1989 has been Director of the Institute for Public Policy Research. He was Director of the Nuffield Foundation from 1981–89, Director of the Outer Circle Policy Unit from 1978–80, and taught in the Politics Department at the University of Edinburgh from 1968–76.

Bhikhu Parekh is Professor of Political Theory at the University of Hull. He is also Deputy Chairman of the Commission for Racial Equality; Ex-Vice-Chancellor, University of Baroda, India, and author of nearly a dozen books.

Index

achievement
  see also Afro-Caribbean children;
    Bangladeshi children; Pakistani
    children; Turkish children;
    underachievement; West Indian
    children
  and multicultural education, 212
  and self-esteem, 108-11
  and social background, 197-8
ACT Schools Authority [Australia], 47
AEAC
  see Australian Ethnic Affairs Council
Afro-Caribbean children
  see also West Indian children
  and culture, 17
  and language, 17
  in special schools, 197
  and underachievement, 232-3, 234
Afro-Caribbean Education Research
    (ACER) project, 211
Agenda for Multicultural Teaching; 147
Ahmed Iqbal Ullah, 177, 184
'Aide-Memoire for the Inspectorate', 147
Almond, H.H., 30
American Association of Colleges for
    Teacher Education, 133
Anglo-Australian students
  in Australian schools, 4-5, 78-95
  and ethnic minorities, 4-5, 71-95
  and self-deprivation syndrome, 94
Annual School Census [Education
    Department, Victoria], 78
anti-racism
  see also anti-racist education
  and curriculum, 19-20
  definition of, 3, 15
  and equality of opportunity, 18
  and multicultural education, 7, 11-25,
    143, 178-9

and selection processes, 19
and teacher awareness of racism, 20
anti-racist education (ARE)
  see also anti-racism; multicultural
    education
  in all schools, 182-8
  in colleges of further education, 186-8
  conceptions in Britain of, 177, 178-81
  core concepts for, 184
  and ideology, 183
  and learning, 177, 181-8
  and learning about collaboration,
    184-5
  and learning new perspectives, 184-5
  and learning about rights, 184-5
  in predominantly white areas, 176
  principles of, 182-4, 187
  and selection, 177, 181-8
  and social inequalities, 7, 184, 187
  and social relations, 7, 183-4, 187
ARE
  see anti-racist education
Asian children
  see also Indo-Asian students
  and achievement, 4-5, 57
  and culture, 17, 21
  and culture clash, 137
  and ethnic success ethic, 5, 69, 94
  and language, 17, 21
  and underachievement, 2
Association for All Speech Impaired
    Children, 201
Association of American Colleges, 113
Atkins, M.
  see Craft and Atkins
Australia as a Multicultural Society, 43
Australia
  see also entries for particular states and
    territories

Schools' Year Twelve and Tertiary
    Entrance Certificate (STC), 79
Secondary Examinations Council (SEC),
    134–5
Seeley, J.E., 32
Seeley Service, 36
Select Committee on Race Relations and
    Immigration (SCRRI), 1, 132, 181
selection
    in multi-ethnic schools, 181–2
    in predominantly white schools, 182
self-esteem
    and academic achievement, 108–11
Selman, L., 180, 184
sexism
    and culturally legitimate
        discrimination, 88–9
    and ethnicity, 88–90
    within ethnic groups, 88–90
    in the workplace, 90
Skipper, 36
Sleeter, C.
    see Grant and Sleeter
social class
    and cultural values, 31–2
    and equality of opportunity, 12
social closure, 72–3, 75, 78–9
social reproduction theory, 72
South Africa
    apartheid and multiculturalism in, 14
South Australia
    see also Australia
    multicultural education in, 49–50
Spastics Society, 201
special educational needs
    and curriculum reform, 194–6
    and 'deficit' model, 8, 194
    and educational reform, 206
    and home-school relationships, 202–3
    and integration, 200–2
    and local education authorities, 206
    and multicultural education, 7–8,
        192–208
    and permeation model, 205
    and professional ignorance, 198–9
    schools and, 193–4
    and separate provision, 199–202
    and social disadvantage, 197–8
    and teacher education, 8, 203–5
    and whole school policies, 194–6
special schools, 197, 200–2
    overrepresentation of ethnic minorities
        in, 197
Stalky and Co., 35

STC
    see Schools' Year Twelve and Tertiary
        Entrance Certificate
structural-functional perspective, 75
student teachers
    see also initial teacher training; teacher
        education
    and assimilation concept, 6, 156–7,
        159, 162, 163, 165, 169–71, 172–3
    and concepts of multiculturalism, 6–7,
        154, 156, 158, 159
    and cultural pluralism, 6–7, 156–7,
        159, 162, 165, 169–71, 173
    ethnocentricity of, 6–7, 154–5, 157,
        158–61, 162–3, 164–5, 166–9
    and feelings toward ethnic minority
        groups, 6–7, 154, 155–6, 157–9
    home region and levels of prejudice of,
        161–2, 163
    and integration concept, 6, 156–7,
        159, 162, 163, 165, 169–71, 172–3
    and knowledge of ethnic minority
        groups, 6–7, 154, 155, 157, 158–9,
        160–1, 162–3, 165, 166–9, 172
    and perceptions of ethnic minorities in
        Britain, 6–7, 151–74
    and prejudice, *see* student teachers,
        ethnocentricity of
    and race awareness courses, 165
    sex and levels of prejudice of, 161
    survey of, 154–73
Study of Man, The, 138–9
Swann, Lord, vii, 4, 69
    see also Education for All, Swann
        Committee
Swann Committee
    see also Education for All [Report of the
        Committee]
    Afro-Caribbean members of, 232–3
    Asian members of, 233
    and commissioning of research, 212
    and difficulties of research in a plural
        society, 8, 209–26, 234
    establishment of, 21
    and sensitivity of research issues, 8,
        210–11
    terms of reference of, 230–2
Swann Report
    see Education for All

Tarzan stories, 35
Tarzan the Untamed, 36
Taylor, M., 233